M000073165

AFRICAN NATURE NOTES AND REMINISCENCES

Library of African Adventure
Mike Resnick, series editor

African Nature Notes and Reminiscences
by Frederick Courteney Selous
King of the Wa-Kikuyu by John Boyes
**Elephant Hunting in East Equatorial Africa* by Arthur H. Neumann

*forthcoming

African Nature Notes
and
Reminiscences

BY

FREDERICK COURTENEY SELOUS, F.Z.S.
GOLD MEDALLIST OF THE ROYAL GEOGRAPHICAL SOCIETY

WITH A "FOREWORD" BY
PRESIDENT ROOSEVELT

AND ILLUSTRATIONS BY
E. CALDWELL

INTRODUCTION BY
MIKE RESNICK, SERIES EDITOR
The Library of African Adventure

ST. MARTIN'S PRESS
NEW YORK

Library of Congress Cataloging-in-Publication Data

Selous, Frederick Courteney.
African nature notes and reminiscences / Frederick Courteney Selous ; foreward by Theodore Roosevelt.
p. cm. — (The Library of African adventure)
Originally published: London : Macmillan, 1908.
ISBN 0-312-09241-5 : $22.95
1. Big game hunting—South Africa—Anecdotes. 2. Natural history--South Africa. 3. Selous, Frederick Courteney, 1851–1917--Anecdotes. 4. Hunters—South Africa—Anecdotes. I. Title. II. Series.
SK251.S44 1993
508.968—dc20 93-12548 CIP

First Edition: June 1993

10 9 8 7 6 5 4 3 2 1

TO

THEODORE ROOSEVELT

PRESIDENT OF THE UNITED STATES OF AMERICA

THIS BOOK IS RESPECTFULLY DEDICATED

NOT ONLY BECAUSE IT WAS ENTIRELY OWING TO HIS

INSPIRATION AND KINDLY ENCOURAGEMENT

THAT IT WAS EVER WRITTEN

BUT ALSO BECAUSE BOTH IN HIS PRIVATE AND PUBLIC LIFE

HE HAS ALWAYS WON

THE SINCERE ADMIRATION AND ESTEEM

OF

THE AUTHOR

"UNFORTUNATELY, ONE OF THESE TERRIFIC BLOWS, VERY PROBABLY THE FIRST AIMED AT THE LEOPARD WHICH SEIZED THE CALF, HAD STRUCK THE LITTLE CREATURE ON THE LOINS AND BROKEN ITS BACK."—*Page* 220.

INTRODUCTION TO THIS FACSIMILE EDITION

The book you are holding was written by presidential decree.

That's right. Theodore Roosevelt was so taken with the writings of Frederick Courtney Selous that he frequently invited him to the White House as a guest, where affairs of state were put on the back burner while the two naturalists discussed African animals and hunting far into the night. Roosevelt kept urging Selous to write one more book, and when Selous finally agreed, Roosevelt thanked him by writing the introduction to it on the letterhead of the President of the United States.

Selous is generally acknowledged as the greatest African hunter of all time—but while he was first and foremost a hunter, he was also a man of many other accomplishments. He was a trusted lieutenant of Cecil Rhodes, who gave him full credit for opening Rhodesia and winning the Second Matebele War. He was a close personal friend of Roosevelt. He was a naturalist whose careful observations and succinct writings were read by layman and scholar alike. The African wing of the British Museum of Natural History is named after him, and a bust of him is prominently displayed. The largest animal reserve in the world, Tanzania's Selous Reserve, bears his name. The crack special forces unit in the Zimbabwe War of Independence was the Selous Scouts. There was even a stakes-winning American racehorse who carried his name not too many years ago.

He has also been a constant source of inspiration to those who write about the exotic lands where he spent most of his life. He was the model for H. Rider Haggard's Alan Quatermain, the first of whose adventures were published in 1885, and more than a century later he was still appearing in such diverse places as an Indiana Jones television adventure and my own science fiction novelette "Every Man a God," as well as my novel *Purgatory* (Tor, 1993) where he appears, thinly disguised, as "T. J. Fuentes."

What kind of a man makes such a lasting impression, reaching over the generations to people who were born decades after he himself died?

Selous was born in London on New Year's Eve of 1851. We don't know much about his youth except that he was continually in trouble with his headmaster for cutting classes and collecting birds' eggs from private land (his passion for birds' eggs remained with him throughout his life, and his collection, while not the largest, was considered to have some of the finest specimens in the world.) We also know that he read Baldwin's *African Hunting from the Natal to the Zambezi,* and that it shaped his life, for from that day forth he had only one desire: to become a big game hunter in Africa.

Success did not come readily to Selous upon his arrival in the Dark Continent. His rifle was stolen before he had a chance to fire it, and his first trip inland in search of game was a dismal failure. Undaunted, he went deeper into the unexplored interior, and became one of the first hunters to reach the capitol of the mighty Lobengula, king of the Matabele. When he asked Lobengula's permission to hunt elephant on Matabele land, the king found the notion of such a young boy facing such huge creatures uproariously funny. He asked Selous if he had ever so much as seen an elephant, and Selous answered truthfully that he hadn't. That struck the King's funnybone again, and he gave his permission, doubtless sure that the young Londoner would die beneath the feet and tusks of the first elephant he encountered.

It was all the encouragement Selous needed. He promptly collected 450 pounds of ivory from bulls he shot, traded with the Matabele for another 1,200 pounds, and made a quick profit of some three hundred pounds, a sum that enabled a man to live like royalty in Africa in 1870.

He continued hunting for his livelihood through 1888, spending most of his time in Southern Africa (and especially those areas now known as Botswana and Zimbabwe), but then became closely involved with Cecil Rhodes' efforts to occupy Mashonaland, shortly to become known as Southern Rhodesia (and, still later, Zimbabwe). Rhodes initially felt he could overrun Logenbula's army with a small force of hardened veterans, but Selous, who knew both Logenbula and the territory far better, convinced him that this would be suicidal, and talked Rhodes into building a road *around* the Matabele territory and then going north to the Portuguese frontier.

The scheme worked, and Mashonaland soon came peacefully under British rule. (Actually, *officially* it came under the rule of the British South Africa Company, but in practice they were one and the same.) It was entirely due to Selous' innovative suggestion, and his willingness to implement it, treating with the various tribes while the road was under construction, that Rhodes was able to annex Mashonaland. Although Rhodes himself called Selous "the man above all others to whom we owe Rhodesia to the British Crown," he actually treated Selous rather shabbily, breaking a number of promises to him and finally refusing to see him at all, now that his usefulness was seemingly at an end.

"Seemingly" was the key word, for in 1893 the Matabele, known for their warlike nature and inhospitability toward intruders, took up arms against the colonists. Selous acted as Chief of Scouts, heading a column of 700 white irregulars and a handful of disenchanted Matabele, and within a year had put down the insurrection, getting wounded in the process. Again, once the perceived need for him was no longer there, he became the invisible man to Rhodes.

Selous returned to England in 1894, where, because of his first book and his part in the Matabele war, he found himself a hero and a celebrity. He took time off to court and marry Marie Maddy and write up his experiences in the service of Cecil Rhodes, *Sunshine and Storm in Rhodesia,* then went on an Asian hunting expedition.

Shortly thereafter, he linked up with Rowland Ward, the taxidermist-turned-publisher, and for the first time in his life he no longer had to hunt for a living; from this point forward, his writing generated enough income for him to go where he wanted and do what pleased him. Which meant that he still hunted, but now it was for trophies, for museums, and for pleasure.

(One of the great disappointments facing the visitor to the Selous section of the British Museum of Natural History is the absence of the many excellent trophies Selous' widow turned over to them. The last time I was there they were all stored away—still in excellent condition—in a sub-basement, near the record tusks of the fabled Kilimanjaro Elephant. When I asked why they were not on display, the answer seemed ridiculous: Selous did not kill these animals on license, and therefore they were illegally poached. The argument would hold a lot more water if they had *had* hunting licenses back then.)

By the time his *Sport and Travel East and West* appeared, he had struck up a correspondence with Theodore Roosevelt, one that would last throughout the rest of his life. He paid a number of visits to the White House, exchanged observations about wildlife with the enthusiastic President, and finally wrote *African Nature Notes and Reminiscences* at Roosevelt's behest.

"Mr. Selous," wrote the President, "is much more than a mere big-game hunter, however; he is by instinct a keen field naturalist, an observer with a power of seeing and remembering what he has seen; and finally he is a writer who possesses to a very marked and unusual degree the power vividly and accurately to put on paper his observations. . . . His book is a genuine contribution alike to hunting lore and to natural history." Fine praise indeed, coming from literally the most popular man in the world at the time.

As far as I have been able to determine, Roosevelt and Selous only had one serious argument during their years of comradery. Selous was a believer in the theory of protective coloration; Roosevelt felt that the zebra was living proof that protective coloration was a crock, since anyone who has been to Africa will tell you that a zebra stands out like a sore thumb from a good half-mile away. How, demanded Roosevelt, can its coloration be called protective, when it is the easiest plains animal to spot?

Selous never won that argument, though had Roosevelt lived another forty or fifty years and seen some of the first serious documentary film footage of lions making kills, he would have realized that the zebra's stripes may make it stand out from 800 yards away, but when racing away in a herd it is almost impossible for the lion to pick a single zebra out from among all those stripes.

It is commonly believed that Selous acted as Roosevelt's white hunter during the ex-President's 1909–1910 safari—the famous photo of Roosevelt and Selous sitting on the front of the engine, just above the cow-catcher, on the train ride from Mombasa to Nairobi has done nothing to dispel the notion—but this is not the case. Selous is the one who talked him into it, and outfitted it, making all the necessary arrangements for the first major safari in history, including the hiring of 500 porters, but his domain was Southern Africa, and he felt that Roosevelt needed men around him who knew East Africa. To that end, he wisely engaged William Judd and R. J. Cunninghame as Roosevelt's guides and hunters.

Selous continued hunting all over the world and collecting his birds' eggs until World War I broke out in 1914. Though sixty-three years old, he immediately volunteered for service and was sent to East Africa as a lieutenant, where he found himself serving with Richard Meinertzhagen, another old-time hunter (and the author of *Kenya Diary*).

The Fusiliers were as idiosyncratic in personnel as Roosevelt's Rough Riders, and they were sent out after the brilliant German commander, Paul von Lettow-Vorbeck, chasing him fruitlessly all over Tanganyika. Within half a year they had lost more than a third of their 1,100 men, more to disease than to battle, and within another six months they were down to less than 450 men. Selous, the hardened old Africa hand, withstood every disease that knocked out his younger, stronger comrades. He shrugged off malaria, avoided dysentery, seemed immune to bilharzia—but there was one physical problem he couldn't ignore, though he did his best: hemorrhoids. He held out for more than a year, saddling up every morning, treating them with ointment in the evenings, but finally he could stand the excruciating pain no longer, and in June of 1916 he was sent home for hemorrhoid surgery, hardly a common procedure back then. It proved successful and, amazingly, he was back in Africa again in August.

This time he had a battalion of 1,400 men, but once again disease and von Lettow-Vorbeck took a tremendous toll, and by December he was down to under 600 men, more than 200 of them unfit for duty. The British finally caught up with the Germans just after New Year's Day of 1917, and engaged in a number of hand-to-hand, bayonet-wielding encounters.

Then came the fateful morning of January 4. Let us turn to Captain R. J. Haines of the South African Forces for an account of it:

"Captain Selous . . . was literally adored by the men. From a boy he had always been a hero of mine.

"The day he was killed, I passed him in the morning with his company. I was driving an armoured machine-gun, as the driver was ill. As I passed him, I shouted out, 'I shall be back and have *tea* with you today, sir,' for we used to joke him about his habit of drinking tea with every meal.

"That was the last I saw of him. There was some fighting in the bush, and when I came back in the afternoon I was greeted with news of his death. I was just in time to see him buried. He was sewn up in a blanket, and buried with five other men of the Royal Fusiliers. I was told he was wounded in the right arm, which was bandaged up, and he remained with the company.

"A little later he was again hit in the mouth and was killed instantaneously and apparently painlessly."

He was buried at approximately latitude 7 degrees south, longitude 38 degrees east, in the heart of what is now the Selous Reserve. His place was taken by Major P. J. Pretorius, himself an elephant hunter of great renown.

Selous left a lot of legacies. Not the least was his trophy collection, which his widow turned over to the Natural History Museum. More important was his writing, which always strove for accuracy, and disdained heroic description (though many of the events, no matter how much he tried to downplay them, came across as heroic for the very simple reason that they *were* heroic).

Most important of all, I think, was the sense of proportion and rationality he brought to hunting through both his example and his writings. Given his status as the most famous of African hunters, and his access to the public through his arrangement with Rowland Ward, he could have perpetuated many of the myths of both Africa and hunting. Instead he described the life of the African hunter as it really was, debunking the braggarts, meticulously observing the intricate patterns of Nature, examining the native populace with an understanding not often seen before, and relating his adventures with a combination of honesty and modesty.

He was quick to dispute what he considered inaccuracies in the works of others. For example, where David Livingstone had written that one feels no pain while being mauled by a lion, Selous, who had undergone maulings himself, pointed out that it hurt like hell (though it may be that

Livingstone was in shock, while the more self-reliant Selous was struggling to free himself).

He also judged men by their merits and not their color, which was rarer than you might think for a man of his era and in his situation, and his observations and experiences led him to conclude that the Zulus were far more admirable and curageous than the Boers, a statement that might have gotten him jailed in 1879 (or in 1979, come to think of it).

When other hunters and writers claimed that there were distinct subspecies of lion and black rhinoceros, Selous refused to take their word for it, and set out to learn the truth for himself. He shot samples of each, measured them, weighed them, had the pelts and horns analyzed, meticulously drew pictures of each, and concluded that neither animal possessed any subspecies—a conclusion that science has since verified.

He was dubious of all unsubstantiated claims to world-record status by hunters, remarking wryly that "Animals shrink before the tape measure."

One would think that he ranked among the leading killers of African fauna, but in fact that is far from the case. He was extremely selective (his lifetime total of lions, for example, was thirty-one, most killed for pelts, a few for meat, of which he was inordinately fond), and, in his own words, "I never killed an animal for mere sport."

But while he didn't kill for sport, he was a sportsman to the core, a man of whom Roosevelt later said, "There was never a more welcome guest at the White House than Frederick Selous." He not only encouraged the President to come to Africa on safari, but used to delight the Roosevelt children by acting out the parts of all the animals he had encountered.

His friend and biographer, John G. Millais, summed up his character thus:

"Perhaps Selous' chief success as a hunter lay in his untiring energy and fearless intention to gain some desired object. He brought the same force into play in pursuit of a bull elephant as of a small butterfly, and allowed nothing to stand in his way to achieve success. Time, distance, difficulty, or danger were all things that would be conquered by a man of strong will, and his bodily strength was such that even to the end he almost achieved the virility of perfect youth."

Roosevelt added that "It is well for any country to produce men of such a type; and if there are enough of them the nation need fear no decadence."

When Selous left England as a young man, he wrote, "If I can't get good shooting and fishing in this world, I'll get it in the next."

Well, he certainly got it here . . . and given his determination, one suspects that he is currently stalking a herd of elephants across some heavenly savannah.

—MIKE RESNICK

PREFACE

THE chapters comprised in the present volume were written at various times during the last ten years. Some of them have already appeared in print in the pages of the *Field*, *Land and Water*, and other papers, but the majority have remained in manuscript until now. The greatest part of the matter in the chapters on the "Lion" was written some years ago, and was intended to be the commencement of a book dealing entirely with the life-history of South African mammals. When, however, I was asked by Mr. Rowland Ward to contribute to a book he was about to publish on the *Great and Small Game of Africa*, all the articles in which would be written by men who had personally studied the habits of the animals they described, I gave up the idea of myself writing a less comprehensive work on similar lines, and became one of the chief contributors to Mr. Ward's large and valuable publication.

My manuscript notes on the lion and some other animals were then consigned to the seclusion of a drawer in my study, from which they would probably never again have emerged had it not been for the fact that during the autumn of 1905 I had the honour to be the guest of President Roosevelt at the White House in Washington.

I found that President Roosevelt's knowledge of wild animals was not confined to the big game of North America, with which he has made himself so intimately acquainted by long personal experience, but that he also possessed a most comprehensive acquaintance with the habits of the fauna of the whole world, derived from the careful study of practically every book that has been written on the subject.

In the course of conversation, President Roosevelt remarked that he wished I would bring out another book, adding to the natural history notes which I had already written on the big game of South Africa; and on my telling him that I had some manuscript notes on the lion and other animals which I had once intended to publish, but had subsequently put on one side, he requested me to let him see them. On my return to England I at once posted these articles to President Roosevelt, who was kind enough to say that he had found them so interesting that he earnestly hoped I would add to them and bring out another book. Thus encouraged, I set about the revision of all my recent writings dealing with the natural history of South African animals which had not been published in book form, and after arranging them in chapters, sent the whole of the manuscript to President Roosevelt, at the same time asking him to be good enough to look through them, if he could find the time to do so, and telling him that if he thought them of sufficient interest to publish in the form of a book, how much I should appreciate it, if he were able to write me a few lines by way of introduction, since the publication of the book would be entirely due to the kind encouragement and inspiration I had received from himself. This request met with a most kind and generous response, for which I shall ever feel most grateful, for, in the midst of all his multifarious and harassing public duties, President Roosevelt contrived to find the time to write an introduction to my book, which adds to it a most interesting and valuable chapter.

The title I have given to my book, *African Nature Notes and Reminiscences*, though it perhaps lacks terseness, nevertheless exactly describes its scope, and although the chapters dealing with the "Tse-tse" Fly and the subject of Protective Coloration and the Influence of Environment on large mammals may have no interest except for a small number of naturalists, I trust that much of the matter contained in the remaining seventeen articles will appeal to a much wider public.

I must once more acknowledge my indebtedness to President Roosevelt, not only for the very interesting "Foreword" he has contributed to this book, but also for the constant encouragement he has given me during its preparation.

My best thanks are also due to Mr. Max C. Fleischmann of Cincinnati for the very remarkable account which will be found at the end of Chapter X. of the struggle between a crocodile and a rhinoceros, of which he was an eye-witness; as well as to my friend Mr. E. Caldwell for the great pains he has taken to render the ten illustrations emanating from his able pencil as lifelike as possible.

As it is possible that some of those who may glance through this book may be versed in South

African languages, and may remark that I have sometimes represented the Masarwa Bushmen as speaking in the Sechwana language, and at others in the dialect spoken by the Matabele, it may perhaps be as well to explain that whilst the greater part of the Bushmen living between the Limpopo and the Zambesi were the serfs of Bechwana masters, a few of those living near the western border of Matabeleland had become the vassals of certain Matabele headmen, by whom they were employed as hunters and trappers. Besides their own language — which is almost impossible of acquirement by a European—all the Bushmen I ever met spoke that of their masters as well. This was usually Sechwana, but sometimes Sintabele—the language of the Matabele people.

F. C. SELOUS.

WORPLESDON, SURREY,
Dec. 31, 1907.

FOREWORD

Mr. Selous is the last of the big-game hunters of South Africa; the last of the mighty hunters whose experiences lay in the greatest hunting ground which this world has seen since civilized man has appeared therein. There are still many happy hunting grounds to be found by adventure-loving wilderness wanderers of sufficient hardihood and prowess; and in Central Africa the hunting grounds are of a character to satisfy the most exacting hunter of to-day. Nevertheless, they none of them quite equal South Africa as it once was, whether as regards the extraordinary multitude of big-game animals, the extraordinary variety of the species, or the bold attraction of the conditions under which the hunting was carried on.

Mr. Selous is much more than a mere big-game hunter, however; he is by instinct a keen field naturalist, an observer with a power of seeing, and of remembering what he has seen; and finally he is a writer who possesses to a very marked and unusual degree the power vividly and accurately to put on paper his observations. Such a combination of qualities is rare indeed, and the lack of any one of them effectually prevents any man from doing work as valuable as Mr. Selous has done. No ordinary naturalist fills the place at all. Big game exists only in the remote wilderness. Thru-out historic time it has receded steadily before the advance of civilized man, and now the retrogression

—or, to be more accurate, the extermination—is going on with appalling rapidity. The ordinary naturalist, if he goes into the haunts of big game, is apt to find numerous small animals of interest, and he naturally devotes an altogether disproportionate share of his time to these. Yet such time is almost wasted; for the little animals, and especially the insects and small birds, remain in the land long after the big game has vanished, and can then be studied at leisure by hosts of observers. The observation of the great beasts of the marsh and the mountain, the desert and the forest, must be made by those hardy adventurers who, unless explorers by profession, are almost certainly men to whom the chase itself is a dominant attraction. But the great majority of these hunters have no power whatever of seeing accurately. There is no fonder delusion than the belief that the average old hunter knows all about the animals of the wilderness. The Bushman may; but, as Mr. Selous has shown, neither the average English, Boer, nor Kafir hunter in South Africa does; and neither does the white or Indian hunter in North America. Any one who doubts this can be referred to what Mr. Selous has elsewhere said concerning the rhinoceroses of South Africa and the astounding misinformation about them which the average South African hunter of every type believed and perpetuated; and in my own experience I have found that most white and Indian hunters in the Rocky Mountains are just as little to be trusted when, for instance, they speak of the grizzly bear and the cougar—two animals which always tend to excite their imaginations. Finally, the few accurate observers among the men who have seen much of big game are apt wholly to lack the power of expression, and this means that their knowledge can benefit no one. The love of nature, the love of outdoor life, is growing in our race, and it is well that it should grow. Therefore we should prize exceedingly all contributions of worth to the life-histories of the great, splendid, terrible beasts whose lives add an immense majesty to the far-off wilds, and who inevitably pass away before the onrush of the greedy, energetic, forceful men, usually both unscrupulous and short-sighted, who make up the vanguard of civilization.

Mr. Selous has hunted in many parts of the world, but his most noteworthy experiences were in Africa, south of the Zambezi, when the dry uplands, and the valleys of the dwindling rivers, and the thick coast jungle belt, still held a fauna as vast and varied as that of the Pleistocene. Mighty hunters, Dutch and English, roamed hither and thither across the land on foot and on horseback, alone, or guiding the huge white-topped ox-wagons; several among their number wrote with power and charm of their adventures; and at the very last the man arose who could tell us more of value than any of his predecessors.

Mr. Selous by his observations illustrates the great desirability of having the views of the closet naturalist tested by competent field observers. In a previous volume he has effectively answered those amiable closet theorists who once advanced the Rousseau-like belief that in the state of nature hunted creatures suffered but little from either pain or terror; the truth being that, in the easy conditions of civilized life, we hardly even conceive of pain and horror as they were in times primeval; while it is only in nightmares that we now realize the maddened, hideous terror which our remote ancestors so often underwent, and which is a common incident in the lives of all harmless wild creatures. In the first two chapters of the present volume, Mr. Selous' remarks on the fallacy of much of the theory of protective coloration are excellent.

The whole subject is one fraught with difficulty and deserving of far more careful study than has ever yet been given it. That the general pattern of coloration, so to speak, of birds and mammals of the snowy North as compared to the South, of a dry desert as compared to a wet forest region, is due to the effect of the environment I have no question; and Mr. Selous' observations and arguments show that the protective theory has been ridiculously overworked in trying to account for coloration like that of the zebra and giraffe, for instance; but there is much that as yet it is difficult to explain.

The most conspicuous colors of nature, for instance, are, under ordinary circumstances, black and white. Yet we continually find black, and sometimes white, animals thriving as well as their more dull-colored compeers under conditions that certainly seem as if they ought to favor the latter. The white goat of the Rocky Mountains may be helped by its coloration in winter, but in summer its white coat advertises its presence to every man or beast within range of vision, and this at the very time when the little white kids are most in need of protection. Eagles are formidable foes of these little kids, and undoubtedly their white color is a disadvantage to them in the struggle for existence, when they are compared with the dull-colored lambs of the mountain sheep of the same general habitat. The sheep tend to become mainly or entirely white at the northern portion of their range —thereby becoming exceedingly conspicuous in summer—but change to grays and browns from the semi-Arctic regions southward. The goats, however, remain white everywhere.

Again, birds and mammals of the far North tend to be white, but one of the typical far northern birds is the jet black raven. It is hard to believe that the color of the snowy owl assists it in getting its prey, or that its color hampers the raven. The northern weasels and northern hares of America both turn white in winter. Thru most of their range the various species of these weasels and hares exist side by side with the close kinsmen of the weasel, the mink and the sable, and at the southern boundary of their range side by side with the small gray rabbits; none of which change their color any more than the lynx and fox do, and yet in the struggle for life seem to be put to no disadvantage thereby. The Arctic hare changes color as does the ptarmigan. The ordinary snow-shoe rabbits and jack-rabbits of the woods and plains south of the Arctic hare region also change their color; but the grouse which inhabit the same woods or open plains, such as the ruffed, the sharp-tailed and the spruce, unlike their northern kinsman, the ptarmigan, undergo no seasonal change. Around my ranch on the Little Missouri, the jack-rabbits all turned white in winter; the little cotton-tail rabbits did not; yet as far as I could see both species were equally at home and fared equally well.

When a boy, shooting on the edges of the desert in Egypt, I was imprest with the fact that the sand grouse, rosy bullfinches, sand larks and sand chats all in the coloration of their upper parts harmonized strikingly with the surroundings, while the bold black and white chats were peculiarly noticeable, and yet as far as I could see held their own as well in the struggle for existence. But as regards the first-named birds it seemed to me at the time that their coloration was probably protective, for in the breeding season the males of some of them showed striking colors, but always underneath, where they would not attract the attention of foes.

Mr. Selous also shows that the "signal" or

"mutual recognition" theory of coloration has been at the least carried to an extreme by closet naturalists. The prongbuck of North America has the power of erecting the glistening white hairs on its rump until it looks like a chrysanthemum; but there seems scarcely any need of this as a signal; for prongbucks live out on the bare plains, never seek to avoid observation, are very conspicuous beasts, and have eyes like telescopes, so that one of them can easily see another a mile or two off. According to my experience—but of course the experience of any one man is of limited value, and affords little ground for generalization—the "chrysanthemum" is shown when the beast is much aroused by curiosity or excitement.

Mr. Selous' chapters on the lion possess a peculiar interest, for they represent without any exception the best study we have of the great, tawny, maned cat. No one observer can possibly cover the entire ground in a case such as this, for individual animals differ markedly from one another in many essential traits, and all the animals of one species in one locality sometimes differ markedly from all the animals of the same species in another locality (as I have myself found, in some extraordinary particulars, in the case of the grizzly bear). Therefore, especially with a beast like the lion, one of the most interesting of all beasts, it is necessary for the naturalist to have at hand the observations of many different men; but no other single observer has left a record of the lion of such value to the naturalist as Mr. Selous.

One of the most interesting of Mr. Selous' chapters is that containing his notes on wild dogs, on hunting hounds, and on cheetahs. Especially noteworthy are his experiences in actually running down and overtaking by sheer speed of horse and hound both the wild dog and the cheetah. These experiences are literally inexplicable with our present knowledge; and therefore it is all the more valuable to have them recorded. Mr. Selous' own account of the speed of wild dogs and the statements of many competent observers about cheetahs—as for instance, of that mighty hunter, Sir Samuel Baker—make it clear that under ordinary circumstances both wild dogs and cheetahs, when running after their game, go at a speed far surpassing that of a horse. Yet in these instances given by Mr. Selous, he and his companions with their camp dogs once fairly ran down a pack of wild dogs; and twice he fairly ran down full-grown cheetahs. In the last case it is possible that the hunted cheetah, not at first realizing his danger, did not put forth his full speed at the beginning, and, not being a long-winded animal, was exhausted and unable to spurt when he really discovered his peril. But with the hunting dogs it is hard to imagine any explanation unless they were gorged with food. In coursing wolves with greyhounds, I have noticed that the dogs will speedily run into even an old dog wolf, if he is found lying by a carcase on which he has feasted, under conditions which would almost certainly have insured his escape if he had been in good running trim. I once saw a cougar, an old male, jump from a ledge of rock surrounded by hounds and come down hill for several hundred yards thru the snow. The hounds started almost on even terms with him, but he drew away from them at once, and when he reached the bottom of the hill, was a good distance ahead; but by this time he had shot his bolt, and after going up hill for a very few yards he climbed into a low evergreen tree, which I reached almost as soon as the hounds. His lungs were then working like bellows, and it was obvious he could have gone no distance further.

The book of nature has many difficult passages, and some of them seem mutually contradictory. It is a good thing to have capable observers who can record faithfully what they find therein, and who are not in the least afraid of putting down two observations which are in seeming conflict. Allied species often differ so radically in their habits that, with our present knowledge, not even a guess can be made as to the reason for the difference; this makes it all the more necessary that there should be a multitude of trustworthy observations. Mr. Selous points out, for instance, the extraordinary difference in pugnacity between the fighting roan and sable antelopes, on the one hand, and on the other, the koodoo and the mild eland. There is quite as great difference between far more closely allied species, or even between individuals of one species in one place and those of the same species in another place. Sometimes the reasons for the difference are apparent; all carnivores in India, with its dense, feeble population, would at times naturally take to man-killing. In other cases, at least a guess may be hazarded. The wolf of America has never been dangerous to man, as his no larger or more formidable brother of Asia and Europe has been from time immemorial; yet the difference may be accounted for by the difference of environment. But it is hard to say why the cougar, which is just about the size of the great spotted cats, and which preys on practically the same animals, should not be dangerous to man, while they are singularly formidable fighters when at bay. The largest cougar I ever killed was eight feet long and weighed over two hundred pounds. Very few African leopards or Indian panthers would surpass these measurements, and this particular animal had been preying not only on deer, but on horses and cattle; yet I killed him with no danger to myself, under circumstances which would probably have insured a charge from one of the big spotted cats of Africa or Asia, or, for the matter of that, from a South American jaguar. And by the way, in reading of the ravages committed by leopards among the hounds of the sport-loving planters of Ceylon, it has always seemed to me strange that these planters did not turn the tables on the aggressors by training packs especially to hunt them. Such a pack as that with which I have hunted the cougar and the black bear in the Rocky Mountains would, I am sure, give a good account of any leopard or panther that ever lived. All that would be needed would be a good pack of trained hounds and six or eight first-class fighting dogs in order, as I thoroly believe, completely to clear out the leopard from any given locality.

Mr. Selous' notes on the Cape buffalo and tsetse fly are extremely interesting. But indeed this is true of all that he has written, both of the great game beasts themselves and of his adventures in hunting them. His book is a genuine contribution alike to hunting lore and to natural history. It should be welcomed by every lover of the chase and by every man who cares for the wild, free life of the wilderness. It should be no less welcome to all who are interested in the life-histories of the most formidable and interesting of the beasts that dwell in our world to-day.

THEODORE ROOSEVELT.

THE WHITE HOUSE,
May 23, 1907.

CONTENTS

CHAPTER I

NOTES ON THE QUESTIONS OF PROTECTIVE COLORATION, RECOGNITION MARKS, AND THE INFLUENCE OF ENVIRONMENT ON LIVING ORGANISMS

CHAPTER II

FURTHER NOTES ON THE QUESTIONS OF PROTECTIVE COLORATION, RECOGNITION MARKS, AND THE INFLUENCE OF ENVIRONMENT ON LIVING ORGANISMS

CHAPTER III

NOTES ON THE LION

CHAPTER IV

NOTES ON THE LION (*continued*)

CHAPTER V

NOTES ON THE LION (*concluded*)

CHAPTER VI

NOTES ON THE SPOTTED HYÆNA

CHAPTER VII

NOTES ON WILD DOGS AND CHETAHS

CHAPTER X

NOTES ON THE BLACK OR PREHENSILE-LIPPED RHINOCEROS

CHAPTER XI

NOTES ON THE GIRAFFE

CHAPTER XII

A JOURNEY TO AMATONGALAND IN SEARCH OF INYALA

CHAPTER XIII

A JOURNEY TO AMATONGALAND (*concluded*)

CHAPTER XIV

NOTES ON THE GEMSBUCK

CHAPTER XV

SOME CURIOUS HUNTING EXPERIENCES

CHAPTER XVI

FURTHER CURIOUS HUNTING EXPERIENCES

CHAPTER XVII

INCIDENTS OF A JOURNEY THROUGH THE NORTHERN KALAHARI

CHAPTER XVIII

THE LAST OF SOUTH AFRICA'S GAME HAUNTS

CHAPTER XIX

HOW I SPENT CHRISTMAS DAY 1879

CHAPTER XX

NOTES ON THE MASARWA: THE BUSHMEN OF THE INTERIOR OF SOUTH AFRICA

ILLUSTRATIONS

CHAPTER I

NOTES ON THE QUESTIONS OF PROTECTIVE COLORATION, RECOGNITION MARKS, AND THE INFLUENCE OF ENVIRONMENT ON LIVING ORGANISMS

Harmony of colour in nature—Theory of protective coloration—Sexual selection — Conspicuous colours not harmful — The influence of environment—The leucoryx—The Barbary sheep—The Sardinian moufflon—African butterflies—Coloration of the musk-ox and caribou—Arctic hares and foxes—Coloration of mammals in the Yukon Territory—The chamois in winter—Examples of conspicuous coloration in African mammals—Colour not always protective—Carnivorous animals usually hunt by scent—Wild dogs and wolves—Wild dog and sable antelope—Sense of smell in herbivorous animals—Sight of antelopes—Experience with waterbuck—Dull sight of caribou—Demeanour of wild animals when alarmed—Small antelopes—Lions—Large antelopes—Difficulty of seeing wild animals sometimes exaggerated—Powers of sight of Bushmen—Colour not protective against animals which hunt by night and by scent—Animals in motion easy to see—Restlessness of wild animals—Lions attacking bullocks—Zebras the principal prey of lions since the disappearance of buffaloes—Appearance of zebras—Undoubtedly conspicuous animals in open country—Zebras by moonlight—Strong smell of zebras—Conspicuous antelopes in East Africa—Effect of the juxtaposition of black and white—Bold coloration of the sable antelope.

ALTHOUGH there are certain striking exceptions to the general rule, yet, broadly speaking, it cannot be gainsaid that living organisms are usually coloured in such a way as to make them difficult of detection by the human eye amongst their natural surroundings. Every collecting entomologist knows how closely certain species of butterflies when resting with closed wings in shady forests resemble dead leaves, or moths the bark of trees. Birds too, especially those which nest on the ground, often harmonise with their surroundings in a most marvellous way.

In the open treeless regions within the Arctic Circle, as well as on bare mountain ranges, nearly all the resident species of animals and birds turn white in winter, when their whole visible world is covered with an unbroken mantle of pure white snow, and become brown or grey during the short period of summer.

In treeless deserts again within the tropics, where the rainfall is very scanty and the climate excessively hot and dry, with intense sunlight throughout the year, all resident living organisms, mammals, birds, reptiles, and insects, are found to be of a dull coloration which harmonises in the most wonderful way with the sandy or stony soil on which they live. It is also very often the case that animals which live in forests where the foliage is not too dense to allow the sun to penetrate are spotted or striped, whilst those which live in really thick jungle or amongst deep gloomy ravines are of a uniform dark coloration.

Now a most interesting question arises as to the true causes which have brought about the extraordinary variations of colour to be seen in living organisms inhabiting different parts of the world.

It is, I believe, the general opinion of modern naturalists that, putting aside cases where brilliant colours may have been produced amongst birds and insects by the action of the law of sexual selection, the coloration of all living organisms is protective, "serving," as that distinguished naturalist Mr. Alfred Russel Wallace puts it, when discussing the subject of the coloration of mammals, "to conceal herbivorous species from their enemies, and enabling carnivorous animals to approach their prey unperceived."

Many very striking facts can be adduced in support of this theory, and no doubt it is of advantage to most species of mammals, birds, reptiles, and insects to harmonise in colour with their surroundings; but there are many instances in nature, especially amongst birds and insects, where a very striking and conspicuous coloration does not appear to have been prejudicial to the life of a species.

The highly decorative but very conspicuously coloured plumage to be seen in the males of many species of birds, especially during the breeding season, was considered by the immortal Darwin to be due to the influence of sexual selection, and whatever may be urged against the correctness of this theory, it is supported by a long array of indisputable facts.

Great, however, as is the divergence between the plumage of the males and females in many species of birds, not only during the breeding season, but in a great number of cases at all times of year, and however gaudy and conspicuous the coloration of the former may be compared with that of the latter, such conspicuous coloration never appears to be prejudicial to the life of a species, though in some cases the brighter coloured male assists the female in incubation, and it would thus appear that in all such cases the sombre coloured plumage of the female was not absolutely necessary for purposes of protection against enemies.

I therefore think that if it is admitted that bright and conspicuous colours have been evolved in living organisms through the action of the law of sexual selection, without detriment to the life of the species in which such conspicuous colours are shown, it must be conceded that a coloration harmonising with its surroundings is not a necessity of existence in all cases to all species of mammals, birds, reptiles, and insects, and that it is therefore quite possible that where living organisms agree very closely in colour with their surroundings, such harmonious coloration may have been produced by some other agency than the need for protection by colour, and I would suggest that in addition to the influence exerted in the evolution of colour in living organisms by the action of sexual selection, and the necessity for protection against enemies, a third factor has also been at work, which I will call the influence of environment.

It is worthy of remark, I think, that in hot, dry deserts, where the climatic conditions are stable, and where the general colour of the landscape is therefore very much the same all the year round, *all* the resident species of mammals, birds, reptiles, and insects are what is called protectively coloured, that is to say, they are *all* of a dull brown or greyish coloration,[1] which harmonises beautifully with their parched, dull-coloured environment. In the leucoryx, the Saharan representative of the gemsbuck of South-Western Africa, all the black markings which are so conspicuous in the latter animal have disappeared or become pale brown, whilst the general colour of the body has been bleached to a dirty white. Now, no one can persuade me that if the leucoryx were coloured exactly like its near relative the gemsbuck, it would suffer one iota more, in the open country in which it lives, from the attacks of carnivorous animals than it does at present, and I therefore believe that the faded

[1] The cock ostrich is, I think, the only exception to this rule, and in the case of this remarkable bird the influence of sexual selection has probably been more potent than that of a dull-coloured, monotonous environment.

colour of the leucoryx, as compared with that of the gemsbuck or the beisa antelope, has not been brought about in order to serve as a protection against enemies, but is directly due to the influence of its desert environment, and constant exposure to strong sunlight on treeless plains. Again, from the point of view of a carnivorous animal hunting for food by daylight and by sight, no two countries could be more alike than the open karoos of the Cape Colony and the plains in the neighbourhood of Lakes Nakuru and Elmenteita in British East Africa, where the grass is always kept very short by the large herds of game, as well as by the cattle, sheep, and goats belonging to the Masai, which pasture there. Before the advent of Europeans, the carnivorous animals inhabiting the Cape Colony were exactly the same as those found to-day in East Africa, viz. lions, leopards, chetahs, wild dogs, and hyænas. In both districts lions were once numerous, and in both zebras formed the principal food of these carnivora. But whereas *Equus granti*, the form of zebra found on the plains near Lake Nakuru, is the most brilliantly coloured representative of the genus to which it belongs, with jet black stripes on a pure white ground, the now extinct form of zebra—*Equus quagga*—which once abounded on the plains of the Cape Colony, was of a dull grey brown in ground colour, with darker brown stripes on the head, neck, and fore-part of the body alone. Now, these two races of zebras, both living on bare, open plains, could not both have been coloured in the best possible way to escape being seen by the lions which constantly preyed upon them. If, as has been contended, the juxtaposition of the black and white stripes in Grant's zebras renders these animals not only inconspicuous, but almost invisible under strong sunlight on an open plain, and is, in fact, the supreme triumph of protective coloration in large mammals, why had the quaggas of the Cape Colony become dull brown, for they also lived on open plains in strong sunlight, and needed protection from the lions every bit as much as their congeners of East Africa? Moreover, I think all naturalists and embryologists are agreed that *Equus quagga* was the descendant of boldly striped ancestors.

To my mind the loss of stripes in the quagga was entirely due to the environment in which this species had lived for long ages; for on the karoos of the Cape Colony everything is of one dull brown colour, whether on hill or plain, and no shade is to be found anywhere, for the whole country is without trees. The air, too, is intensely hot and dry, and the rainfall scanty. In these semi-deserts of South-Western Africa, not only did the quaggas lose their black stripes, but the elands also lost the white stripes of their immediate ancestors, whilst the blesboks had already lost much of the white to be seen in the body colouring of the bonteboks, from which they are descended, and had become of a much duller colour generally. In East Africa, however, the plains are surrounded by well-wooded hills, which give some colour to the landscape, whilst the rainfall every year is heavy. If it is not the influence of their several environments which has brought about the differences between the well-striped elands and zebras of East Africa and their dull-coloured relatives that once lived in the karoos of the Cape Colony, the theory of protective coloration must be equally at fault, for in spite of the fact that in both countries both races of these animals have been hunted by lions from time immemorial on open plains, and under precisely similar conditions, they developed very different schemes of coloration.

The Barbary sheep, again, which inhabits the dry

hills bordering the deserts of Northern Africa, where the vegetation is parched and scanty at all seasons of the year, and the rocks of a red brown colour, is itself of a uniform reddish brown which harmonises exactly with its surroundings, and makes it very difficult to detect when lying at rest amongst rocks. This perfect harmony of coloration with its surroundings in the Barbary sheep may have been brought about by the need of protection from enemies, but seems to me far more likely to have been caused by the influence of the colour of its environment, for its four-footed foes hunt by scent and by night far more than by sight during the daytime.

The male moufflon of Sardinia, which lives in a temperate climate where the colours of its surroundings are much brighter and more diversified than is the case in the habitat of the Barbary sheep, is a much more conspicuously coloured animal than the latter, or than the females of its own kind. As the females and young of the Sardinian moufflon, which are of a uniform brown colour, are more difficult to see than the males in their somewhat conspicuous autumn and winter coats, the latter cannot be said to be protectively coloured. Either through the influence of sexual selection or that of an environment the general colour of which varies very greatly at different seasons of the year, the male of the Sardinian moufflon becomes during autumn and winter conspicuously coloured compared with the female, without detriment, however, to the well-being of the species.

During my long sojourn in the interior of South Africa, I made large collections of butterflies. There was one species (*Precis artaxia*, Hewits) which always puzzled me. This handsome insect is only found in shady forests, is seldom seen flying until disturbed, and always sits on the ground amongst dead leaves. Though handsomely coloured on the upper side, when its wings are closed it closely resembles a dead leaf. It has a little tail on the lower wing which looks exactly like the stalk of a leaf, and from this tail a dark brown line runs through both wings (which on the under sides are light brown) to the apex of the upper wing. One would naturally be inclined to look upon this wonderful resemblance to a dead leaf in a butterfly sitting with closed wings on the ground amongst real dead leaves as a remarkable instance of protective form and coloration. And of course it may be that this is the correct explanation. But what enemy is this butterfly protected against? Upon hundreds of different occasions I have ridden and walked through the forests where *Precis artaxia* was numerous, and I have caught and preserved many specimens of these butterflies, but never once did I see a bird attempting to catch one of them. Indeed, birds of all kinds were scarce in the forests where these insects were to be found. I now think that the form and colour of the under wings of *Precis artaxia* have more probably been produced by the influence of its environment than by the need for protection.

During the rainy season in South Africa, the open glades in the forests bordering the rivers are gay with multitudes of brightly coloured butterflies of many different species, and after a night's rain butterflies of various kinds may often be seen settling in masses round pools of water along waggon roads. Most of these butterflies are conspicuously coloured, though they are in perfect harmony with the sunlit flowers which spring up at the time of year when they appear. I cannot, however, believe that the need for protection against birds or other enemies has had anything whatever to do with the determination of their various colours, as in all my experience (and I have been all my life a close observer of nature) I have never once seen a bird feeding upon butterflies in Africa.

The coloration of certain animals in the Arctic and sub-Arctic Regions is somewhat remarkable, as at certain seasons it is conspicuously out of harmony with its surroundings, and cannot therefore be protective. The musk ox retains it dark brown coat the whole year round, although it lives almost constantly amidst a snowy environment. Mr. Wallace tells us that the reason why the musk ox does not turn white is because it has no enemies to fear, and therefore has no need of a protective coloration. He says: "Then we have that thoroughly Arctic animal the musk sheep, which is brown and conspicuous; but this animal is gregarious, and its safety depends on its association in small herds. It is therefore of more importance for it to be able to recognise its kind at a distance than to be concealed from its enemies, against which it can well protect itself so long as it keeps together in a compact body." As, however, according to the experience of Arctic travellers, large numbers of young musk oxen are annually killed by wolves, this explanation of a case in which an animal is manifestly not protectively coloured does not seem altogether satisfactory. Mr. Wallace, it may be noted, calls special attention to the coloration of the giraffe, which he considers to be protective; yet nothing, I think, is more certain than that a far smaller percentage of giraffes are killed annually by lions in Africa than of musk oxen by wolves in Arctic America. If this is so, the musk ox has more need of protective coloration than the giraffe. The musk ox is, I think, the only one amongst the few truly Arctic mammals which does not turn white during the winter months, for, unlike the barren ground caribou, it does not migrate southwards in the autumn to the dark spruce forests, which change of habitat no doubt has had an influence on the colour of the latter animals; since Peary's caribou, the most northerly form of the genus, whose habitat lies far within the Arctic Circle, where trees of any kind are non-existent, is almost absolutely white in colour. In spite, however, of the fact that the caribou inhabiting Ellesmere Land and the adjacent land masses are white, and therefore harmonise well in colour with the snowy wastes amongst which they live, they form the principal food of the white wolves inhabiting the same regions, which hunt them by scent and run them down just as easily as the grey and black wolves of Alaska capture the dark-coloured and very conspicuous caribou which frequent the mountain ranges of that country. It appears to me that the colour of a caribou's coat, whether it be white, black, or brown, cannot afford it any protection against wolves, which probably possess as keen a sense of scent as any animals in the world, and must surely hunt entirely by scent during the long dark months of the Arctic winter. If this is so, then the great diversity in the coloration of the various species of caribou inhabiting the North American Continent must be due to some other cause than the necessity for protection against wolves, practically their only four-footed enemies.

Speaking of other Arctic animals, Mr. Wallace believes that the Arctic fox *of necessity* turns white in winter in order to enable it to capture the white Arctic hares upon which it chiefly lives. Very little, however, is known as to the life-history of these two animals. But if the Arctic foxes hunt by scent, as they almost certainly do, during the constant darkness of the long Arctic winter, and the hares burrow beneath the snow, and are caught as a rule when completely hidden from sight below its surface, I think it is arguable that the influence of environment has been at least as potent a factor in bringing about the white coloration of these animals in winter as the necessity for protective coloration. At any rate, in Alaska and the Yukon Territory of Canada, where the country is covered with snow for more than half the year, and where the hares are white throughout the long winter, the foxes are red, black, or a mixture of these two colours, all the year round, and the lynxes grey ; yet these two species of carnivorous animals depend almost entirely on the hares for their food supply. It is somewhat remarkable that in the sub-Arctic forests of Alaska and the Yukon Territory, where the cold is intense and the ground covered with snow for so many months of every year, only the hares and the stoats amongst mammals turn white in winter. But in these countries the land is covered for the most part with dark spruce forests, the influence of which —if there is anything in the influence of environment—may have been greater in determining the coloration of the mammals of this district than that of the snow-covered ground.

During winter in the Yukon Territory, moose turn very dark in colour on the under parts of the body, and at this season of the year leave the thick forests and live in the comparatively open valleys amongst willow and birch scrub, where they are said to stand out like haystacks amidst their snowy surroundings. The local race of caribou (*Rangifer osborni*), which live all the year round on the treeless mountain plateaus, are very dark in colour (with the exception of their necks), and, as I myself can testify, stand out very plainly when the open ground they frequent is covered with snow. Of the various races of wild sheep inhabiting the mountains of Alaska, the Yukon Territory, and Northern British Columbia, some are white all the year round, and therefore very conspicuous in summer when there is no snow on the ground, though difficult to detect in the winter; some are grey, with white heads, necks, and rumps; whilst others are nearly black, and therefore very conspicuous in winter. Of the predatory animals the large timber wolves are, as a rule, pale greyish brown with black hairs on their backs and shoulders, but a considerable number are quite black; the foxes are either red or black, or of the intermediate coloration known as "cross"; whilst the wolverines, martens, and minks are rich dark brown, and the lynxes neutral grey. The stoat or ermine is the only carnivorous animal which turns white in winter in these countries.

It would thus appear that in the sub-Arctic Regions of North America the coloration of mammals does not obviously serve the purpose of concealing the herbivorous species from their enemies, or of enabling carnivorous animals to approach their prey unperceived. To come nearer home, we find that whereas in the Alpine regions of Europe the mountain hare turns white in winter, the chamois living in the same snow-covered ground becomes deep black. It is true that in winter chamois often leave the open mountains and live amongst the higher forests, where it may be said that their dark colour harmonises well with the dark foliage of the spruce trees; but I have hunted chamois in December in the mountains of Transylvania, when they were in full winter coat, and I certainly found that their dark coloration often made them conspicuous.

Turning to Africa, we have many instances of what seen in the open and at short range cannot possibly be called anything but conspicuous coloration, such as the jet black and pure white striping of the East African form of Burchell's zebra; the deep glossy black body and neck, with snow-white belly and parti-coloured face, of the sable antelope;

the black and white face of the gemsbuck; the pure white face and rump of the bontebok, combined with the beautiful dark brown neck and sides and lilac tinted back; or the juxtaposition of the black and white in Thomson's gazelle—only to mention a few of the most noteworthy examples.

To me it seems that the influence of environment might very well be deemed sufficient of itself to cause all animals that have lived for long ages in treeless deserts under constant strong sunlight to assume the dull brown coloration which they undoubtedly possess; whilst Arctic conditions might be expected to cause the whitening of an animal's hair in the winter, or the play of the sun's light through the leaves and branches of trees and bushes to be responsible for a spotted or striped coat. In the case of a combination of black and white—the two most conspicuous colours in nature—such as may be seen in the adult cock ostrich or male sable antelope, why should it not be supposed that the law of sexual selection has come into play, as it probably has done in the production of the lion's mane and the exaggerated size of the horns in the male koodoo.

Having spent many years of my life in the constant pursuit of African game, I have certainly been afforded opportunities such as have been enjoyed by but few civilised men of becoming intimately acquainted with the habits and life-history of many species of animals living in that continent, and all that I have learnt during my long experience as a hunter compels me to doubt the correctness of the now very generally accepted theories that all the wonderfully diversified colours of mammals —the stripes of the zebra, the blotched coat of the giraffe, the spots of the bushbuck, the white face and rump of the bontebok, to mention only a few —have been evolved either as a means of protection from enemies or for the purpose of mutual recognition by animals of the same species in times of sudden alarm. Sexual selection and the influence of environment must, I think, have been equally potent factors in the evolution of colours in mammals, birds, reptiles, and insects.

In all recent articles which I have read by well-known naturalists on these subjects, it appears to be assumed that both carnivorous and herbivorous animals trust entirely to their sense of sight, the former to find their prey, and the latter to detect and avoid the approach of their enemies. Yet nothing is more certain than that all carnivorous animals hunt almost entirely by scent, until they have closely approached their quarry, and usually by night, when all the animals on which they prey must look very much alike as far as colour is concerned.

The wild dogs of Africa and the wolves of northern latitudes are not so completely nocturnal, it is true, as the large Felidae, but the former I know, and the latter I have every reason to believe, hunt, as a rule, by night and only occasionally in the daytime. In both these animals the sense of smell is enormously developed, and must be of far greater use to them in procuring food than the sense of sight, however acute that may be. In all my wanderings I have only seen African wild dogs chasing game in the daytime on four occasions. I once saw a single wild dog chasing a sable antelope in the daytime. This wild dog—which was, however, then too far away to enable me to see what it was —first ran past the sable antelope and behind it from where I was watching. It must then have been running on the trail, with its nose on the ground, and must have passed quite close to the animal it was pursuing without seeing it. Its nose, however, kept it on the antelope's tracks and soon brought it to close quarters, and then of course it continued the chase by sight. Now if this is the usual proceeding of African wild dogs, and I am convinced that it is, the value of assimilative coloration to animals on which the wild dog preys cannot be very great.

But not only do all carnivorous animals hunt by scent, and rely far more upon their olfactory organs than upon their keenness of sight to procure food, but, as all practical hunters very well know, the sense of smell is also very highly developed in all, or at any rate in most, of the animals on which the carnivora prey, and personally I am persuaded that all browsing and grazing animals in Africa trust as much to their noses as to their eyes both to avoid danger and to find members of their own species. The eyes of antelopes are quick to detect a moving object, but they are by no means quick to notice any unusual colour in a stationary object. I will relate an anecdote illustrating this point.

Early in 1883, I reached the spot on the Hanyani river in Mashunaland where I intended to establish my hunting camp for the season. Whilst my Kafirs were chopping down trees to build the cattle enclosures, I climbed to the top of the ridge at the foot of which I was having my camp made.

It was late in the afternoon, and I was sitting on a rock looking over the open country to the south, when I heard a slight noise, and turning my eyes saw a fine male waterbuck coming towards me up the ridge. I sat perfectly still, and it presently walked slowly past within three yards of me and then went on along the ridge, into the forest beyond. As it passed me I noticed its shining wet nose, and the way in which its nostrils kept constantly opening and shutting at every step. It was evidently listening to the noise that my Kafirs were making chopping down small trees at the foot of the ridge, but as it could not get their wind did not take alarm.

Of course, if I had made the very slightest movement, this waterbuck would have seen me instantly; but had it possessed much sense of colour, the contrast between the red brown of my sunburnt arms and face and the light-coloured shirt I was wearing would have attracted its attention, as I was sitting on a stone, on the top of a ridge which was quite free from trees or bush. I have never had any other African antelopes pass so close to me as this without seeing me, but many have fed slowly past me, as I sat watching them, with a tree or a bush behind me but nothing between myself and them, at distances of from 20 to 50 yards.

Both in Newfoundland and in the Yukon Territory of Canada, I have had caribou walk almost over me when sitting in front of them on their line of march on ground devoid of any cover whatever. In such cases, of course, the wind was blowing from these animals towards where I was sitting, and I remained absolutely motionless.

As a rule, when wild animals notice something suspicious approaching, say a man on horseback, and cannot get the scent of it, they run off before it gets near them or circle round to try and get the wind of it. But the smaller African antelopes, steinbucks, duikers, oribis, and reedbucks will occasionally, while keeping their eyes fixed on the unfamiliar object, crouch slowly down, and then, with their necks stretched along the ground, lie watching. I have ridden past a few oribis, steinbucks, and reedbucks within a few yards, as they lay absolutely motionless on the ground watching me. To pull in one's horse with the intention of shooting such a crouching antelope was the instant signal for it to jump up and bound away. Lions too, when they see a human being and imagine that they themselves have not been observed, will often lie flat on the ground watching, and will not move until very closely approached. I imagine that these carnivora secure nearly all their prey by approaching herds of game below the wind, and when they have got pretty near lying flat on the ground, perfectly motionless except for the twitching of the end of their tails, which they never seem able to control, and then waiting till one or other of the unsuspecting animals feeds close up to them, when they rush upon and seize it before it has time to turn. If a lion, however, fails to make good his hold with one of his forepaws over the muzzle of a buffalo or one of the heavier antelopes, and cannot fix his teeth in their throats or necks, they often manage to throw him off and escape.

It is perhaps worthy of remark that I have never known a case of one of the larger antelopes trying to escape observation by lying down. Gemsbucks, roan and sable antelopes, elands, koodoos, hartebeests, indeed all the large African antelopes, directly they see anything suspicious, face towards it, and stand looking at it, holding their heads high, and not in any way shielding their bodies and only exposing their faces to view, which, when marked with black and white, as in the case of the gemsbuck and roan antelope, are supposed, though quite erroneously, to render these animals invisible.

I am inclined to think, but it is only my personal opinion, that the difficulty of seeing wild animals in their natural surroundings has been greatly exaggerated by travellers who were not hunters, and whose eyesight therefore, although of normal strength, had not been trained by practice to see animals quickly in every kind of environment.

I am quite sure that to a South-African Bushman

there is no such thing as protective coloration in nature. If an animal is behind a rock or a thick bush, he of course cannot see it, but his eyes are so well trained, he knows so exactly the appearance of every animal to be met with in the country in which he and his ancestors have spent their lives as hunters for countless ages, that he will not miss seeing any living thing that comes within his range of vision no matter what its surroundings may be. Bantu Kafirs are often called savages, and their quickness of sight extolled; but Kafirs are not real savages, and though there are good hunters amongst them, such men will form but a small percentage of any one tribe. To realise to what a pitch of perfection the human eyesight can be trained, not in seeing immense distances but in picking up an animal within a moderate range immediately it is physically possible to see it, it is necessary to hunt with real savages like the Masarwa Bushmen of South-Western Africa, who depend on their eyesight for a living.

Now, if carnivorous animals had throughout the ages depended on their eyesight for their daily food as the Bushmen have done, which is what naturalists who believe in the value of protective coloration to large mammals must imagine to be the case, surely their eyesight would have become so perfected that no colour or combination of colours could have concealed any of the animals on which they habitually preyed from their view. As a matter of fact, however, carnivorous animals hunt as a rule by scent and not by sight, and usually at night when herbivorous animals are moving about feeding or going to drink. At such a time it appears to me that the value of a coloration that assimilated perfectly with an animal's natural surroundings during the daytime would be very small as a protection from the attacks of carnivora which hunted by night and by scent.

Reverting again to the question of quickness of eyesight, I will say that, although a Boer or an English hunter can never hope to become as keen-sighted as a Bushman, his eyes will nevertheless improve so much in power after a few years spent in the constant pursuit of game, that the difficulty of distinguishing wild animals amongst their native haunts will be very much less than it was when he first commenced to hunt, or than it must always be to a traveller or sportsman who has not had a long experience of hunting.

However difficult an animal may be to see as long as it is lying down or standing motionless, as soon as it moves it becomes very apparent to the human eye; and, as I have had ample experience that any movement made by a man is very quickly noticed by a lion, leopard, hyæna, or wild dog, I am quite sure that all these carnivora, if lying watching for prey by daylight, would at once see any animal moving about feeding anywhere near them; and all herbivorous animals move about and feed early in the morning and late in the evening, the very times when carnivorous animals would be most likely to be looking for game by daylight.

During the heat of the day carnivorous animals are very seldom seen, as at that time they sleep, and most herbivorous animals do the same. But even when resting, wild animals are seldom motionless. Elephants and rhinoceroses are constantly moving their ears, whilst giraffes, elands, buffaloes, zebras, and other animals seldom stand for many seconds together without swishing their tails. All these movements at once attract the attention of the trained human eye, and I am very sure would be equally apparent to the sight of a lion or a leopard, were these animals to hunt by sight and during the daytime. But, speaking generally, they do not do so, though doubtless should antelopes or other animals unconsciously feed close up to where a lion happened to be lying resting and waiting for night before commencing active hunting, he would very likely make a rush and try and seize one of them if he could. Upon two occasions I have had my bullocks attacked in the middle of the day, once by a single lioness, and on the other occasion by a party of four lions, two lions and two lionesses. But how many old hunters have seen lions actually hunting in the full light of day? Personally, in all the long years I was hunting big game in Africa—years during which I must have walked or ridden many thousands of miles through country full of game, and where lions were often numerous—I only once saw one of these animals hunting by daylight. This lion was pursuing four koodoo cows on a cool cloudy winter's morning.

As a rule, lions do not commence to hunt before darkness has set in. They then seek their prey by scent, either smelling the animals directly or following their tracks. They understand as well as the most experienced human hunter the art of approaching game below the wind, when hunting singly; but when there are several lions hunting together, I believe that some of them will sometimes creep close up to a herd of game below the wind, whilst one or more of their number go round to the other side. The buffaloes, zebras, or antelopes at once get the scent of these latter, and run off right on to the lions lying waiting below the wind, which then get a good chance to seize and pull down one of the frightened animals. As lions have played this game with my cattle upon several occasions, I presume that they often act in the same way with wild animals.

No matter how dark the night may be, a lion has no difficulty in seizing an ox, a horse, or a donkey exactly in the right way, and I have no doubt that he does the same in the case of all the different kinds of game upon which he preys. Now that the buffaloes have been almost exterminated by the rinderpest in most parts of Africa, the zebra undoubtedly forms the favourite food of the lion. For every zebra that is killed by daylight probably at least a hundred are killed during the night, when, except by moonlight, they would appear to a lion very much the same, as far as coloration goes, as a black ox, a dark grey wildebeest, or a red hartebeest, all of which animals look black by night if they are near enough to be seen at all.

I have had innumerable opportunities of looking at wild zebras, and when met with on open ground they certainly have always appeared to me to be very conspicuous animals, except just at dawn and late in the evening, when they are not so easy to see as animals of some uniform dark colour, such as hartebeests.

In Southern Africa, between the Limpopo and the Zambesi rivers, Burchell's zebras used to be very plentiful in all the uninhabited parts of the country, and although they were often met with feeding or resting in districts covered with open forest or scattered bush, I found them always very partial to open ground, where they were as plainly visible as a troop of horses. In East Africa the local race of Burchell's zebra is remarkable for the whiteness of the ground colour of the body and the intense blackness of the superimposed stripes. These beautiful animals congregate in large herds on the bare open plains traversed by the Uganda Railway, and probably form the chief food of the lions living in that district.

When in East Africa a few years ago, I took special note of the appearance of zebras at different distances on the open plains between Lakes Nakuru and Elmenteita. I found that in the bright African sunlight I could see with the naked eye the black and white striping of their coats up to a distance which I estimated at about 400 yards. Beyond that distance they looked of a uniform dark colour when the sun was behind them, and almost white when the sun was shining on them. But at whatever distance they happened to be on the open plain between myself and the horizon, their forms showed up quite as distinctly as those of a herd of cattle or horses. Never in my life have I seen the sun shining on zebras in such a way as to cause them to become invisible or even in any way inconspicuous on an open plain, and I have seen thousands upon thousands of Burchell's zebras. Should these animals be approached when standing amongst trees with the leaf on, they are not at all easy to see, and the whisking of their tails will probably be the first thing to catch one's eye; but in open ground, and that is where they are usually met with, no animals could be more conspicuous. I have seen zebras too by moonlight, but that was many years ago, and I did not then take any special note of their appearance; but my impression is that they were no more invisible than other animals, but looked whitish in colour when the moon was shining on them, and very dark when it was behind them. As, however, zebras have a very strong smell, and lions usually hunt them by scent and at night, I cannot think that their coloration, whether it be conspicuous or not, matters very much to them, though I look upon the theory that the brilliantly striped coats of these animals render them in reality inconspicuous as absolutely untenable, as it is not in accordance with fact.

When in East Africa I came to the conclusion that not only the zebras, but also the impala antelopes—which are of a much richer and darker red than in South Africa—were conspicuously coloured,

CHAPTER II

FURTHER NOTES ON THE QUESTIONS OF PROTECTIVE COLORATION, RECOGNITION MARKS, AND THE INFLUENCE OF ENVIRONMENT ON LIVING ORGANISMS

Occasional resemblance of African mammals to natural objects—Hartebeests—Elephants—Giraffes—Coloration of the Somali giraffe—Giraffes not in need of a protective coloration—Koodoos and sable antelopes—Acute sense of hearing in the moose—Possible explanation of large size of ears in the African tragelaphine antelopes—Coloration of bushbucks, situtungas, and inyalas—Leopards the only enemies of the smaller bush-haunting antelopes—Recognition marks—Must render animals conspicuous to friend and foe alike—Ranges of allied species of antelopes seldom overlap—Hybridisation sometimes takes place—Wonderful coloration of the bontebok—Coloration distinctly conspicuous and therefore not protective—Recognition marks unnecessary—Coloration of the blesbok—The blesbok merely a duller coloured bontebok—Difference in the habitat of the two species—The coloration of both species may be due to the influence of their respective environments—The weak point in the theory of protective coloration when applied to large mammals—Hares and foxes in the Arctic and sub-Arctic Regions—The efficacy of colour protection at once destroyed by movement—Buffaloes and lions—General conclusions regarding the theory of protective coloration as applied to large mammals.

CERTAIN observations have been made and theories propounded on the occasional resemblance of African mammals to natural objects, which have never seemed to me to have much significance, although they are often referred to as valuable observations by writers on natural history.

Thus it has been said that hartebeests, which are

red in colour, derive protection from their enemies owing to their resemblance not only in colour but also in shape to ant-heaps, and that giraffes gain an advantage in the struggle for life owing to the fact that their long necks look like tree-trunks and their heads and horns like broken branches.

Well, hartebeests are red in colour wherever they are found all over Africa. Ant-heaps are only red when they are built of red soil. In parts of the Bechwanaland Protectorate, where the Cape hartebeest used to be common, the ant-heaps are a glaring white. In East Africa, in different portions of which territory hartebeests of three species are very numerous, all of which are bright red in colour, red ant-heaps are certainly not a conspicuous feature in all parts of the country, and there were, if my memory serves me, very few ant-heaps of any size on the plains where I met with either Coke's, Neumann's, or Jackson's hartebeests.[1] But even in those districts where the ant-heaps are red in colour, and neither very much larger nor smaller than hartebeests, they are usually of one even rounded shape, and it would only be here and there, where two had been thrown up together forming a double-humped structure, that anything resembling one of these animals could be seen. Such unusual natural objects must be anything but common, and cannot, I believe, have had any effect in determining the bodily shape of hartebeests, though, if the coloration of animals is influenced by their environment, red soil and red ant-heaps may have had their influence on the colour of the ancestral form from which all the various but nearly allied species of hartebeests have been derived.

I was once hunting in 1885 with a Boer friend

[1] The plains along the railway line between Simba and Nairobi, the open country between Lakes Nakuru and Elmenteita, or the neighbourhood of the road between Landiani and Ravine Station.

(Cornelis van Rooyen) near the Umfuli river in Mashunaland. We were riding slowly along, followed by some Kafirs, and driving a donkey carrying corn for the horses in front of us, when we saw what we took to be some boulders of black rock in the open forest ahead, but some distance away, as we were crossing an open valley at the time. In this particular part of the country great boulders of black rock were a common feature in the landscape. Suddenly our donkey pricked his ears, and stretching out his nose, commenced to bray loudly. Immediately one of the black rocks, as we had thought them to be, moved, and we soon saw that what we had taken for rocks were elephants. Our donkey had smelt them before either my friend or myself or any of our Kafirs had been able to distinguish what they were. As, however, elephants are only occasionally encountered in forests through which great boulders of black rock are scattered, I do not believe that these huge quadrupeds have been moulded to the shape of rocks by the need of a protective resemblance to inanimate objects, any more than I think that the abnormal shape of certain ant-heaps has had anything to do with the production of the high wither and drooping hindquarters of the hartebeest.

As to the theory that the long neck and the peculiarly formed head of the giraffe have been evolved in order to protect this remarkable animal against its carnivorous foes, by giving it the appearance of a dead or decayed tree, I personally consider such an idea to be so fantastic and extravagant as to be unworthy of serious consideration.

In the course of my own hunting experience, I have shot a great many giraffes to obtain a supply of food for my native followers, and under the guidance of Bushmen have followed on the tracks of many herds of these animals until I at length sighted them.

In certain parts of the country frequented by giraffes in Southern Africa, large camel-thorn trees (*Acacia giraffae*) grow either singly or a few together amongst a wide expanse of wait-a-bit-thorn scrub, which is from 6 to 12 feet high. From time to time these large trees die and decay, until nothing is left but a tall straight stem, standing up like a telegraph pole (only a good deal thicker) amongst the surrounding scrub. When, whilst following on giraffe spoor through such country, something suddenly comes in view protruding from the bush, perhaps a mile ahead, the Bushmen will stop and take a good look at it. Of course at a very great distance it is impossible for even a Bushman to distinguish between the tall straight stem of a dead tree standing up out of low bush and the neck of a solitary old bull giraffe. But if the latter, it is sure soon to move, unless it is standing watching its human enemies approaching, in which case it will not be very far away, and I have never known a Bushman to mistake a giraffe for a tree at any reasonable distance.

As regards the coloration of the species of giraffe inhabiting South and South-Western Africa, it assimilates very well with its surroundings, when amongst trees and bush; but as giraffes spend a great deal of their time passing through open stretches of country on their way from one feeding-ground to another, they are often very conspicuous animals.

With respect to the Somali giraffe (*Giraffa reticulata*), a photograph taken by the photographer who accompanied one of Lord Delamere's expeditions, showing some of these animals feeding amongst mimosa trees, gives the impression of a most marvellous harmonisation of colour and arrangement of marking with their surroundings. But I cannot help thinking that the facts of the case have been very much exaggerated in this photograph, which has eliminated all colours from the picture except black and white. In life, the foliage of the mimosa is very thin, and I think it probable that the rich dark chestnut blotches divided by white lines of the Somali giraffe would show through it at least as distinctly as would the colours of the southern giraffe in a like position. The Somali giraffe cannot constantly live amongst mimosa trees, as these only grow in valleys near streams or dried-up watercourses, and only cover a small proportion of any country I have yet seen either in South or East Africa.

I must say that I rather distrust the camera as a true interpreter of nature, as I have seen so many photographs of the nests of small birds in bushes in which it was very difficult even for a trained eye to find the nest at all, although in all probability it would have been comparatively easy to detect these nests in the actual bushes in which they were placed.

Speaking of the Somali giraffe, Colonel J. J. Harrison, in a footnote to a photograph of one of these animals shot by himself right out in open country, which appeared in the *Bystander* for January 30, 1907, says: "These handsome coloured giraffes are very striking when seen standing in the sun. Of a rich bright chestnut colour, with pure white rings, they stand out splendidly as compared with the dull grey colouring of the more southern giraffe."

However, it appears to me that to whatever extent the coloration of the various races of giraffes harmonises with their surroundings, that result must have been brought about by the influence of their environment rather than by the need of protective coloration, for I cannot believe that the struggle for life against the attacks of carnivorous animals can have been sufficiently severe to have influenced the colour and the arrangement of markings in giraffes. That lions occasionally attack and kill giraffes is an undoubted fact, and, as I shall relate in a subsequent chapter, I have also known a case of a very young giraffe having been attacked by two leopards; but in South Africa giraffes are found in the greatest numbers in those parts of the country where, except during the rainy season, there is very little surface water, and where other species of game are far from plentiful. Into such districts lions do not often penetrate, and when giraffes are found in country where there is plenty of water, zebras, buffaloes, and antelopes of various kinds will also be numerous, and these animals will certainly be preyed upon in preference. At any rate, my own experience would lead me to believe that although lions can and do kill giraffes upon occasion, they do not habitually prey upon these animals. Moreover, when giraffes are killed by lions, they are in all probability followed by scent and killed in the dark.

Altogether, the theory that the colour of the giraffe has been evolved by the necessity for concealment and protection from the attacks of carnivorous animals does not seem to me to be at all well supported by the life-history of that animal as seen by a practical hunter; but the fact that the coloration of this remarkable animal assimilates very well with the dull and monotonous shades of the trees and bushes in the parched and waterless districts it usually frequents, is a strong argument in favour of there being a law which, working through the ages, tends to bring the colours of all organic beings into harmony with their surroundings, irrespective of any special benefit they may receive in the way of protection from enemies by such harmonious coloration.

Turning to the striped and spotted forest antelopes inhabiting various parts of Africa, I think there is some misconception amongst naturalists who have not visited that country as to the general surroundings amongst which the various species live. The magnificent koodoo, with his long spiral horns, striped body, spotted cheeks, nose marked with a white arrow, and throat adorned with a long fringe of hair, is often spoken of as an inhabitant of dense jungle. This is, however, by no means the case, for although koodoos are never found on open plains, they are, on the other hand, seldom met with in really dense jungle.

The range of the koodoo to the south of the Zambesi extends farther to the south and west than that of the sable antelope, but I think I am justified in saying that up to the time of the deplorable visitation of rinderpest in 1896, wherever, between the Limpopo and the Zambesi, sable antelopes were to be met with, there koodoos were also to be found, and outside of districts infested by the "tse-tse" fly, excepting amongst rocky hills, I have never met with the latter animals in any country where I was not able to gallop after them on horseback.

Living as they do in surroundings so very similar to those frequented by sable antelopes, I have never been able to understand why koodoos should have such much larger ears than the former animals. I have never been struck with the acute sense of hearing in koodoos as I have been in the case of the moose of North America, and I should scarcely think that this sense would often save them from the noiseless approach of such animals as lions or leopards, to which they very frequently fall a prey, judging by the number of the remains of koodoo bulls which I have found that had been killed by the former animals.

I have often wondered whether the large size of the ears observable in the African tragelaphine antelopes, which are all forests dwellers (with the exception of the situtunga, which lives in dense beds of reeds), may not be useful to them by enabling the males and females to hear one another's calls during the mating season. The large ears and exquisite sense of hearing of the moose, which is also a forest-dwelling animal, have undoubtedly been developed for the purpose of enabling the males and females to find one another in the breeding season, and not for protection against the attacks of wolves. I have frequently heard both koodoos and bushbucks calling by night and also in the early morning. The noise they make is a sort of bark or cough.

Antelopes inhabiting open plains are very gregarious, and in the daytime would always be able to find their mates by sight. I have never heard them making anything but low grunting noises. As it is often assumed by naturalists that all bush-haunting species of antelopes have very large ears, it is perhaps worth noticing that in the little blue buck and the red bush duiker of South-East Africa, which both live in dense jungle near the coast, the ears are very small; whilst in the steinbuck, on the other hand, which is always found in very open country and never in thick bush, the ears are very large—both long and broad.

The coloration observable in the different races of bushbucks inhabiting different localities, as well as in the situtunga and inyala antelopes, is, I think, very interesting and suggestive. It may, I think, be taken for granted that all the races of African bushbucks have been derived from an ancestral form which was both striped and spotted; but in the bushbucks found near the coast of the Cape Colony and Natal, the adult males are deep dark brown in colour, often absolutely devoid of any white spots or stripes on face or body, whilst the adult females are yellowish red, with only a few white spots on the flanks. Now these most southerly of the African bushbucks live in really dense bush, and often in deep ravines, where the sun never penetrates. Their habitat too being near the sea-coast, the climate must be damper than in the interior of the continent. In the northern parts of Mashunaland and along the Central Zambesi and Chobi rivers the bushbucks live in forest and bush which is seldom very dense, and through most of which the sunlight plays constantly. In these districts the males are, when adult, beautifully striped and spotted, and the ground colour of their coats is rich red and dark brown, the females being of a dark rich red and also well striped and spotted. The situtunga antelopes live (on the Chobi and Central Zambesi) in immense beds of reeds which are always of one dull monotonous greyish green or brown. The adult animals are, as might be expected by those who believe in the direct influence of environment, of a uniform light brown colour, except that the spots on the cheeks and the arrow-shaped mark across the nose, present in most tragelaphine antelopes, are still discernible. In the inyala antelope, which inhabits thick jungly tracts of bush along the south-east coast of Africa, the adult male is of a deep dark grey in general body colour, with a few scarcely visible vertical white stripes. The young males and the adult females are, however, of a brilliant light red colour, profusely striped and spotted with white. The young of all bushbucks and of the inyala are reddish in ground colour, striped and spotted with white. The fœtal young of the situtunga found in the marshes of the Chobi are of the colour of a dark moleskin beautifully banded and spotted with pale yellow, and it is, I think, a very remarkable fact that these stripes and spots are identical in position with those found on the adult Chobi bushbuck, which is strong evidence, I think, that both these animals are descended from one ancestral form.

Now the only animal that preys habitually on bushbucks, inyalas, and situtungas is the leopard, and as leopards hunt by night and by scent, I cannot believe that the very different outward appearance of the various races of bushbucks inhabiting different parts of Africa is to be accounted for by the theory of protective coloration. The males and females of the Cape bushbuck and of the inyala antelope are very different one from another in the colour of their coats, but this does not seem to be prejudicial to either sex, though there is absolutely no difference in their habits or their habitat. In all the different races of bushbucks, however, with which I am acquainted, the males are much darker in colour than the females, so that it is not so very surprising that in the case of the inyala and the Cape bushbuck the males should have been the first to lose their stripes and spots in a sombre environment. In the case of the Cape bushbuck the adult females have already lost all the stripes and most of the spots of the ancestral form. The female inyala is, however, one of the most distinctly striped and spotted representatives of the tragelaphine group.

I cannot see that facts support the opinion that the uniform dull brown coloration of both sexes of the southern race of situtunga has been brought about for the purpose of protection from carnivorous enemies. During the daytime these animals live in the midst of beds of reeds growing in water where they cannot be approached except by wading; but at night they are often killed by leopards, and perhaps sometimes by lions, whilst feeding just outside the reed beds, on open ground which has perhaps been recently swept by a veld fire, and where young reeds and grass are just sprouting.

At such a time their actual colour can be of no more use in the way of protecting them from their keen-scented feline foes than if it were black or red or grey. To me it seems far more probable that the situtunga has gradually lost the stripes and spots of the ancestral form from which it is derived, and assumed a uniform dull brown coloration, because it has lived for ages amongst reed beds of one dull monotonous colour, than because a uniform brown coat affords it a special protection against carnivorous foes.

I gather from the writings of Mr. A. R. Wallace and other well-known naturalists that, whereas the coloration of all animals is supposed to be due to the need of protection from carnivorous beasts, many species have developed in addition what are known as recognition marks, to enable them to distinguish members of their own species from nearly allied forms, or to help them to quickly recognise and rejoin the members of the herd or family from which they may have been separated.

That many large mammals belonging to different genera, and living in widely separated parts of the globe, are marked with conspicuous patches of white on the rump, neck, or face, or throw up bushy tails when running, showing a large white under surface, is an indisputable fact, though it is not possible to say that the possession of such a conspicuous coloration is absolutely necessary to the well-being of any particular species, because there will nearly always be other species living in the same country, and subject to the attacks of the same predatory animals, in which these so-called recognition marks are absent. However, on the supposition that carnivorous animals hunt by sight, it seems to me that no animal can be said to be protectively coloured which is marked in any way so conspicuously as to be recognisable by others of its own species at a distance, for it would be equally recognisable by all predatory animals, and caribou and white-tailed deer or African antelopes cannot escape from wolves or wild dogs by running like rabbits into burrows.

Personally, I cannot see why large antelopes which live in herds on open plains should require special recognition marks, as in such localities the bulk of an animal's whole body would be plainly visible at a great distance no matter what its colour might be. If an antelope became separated from its fellows by night, all so-called recognition marks would be invisible at a very short distance. It must be remembered, however, that every species of animal has a peculiar and very distinctive smell of its own, and my own observations would lead me to believe that most wild animals recognise one another, as a rule, more by scent than by sight.

It seems difficult to believe that there can be any truth in the theory suggested by Mr. Wallace, that recognition marks have been developed in certain species of large mammals because they are necessary to enable nearly allied species of animals to know their own kind at a glance, and so prevent interbreeding; for the ranges of very nearly allied forms of one genus, such as the various species of hartebeests and oryxes, or the bontebok and the blesbok, very seldom overlap, and so each species keeps true of necessity and without the help of special recognition marks. Where the ranges of two nearly allied species do overlap interbreeding probably will take place.

There seems little doubt that the species of hartebeest known as Neumann's hartebeest has interbred with Jackson's hartebeest in certain districts where the ranges of the two species meet. In the neighbourhood of Lake Nakuru, in British East Africa, I shot, in February 1903, a hartebeest which was not a Jackson's hartebeest, but which closely resembled an animal of that species in the character of its horns and the measurements of its skull, whilst all the others in the same herd appeared to be true Neumann's. I have known too of one undoubted case of the interbreeding of the South African hartebeest (*B. Caama*) with the tsessebe (*Damaliscus lunatus*).

This animal (an adult male) was shot by my friend Cornelis van Rooÿen in Western Matabeleland, where the ranges of the two species just overlap. In coloration it was like a tsessebe, but had the comparatively bushy tail of the hartebeest, whilst its skull and horns (which are, I am glad to say, in the collection of the Natural History Museum at South Kensington) are exactly intermediate between those of the two parent species. This skull has been very unsatisfactorily labelled "supposed hybrid between *B. Caama* and *D. lunatus.*" But as, when I presented it to the Natural History Museum, I gave at the same time a full description of the animal to which it had belonged, which I got from the man who actually shot it, there is no supposition in the matter. If the skull and horns in question are not those of a hybrid between the South African hartebeest and the tsessebe, then they must belong to an animal still unknown to science.

There is, I think, no large mammal in the whole world whose coat shows a greater richness of bloom and a more abrupt contrast of colours than the bontebok, so called by the old Dutch colonists of the Cape because of its many coloured hide, for *bont* means spotted, or blotched, or variegated. The whole neck, the chest, the sides and under parts of the head, and the sides of the body of this remarkable antelope are of a rich dark brown, and the central part of the back is of a beautiful purple lilac; whilst, in strong contrast to these rich dark colours, the whole front of the face, a good-sized patch on the rump, the whole belly, and the legs are of a pure and brilliant white. In life, and when they are in good condition, a wonderful sheen plays and shimmers over the glossy coats of these beautifully coloured animals, which fully atones for the want of grace and refinement in the shape of their heads and the heavy build of their bodies.

Now, a practical acquaintance with the very limited extent of country in which the bontebok has been evolved, and where the survivors of the race still live, makes it quite impossible for me to believe that the extraordinarily brilliant colouring of this species of antelope can have been gradually developed in order to make it inconspicuous and therefore difficult of detection by carnivorous animals, nor can I believe that it has been evolved for the purpose of mutual recognition between individuals of the species; for although the snow-white blaze down the face or the white rump patch might very well subserve such a purpose, I see no necessity, looking to the habitat and the habits of the bontebok, for special recognition marks.

Now, before proceeding further, I think I ought to say a word as to the points of resemblance and the differences between the bontebok and its near ally the blesbok.

In the latter, the wonderful contrasts of colour to be seen in the former are considerably toned down; but the difference between the two species is merely superficial. The general body colour of the blesbok is dark brown, but not so dark as on the neck and sides of the bontebok, and the delicate purply lilac colour of the back in the latter species is altogether wanting in the former. In the blesbok, too, the colour of the rump just above the tail, which in the bontebok is snow-white, is brown, though of a paler shade than any other part of the body. In the blesbok, too, the white face "blaze" is not continuous from the horns downwards as in the bontebok, but is interrupted above the eyes by a bar of brown. The legs, too, in the blesbok are not so white as in the bontebok, and whilst the horns of the latter species are always perfectly black, in the former they are of a greenish colour.

In a word, the differences between the bontebok and the blesbok are confined to the intensity of the colours on various portions of their hides, the former being much more brilliantly coloured than the latter.

Owing to the fact that the early Dutch settlers at the Cape first met with the antelopes which they called bonteboks on the plains near Cape Agulhas, and subsequently at first gave the same name to the nearly allied species which was discovered about one hundred years later in the neighbourhood of the Orange river, although these latter were undoubtedly blesboks and not bonteboks, a great confusion arose between these two nearly allied species, which I think that I was the first to clear up, in the article on the bontebok which I contributed to the *Great and Small Game of Africa*, published by Rowland Ward, Limited, in 1899. I cannot go into all the arguments I then used, but there can be no doubt that the animals which Captain (afterwards Sir Cornwallis) Harris first met with on the bontebok flats near the Orange river, in the Colesburg division of the Cape Colony, were blesboks and not bonteboks, and that all the millions of antelopes of the same species which he subsequently saw to the north of the Orange river and thought to be bonteboks were also all blesboks, and that he never saw a bontebok at all until after his return to the Cape, when he made a special journey to Cape Agulhas to secure specimens of that species, as he was "anxious to ascertain whether the animal rigorously protected in the neighbourhood of Cape Agulhas differed in any respect from that found in the interior, *as pretended by the colonists.*"

I think myself that the correct determination of the true distribution of these two nearly allied species of antelopes is of the utmost importance to the question as to the influence of environment on the coloration of animals.

I imagine that the white-faced bontebok was evolved from the same ancestral form as the topi and the tiang of East and Northern Africa, for the new-born bontebok as well as the blesbok has a blackish brown face, and I believe—however fantastic this belief may appear to be—that the wonderfully rich and varied coloration of this remarkable antelope has been brought about purely through the influence of its exceptional environment. The plains where these animals live lie along the shore of a deep blue sea, the ground beneath their feet is at certain seasons of the year carpeted with wild flowers, which grow in such profusion that they give a distinct colour to the landscape, whilst above them rises a range of mountains of a considerable altitude, the upper parts of which are often covered with a mantle of pure white snow. I cannot imagine how any one who has seen bonteboks on the plains they inhabit can believe that their white rumps, faces, bellies, and legs, contrasting as they do so vividly with the dark rich brown of their sides and necks, can afford them any protection against their carnivorous foes; nor, although a white rump or face is a conspicuous mark, can I see the necessity of recognition marks for animals which live on open plains where the vegetation is short, and where an animal's whole body can be seen at a long distance.

In the blesbok, which also lives on open plains,

the white rump patch so conspicuous in the bontebok has become pale brown, as, I think, through the influence of the dull monotonous colours of the dreary, dull-coloured country in which it lives. Ages ago no doubt the bontebok spread northwards through the karroo into the countries beyond the Orange and the Vaal rivers, but the gradual desiccation of the whole of South-Western Africa, which has been going on for a very long time, must have gradually driven all the bonteboks outside the Cape peninsula northwards to the Orange river, and completely separated them from their relatives still living near Cape Agulhas. These latter have retained all their richness of coloration brought about by the influence of their very striking surroundings, the deep blue of the sea, the snow on the mountains, and the bloom of innumerable wild flowers. The northern herds moved into open plains, in themselves very similar to the plains near Cape Agulhas, but they are never carpeted with wild flowers, nor are they skirted by a deep blue sea, nor ever overlooked by snow-covered mountains. Is it not possible that the differences which exist to-day between the coloration of the bontebok and the blesbok are entirely the result of the absence of any kind of colour but various monotonous shades of brown in the countries in which the latter species has now been living for a long period of time?

Not only has the rich and beautifully variegated body colouring of the bontebok become an almost uniform dark brown in the blesbok, but the snow-white disc on the rump of the former animal has turned to a pale brown in the latter, whilst the area of white on the face and legs of the bontebok has already been considerably contracted in the blesbok.

Personally, I look upon the blesbok as a faded bontebok; faded because it moved northwards out of the richly coloured environment in which it was first evolved into the dull-coloured plains of its present habitat, where it subsequently became isolated owing to the desiccation of the intervening country.

Could the opening up of Africa by the destructive civilised races have been delayed for a few hundred or a few thousand years, the blesbok would no doubt have lost the white blaze down the face as completely as it has lost the white disc over the tail, which is so conspicuous a feature in the coloration of its immediate ancestor, the bontebok. To those who believe that every spot or stripe or patch of colour on every animal is a beautiful illustration of the truth of the theory of protective coloration, this may seem a very fanciful idea. Yet I feel convinced that the influence of environment has played a greater part than is generally believed in the evolution of colour in living organisms. The weak point in the theory of protective coloration when applied to large mammals is the fact that all carnivorous animals are nocturnal and seek their prey habitually by night and by scent, and only occasionally by daylight and by sight.

I submit that the beautiful case in the Central Hall of the Natural History Museum at South Kensington—showing an Arctic fox, in its white winter coat, approaching a Polar hare, also in winter dress, and an ermine (stoat) hunting for ptarmigan (evidently by sight)—gives an entirely false view of the struggle for life as carried on by animals inhabiting the Arctic Regions, for it conveys the idea of the carnivorous animals of those snow-covered wastes hunting for their prey in a bright light and by eyesight alone.

But the truth is that the Arctic winter, during the long continuance of which all living resident creatures, with the exception of the musk ox, become white,[1] is one long night, in the gloom of which the wolves and the foxes and the ermines (stoats) search for and find their prey by scent alone, just as foxes, stoats, and weasels do in this country. As long as a hare gives out any scent at all, a fox will be able to follow and find it. The fact that the hare has turned white in the snow-covered ground in which it is living will not help it as long as it throws out the scent of its species, nor can it be shown that the foxes of the sub-Arctic regions, which never turn white in winter, have any greater difficulty in approaching and killing the white hares on which they live than the white Arctic foxes experience in catching the Polar hares.

There is one other point regarding the protection afforded by colour to large mammals against carnivorous foes which I think has not been sufficiently considered by naturalists, and that is, that no matter how well the colour of an animal may harmonise with its surroundings as long as it remains perfectly still, as soon as it moves "it jumps to the eyes," as the French say, no matter what its colour may be. What is called protective coloration to be effective must be motionless. Movement, even very slight movement, at once destroys its efficacy. But no herbivorous animals can remain constantly motionless. They lie down and rest certainly during the heat of the day, which is, however, just the time when all carnivorous animals are sleeping. At night and in the early mornings and late evenings they move about feeding, and it is at such times that carnivorous animals hunt for their prey. In the dark these latter are undoubtedly

[1] I do not admit that the raven is a truly Arctic bird. Nansen, in *Farthest North*, although he kept careful records of all the birds seen during the three years his expedition lasted, never mentions having seen a raven, which I believe has only penetrated into the Arctic Regions, as an excursionist, in comparatively recent times, following the whaling ships, and living on the carcases of the whales and seals killed.

guided by scent and not by sight, and I cannot see that it matters much to them whether the beasts on which they prey are black or red or grey or spotted or striped; whilst, if they should happen to be still hunting after daylight, any antelopes or other animals feeding and moving about within their range of vision would at once be seen whatever their colour might be. Every old hunter knows how easy it is to overlook any animal, no matter what its colour or surroundings, as long as it is motionless, and how easy it is to see it as soon as ever it moves.

I have never yet heard any explanation given of the black, and therefore most conspicuous, coloration of the Cape buffalo. If any animals needed protective coloration buffaloes certainly did, for in the interior of South Africa they formed the favourite food of the lion, and enormous numbers of them must have been annually killed by these powerful carnivora, which seemed to live with and follow the larger herds in all their wanderings.

It certainly seems very strange to me that giraffes, which are very seldom killed by lions or other carnivora, should have found it necessary to evolve a colour which harmonises with their surroundings, as a protection against such foes, whilst buffaloes, which in many districts used once to form the principal food for the lions living in the same countries, have retained throughout the ages a coloration which is everywhere except in deep shade singularly conspicuous. Altogether, a very long experience of the larger mammals inhabiting Africa and some other parts of the world has convinced me that neither the need of protection against carnivorous foes nor the theory of recognition marks can satisfactorily explain all the wonderful diversity of colour to be seen in the coats of wild animals.

CHAPTER III

NOTES ON THE LION

The lion—Native names for—Character of—Death of Ponto—Picture in Gordon Cumming's book—Death of Hendrik—Number of natives killed by lions—Usual mode of seizure—A trooper's adventure—Poisonous nature of lion's bite—Story of the Tsavo man-eaters—Death of Mr. Ryall—Story of the tragedy—Precautions by natives against lions—Remains of a lion's victim found—Four women killed—Lion killed—Carcase burned—Story of the Majili man-eater—Man-eating lions usually old animals—Strength of lions—Large ox killed by single lion—Buffaloes killed by lions—Ox slowly killed by family of lions—Lions usually silent when attacking and killing their prey—Camp approached by three lions—Various ways of killing game—Favourite food of lions—Giraffes rarely killed by lions—Evidence as to lions attacking elephants—Michael Engelbreght's story—Mr. Arnot's letter describing the killing of an elephant cow by six lions.

Of all the multifarious forms of life with which the great African Continent has been so bountifully stocked, none, not even excepting the "half-reasoning elephant" or the "armed rhinoceros," has been responsible for such a wealth of anecdote and story, or has stirred the heart and imagination of mankind to such a degree, as the lion—the great and terrible meat-eating cat, the monarch of the African wilderness, by night at least, whose life means constant death to all his fellow-brutes, from the ponderous buffalo to the light-footed gazelle, and fear, and often destruction too, to the human inhabitants of the countries through which he roams.

How often has not the single word "Simba," "Tauw," "Shumba," "Silouān," or any other native African synonym for the lion, sent the blood tingling through the veins of a European traveller or hunter; or when whispered or screamed in the darkness of the night in a native village or encampment, brought terror to the hearts of dark-skinned men and women!

When met in the light of day, a lion may be bold and aggressive, retiring, or even cowardly, according to its individual character and the circumstances under which it is encountered; but no one, I think, who has had anything like a long experience of the nature and habits of these great carnivora can doubt that by night, particularly on a dark rainy night, a hungry lion is a terrible and terrifying beast to deal with.

One day towards the end of the year 1878, my friend Mr. Alfred Cross left our main camp on the Umfuli river in Mashunaland, and taking an empty waggon with him, went off to buy corn at some native villages about twenty miles distant. That same afternoon he outspanned early near a small stream running into the Umfuli, as a heavy thunderstorm was threatening. A kraal was made for the oxen, behind which the Kafir boys arranged a shelter for themselves of boughs and dry grass as a protection from the anticipated downpour of rain. They also collected a lot of dry wood in order to be able to keep up a good fire. The waggon-driver, a native of the Cape Colony, made his bed under the waggon, to the front wheel of which Mr. Cross's horse was fastened. As one of the hind oxen kept breaking out of the kraal, it was tied up by itself to the hind yoke close in front of the waggon. The trek chain, with the other yokes attached to it, was then stretched straight out along the ground in front of the waggon. Soon after dark the thunderstorm, which had been gathering all the afternoon, burst forth with terrific violence. The rain fell in sheets, soon extinguishing the fires that had been lighted by the Kafirs, and the blinding flashes of lightning which continually lit up both heaven and earth with blue-white light were quickly succeeded by crashing peals of thunder.

The storm had lasted some time and the rain had almost ceased, when the ox which was tied up all alone to the after yoke of the waggon began to jump backwards and forwards over the disselboom —the waggon pole.

Cross, who was then lying down inside the waggon, raised himself to a sitting position, and whilst calling to the ox to quiet it, crawled forward, and raising the fore sheet, looked out. Just then a vivid flash of lightning lit up the inky blackness of the night just for one brief moment. But the brilliant light revealed to my friend every detail of the surrounding landscape, and showed him with startling distinctness the form of a big male lion lying flat on the ground not ten yards in front of the frightened ox, which it would probably already have seized, had it not been for Cross's loud shouting. The lion had been no doubt creeping silently towards its would-be prey, which had already become aware of its proximity, when my friend's voice caused it to halt and lie flat on the ground watching. By this time Cross's dog, a well-bred pointer, which had been lying on the driver's blankets under the waggon, had become aware that something was wrong—though the lion was no doubt making its approach against the wind—and was standing just behind the ox, growling.

Directly the position of the lion was revealed to him by the lightning, Cross seized his rifle, and calling to the waggon-driver to jump up and hold his horse, took aim in the direction of the crouching brute, waiting for another flash of lightning. This was not long delayed, and showed the lion still lying flat on the ground close in front of the waggon. Cross fired at once. Encouraged by the report of the rifle, poor Ponto rushed boldly forward, past the terrified ox, into the black night, barking loudly. A yelp of fright or pain suddenly succeeded the bold barking of the dog, and poor Ponto's voice was stilled for ever. He had rushed right into the lion's jaws, and had been instantly killed and carried off. Fires were then made up again, but the lion, apparently satisfied with a somewhat light repast, did not give any further trouble. On the following morning Cross could find no part of Ponto but the head. All the rest of him had apparently been eaten.

I remember even to-day, and with perfect distinctness, though I have not seen it for many years, a certain picture in Gordon Cumming's well-known book on African hunting, and the fearful fascination it always had for me when I was a small boy. That picture represented a great gaunt lion in the act of seizing one of the hunter's Hottentot servants—poor Hendrik—as he lay asleep by the camp fire; but it left to the imagination all the horror and agony of mind suffered by the poor wretch, when so rudely awakened at dead of night and swiftly dragged away into the darkness to a cruel death, in spite of the gallant attempts of his comrades to save him.

During the sixty odd years that have elapsed since this tragedy was enacted on the banks of the Limpopo, many a similar incident has taken place. Some of these occurrences have come within the knowledge of, and been described by, European travellers and hunters, yet these have been but isolated cases, and can only represent a very small percentage of the number of natives that have been dragged away from their camp fires, or even killed in their huts, by hungry lions within recent times.

As a rule, I think, a lion seizes a sleeping man by the head, and in that case, unless it is a very old and weakly animal, death must be usually instantaneous, as its great fang teeth will be driven into the brain through the thickest negro skull.

I have known of two instances of men having been seized at night by the shoulder. This, I think, is likely to happen to a sleeping man lying on his side with one shoulder raised, especially if his recumbent form should happen to be covered with a blanket, in which case the most prominent part of him would very likely be mistaken by a lion for his head.

In the early 'nineties of the last century, two troopers of the British South Africa Company's Police started one afternoon from the neighbourhood of Lo Magondi's kraal to ride into Salisbury, the capital of Mashunaland, a distance of about seventy miles. They rode until dark, and then off-saddling their horses, tied them to a tree, and after having had something to eat and cooked a pot of tea, lay down by the side of the camp fire they had kindled, intending to sleep until the moon rose and then continue their journey by its light. About midnight, however, and when it was very dark, for the moon had not yet risen, a prowling lion came up to their lonely bivouac, and, disregarding their horses, seized one of them by the shoulder and at once dragged him away into the darkness. His companion, awakened by his cries, quickly realised what had happened, and snatching up his rifle, ran to his friend's assistance and fired two or three shots into the air in quick succession. This so startled the lion that it dropped its prospective supper and made off. The wounded man, it was found, had received a severe bite in the shoulder when the lion first seized him, but fortunately had not suffered any further injuries, and was able to proceed with his friend to Salisbury as soon as the moon had risen. He had to be sent to the Hospital on his arrival there, as, although his hurts were not very serious, any wound inflicted by the teeth of a lion is, as a rule, very difficult to heal unless carefully attended to at once and cauterised with a strong lotion of carbolic acid. Dr. Livingstone has described how he suffered for years from the bite of a lion; and I have myself seen wounds from the teeth of one of these animals in a horse's neck, which had never been properly attended to, still suppurating thirteen months after they had been inflicted; whilst, on the other hand, I have seen wounds from the bite of a lion, which were cauterised at once, heal up very quickly and never reopen.

Of all the lion stories that I have ever heard or read, I think none equals in dramatic interest the thrilling narrative of Mr. J. H. Patterson's[1] experiences with two man-eaters during the construction of the Uganda Railway in 1898. This very remarkable story, a brief account of which I first read some years ago with the most absorbing interest in the *Field* newspaper, has now, I am glad to say, been incorporated in the record of his experiences in East Africa which Colonel Patterson has recently published under the title of *The Man-Eaters of Tsavo.* Mr. Patterson (as he then was) at last succeeded in ridding the country of both of these dread beasts, but not before they had killed and eaten twenty-eight Indian coolies employed upon the construction of the Uganda Railway, and caused such a panic through the country-side, that at one time it looked as if the building of the railway would have to be abandoned altogether for the time being.

[1] This gentleman greatly distinguished himself in the late South African War, and is now Lieut.-Col. Patterson, D.S.O.

The death of Mr. C. H. Ryall, the Assistant Superintendent of the East African Police Force, who was killed by a man-eating lion inside a railway carriage on the Uganda Railway, is also a most interesting episode, as it shows how extraordinarily bold a hungry lion may become, when in search of prey during the hours of darkness.

When in East Africa a few years ago, I met both the other two Europeans (Mr. Huebner, a German, and Mr. Parenti, an Italian) who were in the carriage with Mr. Ryall when he was killed, and I heard the story of the tragedy from their lips.

The railway carriage in question, which contained a small saloon and an adjoining servants' compartment, had been pulled on to a siding, close to a small station on the Uganda Railway, in order to give its occupants the chance of getting a shot at a man-eating lion which had lately been giving trouble in the neighbourhood—either as it came prowling about during the night or by hunting it up the next morning. There was a small window on each side of the little saloon, and a sliding door at the end of the carriage. Both the windows and the door were wide open. Mr. Ryall took the first watch, and seems to have taken up a position on one of the seats of the carriage, with his back to the open window. His head and shoulders would therefore probably have been visible to the eyes of a nocturnal animal from outside.

Mr. Huebner turned in and went to sleep on one of the top berths in the carriage, and Mr. Parenti made his bed on the floor. It is probable, I think, that Mr. Ryall also went to sleep after a time. What happened afterwards I will now relate as it was told to me by Mr. Parenti. "I was awakened from a sound sleep by the sensation of a weight holding me down on the floor, and for a moment was unable to move. Then the weight was taken off me, and I raised my head with a jerk. My face immediately came in contact with a soft hairy body, and I became conscious of a disagreeable smell. In an instant I realised that there was a lion in the railway carriage, and that at that moment it was killing poor Mr. Ryall, as I heard a sort of gurgling noise, the only sound he ever made."

Mr. Huebner seems to have awakened at the same time, and to have at once jumped down on to the floor of the carriage, where he and Mr. Parenti and the lion were all mixed up together. At this time the weight of the lion and the struggling men combined slightly tipped the carriage to one side, causing the sliding door to close automatically, and thus materially increasing the horror of the situation. Mr. Parenti, as soon as he could collect his thoughts, made his escape from the carriage through the open window opposite to the one against which poor Mr. Ryall had been sitting when the lion seized him, and Mr. Huebner burst open the door communicating with the smaller compartment occupied by Mr. Ryall's two Indian servants, who, having become aware that there was a lion in the other room with the "Sahibs," were holding the door against the crowd with all their strength. Mr. Huebner, however, who is a heavy, powerful man, soon overcame their resistance.

To do it justice, this lion does not seem to have had any wish to make itself unnecessarily disagreeable. It wanted something to eat, but, having got hold of Mr. Ryall, seems never to have paid the smallest attention to any one else. In all probability, I think, it had seen its victim's back and head from outside against the open window, and, coming round to the open door, had entered the carriage and made straight for him, treading on Mr. Parenti's sleeping form as it crossed the floor. It seized Mr. Ryall by the throat just under the jaw, and must have reared itself up, probably resting its fore-paws on the seat of the carriage, to have done so. Mr. Ryall must have been killed by the first bite almost instantaneously, as he never seems to have struggled or made any noise but a low gurgling sound.

The windows of the carriages on the Uganda Railway are small, but after having killed Mr. Ryall, this lion—a big male—succeeded in carrying off his body through the comparatively small opening. It probably never relaxed its hold on his throat until it had got his dead body safely out of the carriage and pulled it away to some distance.

The half-eaten remains of the unfortunate man were recovered the next day nearly a mile away from the railway carriage in which he had met his death; but the lion was nowhere to be found, and in spite of a large reward offered for its destruction, it was some time before this bold and dangerous beast was disposed of. At last, however, it was caught alive in a big cage-trap made by a Mr. Costello, who at that time was the station-master at Makindu, on the Uganda Railway. After having been photographed, this lion was shot. This photograph was shown me by Mr. Costello himself, who told me that the captured animal was old and mangy, with very worn teeth and claws, and a short, scrubby mane. He thought that there could be no reasonable doubt that it was the lion that had killed poor Mr. Ryall, but of course nobody can be absolutely certain on this point.

Natives living in very small communities, in wild districts where game being still abundant, lions also are consequently fairly numerous, are often troubled at night by these animals. In such cases a man-eating lion usually proves to be an old and almost worn-out beast, which having grown too weak to catch and kill its usual prey, has been driven by hunger to approach the haunts of men.

"HE HAD EVIDENTLY BEEN SITTING OR LYING BY A FIRE WHEN CAUGHT."

Urged on by its desperate need, such a lion knows no fear, and will not hesitate to enter a small native village or even to force its way into a hut in search of food.

In 1879, whilst hunting elephants in the country to the east of the Chobi or Quito river, I met with a very primitive tribe of natives living in families or very small communities in isolated villages along the bank of the river. Their huts were of the flimsiest description, being formed of a light framework of poles, over which a few grass mats had been stretched; but the two or three, up to half a dozen, ill-made huts which formed each village were always surrounded and protected by a carefully made stockade, the poles forming which were all sharpened at the end and hardened by having been charred in the fire, and so placed that they slanted outwards and would have been very difficult to surmount from the outside. The natives informed me that they had taken this trouble as a defence against lions.

One morning, in this same district, I came upon most of the skeleton of a man who had been killed and eaten by a lion a few days before. He had evidently been sitting or lying by a fire when caught, and had probably been overtaken by darkness when on his way from one village to another. This man's spears lay close to his bones, so that he must have been holding them in his hand when he was seized. None of my Kafirs would touch them. Apparently it was not etiquette to meddle with the belongings of a dead man, though I think that most of the members of my retinue would not have been above stealing anything they might have found lying about, belonging to a live one.

In April 1878 a lion entered a small Banyai village near the river Umay, in Northern Matabeleland, a short time after I had left it, and, not being able to make its way into any of the huts through the small doorways, all of which had been very carefully barricaded, climbed on the roof of one of them, and tearing away the grass thatching, forced its way in from the top. There were three or four women inside the hut, and it killed them all; but, having gorged itself, was apparently unable to make its escape through the roof again, and was speared to death by the men of the village the next morning through the framework of the hut, after the mud plaster had been removed in places.

A native servant of my own, whom I had left behind in this village, was present when this lion was killed, and he told me that, as soon as it was dead, a huge bonfire was built, on which the carcase of the man-eater was thrown, and the fire kept up until it was quite consumed.

The most cunning and destructive man-eating lion—probably because it was not an old and weakly animal, but in the prime of life—that I ever heard of in South Africa was one which once haunted the neighbourhood of the Majili river, a tributary of the central Zambesi from the north. I gave some account of the doings of this bold and ferocious beast in the course of an article which I contributed to the pages of the *Fortnightly Review* some twenty years ago, and as I have the kind permission of the editor and proprietor of that publication to do so, I will now retell the story as I originally heard it from one of my own native servants shortly after the occurrences related took place.

In the early part of 1886 two half-caste elephant-hunters, Henry Wall and Black Jantje—the latter for several years both before and after this time a trusted servant of my own—crossed the Zambesi at its junction with the Quito or Chobi, in order to hunt elephants in the country to the north between the Majili and Ungwesi rivers.

They soon heard from the natives that there was a man-eating lion in the district which had already killed several people, and they were therefore careful to see that a strong fence was made every night behind their camp, and sufficient dry wood collected to keep up good fires during the hours of darkness. The two half-civilised hunters were accustomed to sleep by themselves within a strong semicircular fence, the open end of which was protected by a large fire. All but one of their native boys—wild Batongas and Masubias—slept together, lying in a row with a strong fence behind them and a succession of fires near their feet. The boy who would not sleep with the others, always lay by one or other of the fires by himself.

One night, Henry Wall, who was a very light sleeper, and had perhaps been dreaming of lions, was awakened, as he afterwards declared, by the sound of a low growl or purr close to him. Springing to his feet, he shouted out, "De leeuw is hier!" ("The lion's here!"); "wake up, Jantje!" But Jantje and all the Kafirs were fast asleep, and it was not until they had been awakened and questioned that it was discovered that the man who had been lying by one of the fires all alone was gone. Where he had gone and why was not left long in doubt, for almost immediately a lion was heard eating his remains close behind the encampment. Henry Wall and Jantje at once fired in the direction of the sound, on which the lion retired to a safer distance with its prey.

As soon as it was broad daylight, the hunters took up the spoor of the lion, which was, they told me, quite easy to follow through the dewy grass. It was not long before they saw it walking slowly along with its head half-turned, holding the dead man by one shoulder, so that his legs dragged at its side. As soon as it became aware that it was being followed, it dropped its prey, and wheeling round, stood looking at its pursuers, twitching its tail and growling angrily.

Henry Wall, who was a very good shot and a cool and courageous man, now tried to fire, but the old, clumsy, muzzle-loading elephant gun he was using only snapped the cap. At this juncture Jantje, who was a little to one side, was unable to fire because there was a bush in his way, and before Henry Wall could get another cap on the nipple of his gun, the Kafir who carried his second weapon fired at and missed the lion, which instantly turned and, running into a patch of bush, made good its escape.

On examination, it was found that the dead man had been seized by the head. He must have been killed instantaneously, as the two upper canine teeth had been driven through the top of the skull, whilst one of the lower ones had entered beneath the jaw and broken the bone. During the night the corpse had been disembowelled and all the flesh eaten off the thighs and buttocks.

A few days later, a native family was attacked not far from the scene of the episode I have just recounted, and almost certainly by the same lion.

All over Africa, wherever game is plentiful, it is customary for the natives, at the season when their crops are ripening, to build huts in their fields, in which they spend the night and endeavour to keep buffaloes, elephants, and all kinds of antelopes out of their corn by shouting and beating tom-toms. The huts are often built on the top of platforms raised ten or twelve feet above the ground and reached by a ladder. The native family in question occupied two huts—a large one built on the ground and a small one on the top of a platform. The large hut was occupied by a woman and her two children, whilst her husband kept watch alone in the little open hut above.

One night the dread man-eater of the Majili came prowling round, and scenting the native on the platform, either sprang up and seized him with its teeth, or more probably, I think, half clambered up by the help of the ladder, and dragged him from his shelter with its claws. At any rate, it bore him to the ground and speedily killed him, but not before he had made a good deal of noise, as reported afterwards by his children. His wife, awakened by the cries of her husband, opened the door of her hut and rushed out, leaving the two children inside. The lion at once left the man, who was then dead, and seizing the woman, quickly killed her. It never returned to the body of the man at all, but ate all the fleshy parts of the woman, retiring into the bush before daylight, and never revisiting the corpses.

All through the dry season this lion kept the natives in the neighbourhood of the Majili river in a constant state of alarm, and whilst adding steadily to the number of its victims, baffled every attempt made to hunt it down and destroy it. After having been away for some months, hunting elephants in the country farther north, Henry Wall and Black Jantje once again camped on the Majili river on their way back to the Zambesi, and for the second time the man-eater paid them a visit. This time Jantje was awake, and hearing, as he told me, a low purring growl, jumped up, calling out, "Daat's de leeuw wieder!" ("That's the lion again!").

At the same time one of the Kafirs stood up holding his hand to his head.

"What's the matter with you?" asked Jantje, going up to him.

"I don't know," answered the man; "something hit me on the head."

At this moment Jantje saw by the light of the fire blood running down his neck, and called out, "Wake, wake, it was the lion I heard! Wake, wake, and see if every one is here!"

It soon appeared that one of the Kafirs was missing, and this is no doubt what had happened. The lion must have crept or sprung in amongst the sleepers, and seizing one of them by the head, must have killed him instantly and carried him off. But in doing so it must have struck the man lying next him on the head with one of its paws, and inflicted a slight scalp wound with one of its claws. The body of the man who had been carried off was not recovered, because, as Henry Wall and Jantje told me, the rest of the Kafirs would give them no assistance in following up the lion the next day.

This dangerous man-eater was at last mortally wounded by the spears of two young men whom it attacked in broad daylight close to a small native village. One of these youths died the same evening from the mauling he received in the encounter, but he had driven his spear into the lion's chest when it attacked him, and his companion had also struck it in the side with a light throwing spear. The next day, all the men from the two or three little villages in the neighbourhood turned out and followed up the bloody tracks of the wounded lion. They had not far to go, for the grim beast lay dead, with the two spears still sticking in it, within a short distance from the spot where it had attacked the two young men the previous day. As is the custom when man-eating lions are killed in the interior of Africa, a great quantity of dry wood was then collected, and a huge fire lighted, on which the carcase was thrown and utterly consumed.

There is one rather curious fact in connection with the history of this notorious man-eating lion which I omitted from the first account I wrote of its doings, but which I will now relate, as it is of interest. Soon after dark on the night of the second attack on their camp, Henry Wall and Jantje and all their boys heard the sudden rush of an affrighted herd of buffaloes, which had been feeding in the open ground between their camp and the Majili river. Suddenly there was the loud and agonised bellow of a buffalo in pain and terror, and they all knew that one of these animals had been seized by a lion. The following morning they found a buffalo cow lying dead not two hundred yards from their camp, with its head twisted in under it and its neck dislocated. It had the claw-marks usual in such cases over the muzzle and on the shoulder, showing the manner in which it had been seized, but after having been killed it had not been touched. The tracks of the lion, however, led from the carcase of the buffalo to the hunters' camp, and I think that there can be no doubt that it was the same animal which killed the buffalo that a few hours later carried off a human being. If so, it proves two things. Firstly, that this man-eating lion must have been in its prime, for it requires a strong and vigorous male lion to kill a full-grown buffalo cow or a heavy bullock neatly and quickly by breaking its neck; and secondly, that it preferred human flesh to that of a buffalo. It must either have seen the gleam of the camp fires for the first time immediately after it had killed the buffalo, and abandoned the carcase in the hope of obtaining more succulent food, or, if it was aware of the neighbourhood of the hunters' camp before it attacked the buffalo, it must have killed the latter out of sheer mischief.

Though similar cases of lions becoming confirmed man-eaters when in the prime of life and still in the enjoyment of their full strength and vigour do from time to time occur—the celebrated Tsavo man-eaters which played such havoc amongst the construction camps on the Uganda Railway were reported to have been far from old—yet it cannot be denied that in the vast majority of cases a lion only takes to killing human beings in its declining years, and when its strength is failing.

On this subject, Dr. Livingstone wrote many years ago: "A man-eater is invariably an old lion, and when he overcomes his fear of man so far as to come to villages for goats, the people remark, 'His teeth are worn, he will soon kill men.' They at once acknowledge the necessity of instant action and turn out to kill him."

Speaking generally, nothing truer could have been written than these sentences; but there are exceptions to every rule, and when a strong and vigorous lion does take to preying upon human beings, it is naturally not so easy to hunt down and destroy as would be an old and weakly beast, whose "teeth are worn."

An adult male lion is probably possessed of greater strength in proportion to its size and weight than any other African animal. It will kill with astonishing ease and dexterity a full-grown buffalo cow or the heaviest bullock, and probably sometimes a buffalo bull or a giraffe. I never remember, however, to have seen the carcase of an old buffalo bull that had palpably been killed by a single lion, whilst I have shot several buffalo bulls that had escaped from lions after receiving very severe wounds from their teeth and claws. I once had a very good opportunity of noting the manner in which a big male lion killed a heavy ox, which would certainly have scaled more than twice its own weight. This ox was killed during the night, but as the lion was immediately driven from the carcase, it had no time to inflict any wound upon it other than those made when it first seized its victim, and the ground being soft from recent rain, every step taken by both the ox and the lion during the brief struggle was plainly visible. The lion had evidently crept close up to where the ox was lying (within forty yards of my waggon), and had either attacked it where it lay or just as it was rising to its feet. It had not jumped upon its victim, but throughout the struggle had always kept its hind-feet on the ground. The only wounds that had been inflicted on the ox were claw-marks on the nose and on the top of the left shoulder-blade, and the lion had evidently seized it by the muzzle with its left paw and on the top of the shoulder with the right, and had simply held it, pulling its head in towards its chest. The ox had plunged forward, dragging the lion with it for a few yards, and had then fallen with its head twisted right under it and its neck dislocated. Whether the lion had broken the ox's neck by its own strength, or whether the dislocation was due to the way in which it fell with its head twisted in under it, I cannot say; but my experience is that when a single lion tries to kill an ox or a buffalo, it invariably seizes it over the muzzle with one paw, and usually succeeds in either breaking its victim's neck or causing it to break it itself by its own weight in falling. When several lions attack an ox or buffalo, they will often bite and tear it all over and take a long time to kill it. Upon several occasions I have listened to the protracted bellowing of buffaloes being thus mauled to death. Upon one occasion a party of five lions stampeded my oxen as they lay round the waggon, and very soon seized and pulled down one of them. The wretched creature bellowed most fearfully, and must have been suffering terribly. Hastily lighting torches of long dry grass, several of my Kafirs and I ran to help it. The blazing grass scared the lions off, and they left the ox before the light of the torches reached them. The wounded animal immediately got up and rushed off again into the darkness, but had not gone far before its loud bellowing told us the lions had got hold of it once more. They took some time to kill it, but its agonised bellowings gradually died away in low moans, until at length all was again quiet. During the approach of these five lions to my camp, and the subsequent chase and long-drawn-out killing of the ox, not one of them made the slightest sound; and as far as my own personal experience goes, with one exception, whenever lions have reconnoitred or attacked my camp at night, and bitten or killed any of my native followers or cattle or horses, they have done all their stalking and killing without making a sound. If disturbed, however, they always growl loudly. On the occasion I have referred to as an exception to this rule, three lions —as we learnt the next morning by the spoor— came quite close up to my bivouac one night in Northern Mashunaland, and one of them gave a very loud roar which woke us all up. I was travelling at the time with a small cart and eight oxen, which were tied to the yokes, and were right in the open, unprotected either by fires or any kind of kraal or fence. My two horses were tied to one of the wheels, and my few native servants and myself were lying close to them, with a small fence of soft bush behind us. The three lions that came so near us in the night could not have been very hungry, or they would assuredly have seized one of my oxen. Perhaps the one that so suddenly roared only did so with the idea of frightening the oxen, and if one of them had broken the raw hide thong with which it was fastened to the yoke, and run off away from our camp, all three of them would very likely have pursued and killed it. Fortunately, neither my oxen nor my horses showed much fear on this occasion, and although the former pulled a bit, they did not break their thongs, and we soon quieted them and then built up some big fires. The lions passed on up the little river near which we were camped, and before long began to roar loudly, a pretty good sign, I think, that they had already dined and were not hunting. Why, when a family of four or five lions are hunting together, one of their number being an old male, they should kill an ox so much less artistically than the old male would have done, if he had been alone, I do no know. Possibly the eagerness of each member of the party renders a scientific attack by any one of them impossible, or perhaps the older lions allow the younger ones to do the killing for practice. There is no doubt, I think, that lions know that the head, throat, and the back of the neck are the most vital spots in all animals on which they prey. Human beings are nearly always seized by the head or neck; horses, donkeys, and zebras are almost invariably killed by bites in the back of the neck just behind the ears, or by bites in the throat; whilst they either dislocate the necks of heavy animals like buffaloes, or hold them in such a way that they can hardly help falling and breaking their own necks. The lion which broke the neck of one of my oxen, as I have described above, escaped punishment when it returned to the carcase the following evening owing to my rifle missing fire. It then visited a mining camp close at hand, and forcing its way into an enclosure in which there were fourteen sheep and goats and one calf, it killed every one of these unfortunate animals. I shot this lion early the following morning and then examined its victims. Every one of them, the calf as well as the sheep and goats, had been killed by a single bite in the head. In each case the upper canine teeth had been driven through the top of the skull or the back of the neck just behind the ears. I once came on a young elephant only a few minutes after it had been killed by a lion. The only wounds I could find were deep tooth-marks in the throat.

Lions kill and eat every kind of wild animal in Africa with the exception of the Pachydermata—though they occasionally catch and kill a young elephant or rhinoceros that has been separated from its mother—but as long as buffaloes and zebras are plentiful in the countries they inhabit, they will kill far more of these than of any other animal. Quaggas and Burchell's zebras probably formed their chief food on the plains of the Cape Colony, the Orange River Colony, and the Transvaal before those countries were settled by Europeans; whilst farther north, where great numbers of buffaloes frequented the neighbourhood of every river, the lions lived almost entirely on these animals, following the herds in all their wanderings, just as in North America the prairie wolves were always in attendance on the bisons. Giraffes are sometimes killed by lions, but according to my experience only very rarely; no doubt because they must be very awkward animals to pull down, and also for the reason that, generally speaking, they inhabit dry, waterless stretches of country, throughout which game is usually only sparsely distributed and into which lions do not penetrate.

Although I have excluded the Pachydermata from the list of animals on which lions prey, there nevertheless seems to be good evidence that these carnivora do sometimes attack and kill good-sized cow elephants.

I well remember an old Boer hunter, Michael Engelbreght, telling me of an unsuccessful attack made by lions on a cow elephant within a short distance of the shooting hole where he was lying one night watching for elephants coming to drink at Tamasanka vley on the old road to the Zambesi. This incident had occurred only a few nights before I met Engelbreght at the vley in question. But it happened so long ago (in 1874) that I cannot remember anything more than that the elephant was held up by the lions for some hours, and that the trumpeting of the former was accompanied by the loud growling of the latter, and that when my informant examined the ground where the combat had taken place, the next morning, he found a great deal of thorn bush trampled down by the elephant, and some blood on the ground. The former, however, although probably it had been badly bitten in the trunk and legs, had kept the lions from its throat, and had finally beaten them off and made good its retreat. Michael Engelbreght was at that time a man of over sixty years of age, and as he had been a hunter from his youth upwards, in the golden days of South African hunting, he must have had a vast experience of the habits of wild animals, but I well remember that he spoke of this incident of an elephant having been attacked by lions as wonderful and almost incredible.

I have, however, heard of another case of an elephant having been attacked and killed by lions.

When passing through Kimberley in 1895, I met my old friend Mr. F. S. Arnot, who has done such splendid work as a pioneer missionary in Central Africa, and who is an absolutely reliable man, and he then told me a story of an elephant having been killed by lions near Lake Mweru. Hearing last year that Mr. Arnot was in England, I wrote and asked him if he would kindly tell me this story again, as I wanted to put it on record. In the course of his answer to my letter Mr. Arnot wrote: "The lion story I told you may appear rather *tall* to some, but when travelling between Lakes Tanganyika and Mweru, in November 1894, and when skirting the northern end of the great Mweru Marsh—a regular elephants' stronghold—my men suddenly left me *en masse*—they were a raw set of men—returning presently with elephant flesh. They then told me that our guides having informed them that they had that morning seen six hungry lions attack and pull down a full-grown cow elephant, just ahead of where we then were, they had left me so suddenly in order to drive the lions off and get some meat. Unfortunately, I did not see the lions myself, but there could be no doubt about the truth of our guides' statement, for I saw the lions' spoor and the carcase of the dead elephant. The tusks were very small, but my men brought them. They may have weighed from four to five pounds each."

As the tusks were so small, this elephant could hardly have been a full-grown cow; but it must have been a good-sized animal, probably a young cow about three-parts grown. It is a great pity that Mr. Arnot did not examine the carcase carefully and ascertain exactly how the elephant had been killed. As the natives, however, asserted positively that they had seen six lions attack and kill it, and as Mr. Arnot is fully convinced that their story was true, I think it ought to be accepted as a fact, especially as cases of full-grown elephants having been killed by tigers in India and Burma have been put on record.

CHAPTER IV

NOTES ON THE LION (*continued*)

Depredations of lions in Mashunaland—Sad death of Mr. Teale—Great slaughter of pigs by a lioness—Mode of entering a cattle kraal—Method of killing prey—Sharpness of lion's claws—Mode of seizing a horse in motion—Lion chasing koodoos—Lions lying in wait for oxen—How a lion charges—Black Jantje's story—Numbing effect of lion's bite — Cruelty in nature—Appearance of wild lions—Colour of eyes—Lions at bay—A crouching lion—A lucky shot—The cat a lion in miniature—A danger signal—Social habits of lions—Troops of lions—Lions on the Mababi plain—Difference between cubs of one litter—Individual differences in lions—Great variation in the development of the mane—Lion probably first evolved in a cold climate—Still found in Europe in the time of Herodotus—Effect of cold on growth of lion's mane.

WHEN a previously uninhabited piece of country is invaded and settled up by a tribe of natives or by Europeans, lions are always very troublesome, as they look upon all the newly introduced domestic animals as some new species of game specially brought into the country for their benefit.

For the first few months after Mr. Rhodes's pioneers entered Mashunaland in 1890, I kept as accurate an account as I could of the number of horses, donkeys, oxen, sheep, goats, and pigs that were killed by lions, and it soon amounted to more than two hundred. During the same time two white men were killed and several others severely injured by lions. The saddest case was that of a young man named Teale, who had come to Mashunaland in the hope of making his fortune by market-gardening. He was outspanned one night near a native village not far from Umtali, where he had gone to buy grain. His four oxen were tied to the yokes, and he with his native driver was sleeping on the ground beneath his two-wheeled cart, when he was seized and carried off by a lion. What the lion did not eat of him, the hyænas probably got, as nothing was ever found but his head and one foot with the boot still on it.

A rather curious incident happened the following year at a farm on the Hanyani river about forty miles from Salisbury. The owner of the farm—from whom I heard this story (which was fully corroborated by his native servants)—was breeding pigs, and had a large number of these animals in a series of pens, separated from one another by low partitions, but all under one thatched roof. One night a lioness managed to force her way into the piggery between two poles, and after having satisfied her hunger, was apparently unable to find her way out again, and either became angry or frightened, or else must have been overcome with an almost insatiable lust for killing. At any rate, she wandered backwards and forwards through the pens and killed almost all the pigs, over a hundred altogether, each one with a bite in the head or the back of the neck. She had only eaten portions of two young pigs. She managed to effect her escape before daylight, but returned the following night, and was shot by a set gun. I saw her skull, which was that of a full-grown lioness with good teeth.

There appears to be a considerable difference of opinion as to the means usually adopted by lions to effect an entrance by night into a cattle kraal or a camp surrounded by a fence. They are often said to leap boldly over high fences and stockades. In my own experience I have not known them do this.

They will walk through any opening in an enclosure, but in the absence of such a means of ingress, I have always found that they got inside by creeping through the fence, even when it was low and very thick and thorny. I have known a lion to walk round and round a stockaded cattle kraal, and at last force its way in by pressing two poles apart and squeezing through the opening thus made. Should lions, however, be disturbed and suddenly fired at whilst feeding on a bullock which they have killed inside an enclosure, they will almost always jump over the fence in their hurry to escape.

I have never seen any evidence of a lion's killing its prey by striking it a heavy blow with one of its paws, and I believe that it always endeavours to kill by biting, and only uses its claws for holding or pulling an animal to its mouth. I have seen both a lion and a lioness bayed by dogs repeatedly throw out their fore-paws like lightning when one of these latter came near them ; but the movement was not in the nature of a blow, but rather an attempt to hook one of the dogs in their claws and draw it to them. Lions, I think, must often lose their prey through the very sharpness of their claws, which cut like knives through the skin and flesh of a heavy animal in motion. I have known several instances of a lion overtaking a horse that had only had a short start. In such a case a lion will not land with a flying leap right on to a horse's back. It gallops close along the ground until it is almost under the horse's tail, and then, rearing itself up on its hind-legs, seizes it on either flank, endeavouring to hold it with the protruded claws of its great fore-paws. But almost invariably in such a case it fails to stop a galloping horse, its claws simply cutting great gashes through skin and flesh. I once saw a lion chasing four koodoos in broad daylight, though on a cold cloudy morning. It was galloping after them flat along the ground as hard as it could go, and looked like an enormous mastiff, especially as, though a male, it had but little mane. On another occasion, late one evening, I saw a lion and two lionesses lying in wait for some cattle of mine which were feeding towards them. Every now and then one or other of the lions would raise its head for a moment above the grass to see that the oxen were still coming on, lowering it again after one quick look. But for my intervention, these lions would probably have lain quite still until one or other of the oxen had fed close up to them, when they would have seized it by the head before it had time to turn. As lions nearly always hunt by scent and by night, they no doubt come up wind and approach as near as possible to a herd of game before making an attack, and probably often lie quite still until some animal feeds right on to them. In a country where game is plentiful, one would imagine that on a dark night lions must have but little trouble in securing food, and this is no doubt the case, as these carnivora become excessively fat wherever game is really plentiful.

When a lion charges, it does not come on in great leaps, nor does it strike its adversary a crushing blow with its paw. It comes along close to the ground like a great dog and bites, often so low that its forefeet can hardly be off the ground. Two Boer hunters of my acquaintance were both of them first bitten in the thigh. Shortly after the opening up of Mashunaland, too, an Englishman and a Dane were both seized in the same way by charging lions when hunting near the Pungwe river, in Portuguese East Africa, the latter dying from his wounds. In 1877 an Englishman was charged by an unwounded lion in Mashunaland and severely bitten in the groin; and in the following year, in the same locality, an old Hottentot servant of mine was badly bitten in the small of the back when running away from a charging lion which he had previously wounded. All these wounds were so low down that they must have been inflicted when the lion's forefeet were on the ground. On the other hand, many cases are on record of men standing facing charging lions being seized by the left forearm and sometimes by the shoulder. I do not remember to have heard of a case of a man being bitten in the head in a frontal charge, but one of my old servants, "Black Jantje," described to me very minutely the way in which he saw from a distance of only a few yards a Bushman killed by a wounded lion. When the lion charged every one ran, and just as "Black Jantje" reached a small tree, it dashed past him and the next instant caught up to a Bushman. It appeared, Jantje told me, to rear itself up, and placing a forepaw on each shoulder, gave the unfortunate savage a bite in the head. There were no wounds on the man's shoulders, but his skull was bitten through, and he was dashed to the ground with such violence that the skin was knocked off both his knees. The wounded lion made no further attack, but walking slowly away to the foot of a neighbouring tree, lay down and presently died within a few yards of its dead enemy. Two cases have come within my experience of lions charging home, and after having thrown their adversaries to the ground with one severe bite, leaving them without further molestation. I have known personally a number of men who had been mauled by lions. Every one of them was bitten, not struck by the lion's paw. Indeed, most of them were absoultely untouched by the lion's claws.

I once made the acquaintance of a fine old Boer hunter with whom I subsequently became very intimate, just after he had been very severely mauled by a lion. On asking him if he had felt much pain when the lion was biting him—he had eleven deep tooth wounds in the one thigh, besides others in the left arm and hand, and described the lion as having "chewed" him — he answered, "Ja, ik at byung sair gekrij" ("Yes, I felt much pain"); and some Kafirs have also told me that they have suffered much when being bitten by lions. It is possible that old Petrus Jacobs and my Kafir informants did really feel some pain at the time when they were being bitten, but in the case of Europeans, at any rate, who probably possess very highly-strung nervous systems, all the first-hand evidence I have been able to gather goes to prove that the bite of a lion or a tiger is practically painless. I imagine that the reason of this is, that the tremendous energy exerted by a lion in biting is equivalent to a heavy blow, which produces such a shock to the nervous system that all sensation is for the time being deadened, as it would be by a heavy blow from a sledge-hammer. I do not think that any kind of wounds from either blows or bullets or bites are likely to give any appreciable pain if inflicted swiftly when the blood is up; but they become painful enough very soon afterwards. When animals are killed quickly by lions, they too probably suffer very little, if at all, but no one who has listened, as I have done, to the bellowing of an ox or a buffalo being killed by inches could possibly say that such an animal's sufferings were not very great. I once had a fine stallion donkey killed by a hyæna within a short distance of my bivouac. It had first been seized between the hind-legs by its foul assailant, and its screams were perfectly heart-rending, and haunted me for a long time afterwards. My Kafirs and I ran to the poor brute's assistance at once, but were too late to save it, as a great hole had been torn in its belly, out of which half its entrails were hanging. No; it is useless for the scientist or the divine to tell an old hunter that there is no cruelty in nature, because the man who has spent many years of his life in a wild country knows by actual experience that such an assertion is not true. But let me return to my lions.

In appearance a full-maned, well-proportioned lion lying in peaceful repose in a European menagerie, gazing placidly and thoughtfully out of sleepy, brownish yellow eyes at the human crowd beyond the bars of its cage, is a truly dignified and majestic-looking animal; and if a fine specimen of a wild lion could be viewed at close quarters and at a moment when it was lying or standing with its massive mane-encircled head well raised, content with itself and all the world, after a good meal, and entirely unconscious of danger, it also would doubtless look both dignified and majestic, though I doubt if it could ever look quite so reposeful as the typical lion of the picture-books; for although wild lions are sometimes caught fast asleep, they are usually alert and watchful. I have spoken of the eyes of lions that have grown up in captivity as being brownish in colour and somewhat sleepy in expression, and that is the impression I have received from looking at the lions in the Zoological Gardens in Regent's Park. On the other hand, I remember the colour of the eyes of wild lions as being of a flaming yellow, which retains its fierce brilliancy for many hours after death. Should a lion be shot through the loins and injured in such a way that, its hindquarters being paralysed, it can be closely approached without danger, its fierce eyes seem ablaze with bright yellow flame, and give complete expression to the awful fury by which it is possessed. It is worth mentioning, I think, that when visiting the Zoological Gardens at Clifton, a couple of years ago, I noticed that the eyes of the lions and tigers there were in most cases of a flaming yellow, as they are, according to my experience, in wild lions. In some of them, however, the eyes were brownish and sleepy-looking.

When walking, wild lions hold the head rather low, lower than the line of the back, and although, when suddenly encountered, they will raise it for a moment to take a look at the intruder, they will soon lower it again and either trot away with a low growl or else stand watching. A wild lion looks his best and his worst, intensely savage but not at all majestic, when standing at bay. I have the pictures of four male lions, that I had chased on horseback and brought to bay, very vividly impressed on my memory. One was wounded, though only slightly, the other three as yet untouched. They all stood fairly facing me, their heads held well down below their mane-crowned shoulders, their fierce yellow eyes gleaming, and their ears laid flat, like the ears of an angry cat or leopard. All the time they stood at bay they kept up a constant succession of loud rumbling growls and flicked their tails continually from side to side, throwing them suddenly into the air before charging with louder, hoarser growls.

In one respect the behaviour of these four angry lions was quite different from that of an angry cat or leopard, or even tiger. There was no suspicion of snarling about them. Their mouths were held slightly open, but instead of the upper lip being drawn up so as to expose the upper canine teeth, it was drawn down so as to completely cover them. They stood thus with their mouths held slightly open, growling savagely and twitching their tails from side to side, until two of them charged before I fired at them, and the other two I fired at and killed before they could make up their minds to charge. Now this abstention from all suspicion of snarling which I remember so well in the case of four different lions when driven to bay, and the fact that I do not carry in my mind the picture of any lion snarling that I have ever shot, makes me wonder whether it is correct to depict an angry lion as snarling like an angry cat or leopard. This is a small matter, no doubt, but one which I think it is worth while inquiring into, as if an angry lion really does not snarl, it differs in this respect from all other members of the cat tribe.

I once galloped almost on to a lion lying flat on the ground in grass only about a foot in height before I saw it. When I at last made it out, I was directly in front of, and probably less than twenty yards away from it. As I pulled my horse in, this lion had its head pressed down on its outstretched paws and its eyes were fixed upon me. Had I ridden by, it would certainly never have moved until I had got out of sight. As I raised my rifle and looked down the barrel to align the sights upon its head, I saw the black tuft of hair at the end of its tail flicked lightly from side to side, and the fore-paws, that had been stretched out straight beyond its nose, drawn slowly under its breast, without its head or body being perceptibly raised. I knew the lion was on the very point of charging, but my horse kept breathing hard and I could not get my sight steadily fixed below its eyes. Then, just as I saw the crouching beast's hind-quarters quivering, or rather moving gently from side to side, I fired, and luckily my bullet struck it just between the eyes, and crashing into its brain, killed it instantly, so that it never moved, but still lay crouching on the ground, struck dead at the very last moment before starting on its charge. Since that time I have on several occasions watched a cat when stalking a bird go through every movement made by that lion —the same apparently involuntary twitching of just the end of the tail, the same drawing-in of the fore-paws beneath the chest, and then the wavy movement of the loins just before the final rush. As lions are very nocturnal in their habits and usually hunt by night, it is, of course, very unusual to see them approach and kill their prey, but from the above related experience I imagine that every movement made by a lion in approaching and finally making a rush upon an antelope or zebra is exactly represented in miniature by a cat stalking a bird or rabbit. It is as well to remember that if a lion, after standing for a short time growling at you and whisking its tail backwards and forwards round its hind-legs, suddenly stiffens it and throws it straight into the air at right angles to the line of its back two or three times, it is a danger-signal and means charging. A lion may often charge without throwing its tail straight up, but I believe that it will never throw its tail up without charging.

The African lion appears to be more gregarious than any other of the Felidae, and the male is certainly addicted to polygamy. Often a lion or a lioness may live and hunt for a time by itself, and very old animals are probably always solitary, as an old lion would be driven away from the females by younger males, and an old female would probably be badly treated by younger animals of both sexes. Sometimes two or even three males will hunt together for a time. More often a male lion may be met with accompanied by from one to four females, some of which latter may be followed by cubs of different ages and sizes. A family party consisting of one old male lion, three or four adult females, and several cubs, some of which may stand almost as high at the shoulder as their mothers, would constitute what the old Boer hunters would have called "en trop leeuws" (a troop of lions). In parts of Africa where game is, or was, very

PLATE SHOWING DIFFERENCES IN THE DEVELOPMENT OF THE MANE IN LIONS INHABITING A COMPARATIVELY SMALL AREA OF COUNTRY IN SOUTH AFRICA.

The skins from which these figures have been drawn are all in the possession of the Author, and are all three those of fully adult animals.

No. 1.—Lion killed on the upper Hanyani river in Mashunaland in June 1880.

No. 2.—Lion killed on the Umzingwani River near Bulawayo.

No. 3.—Lion killed on the Botletlie river, near the Makari-kari Salt-pan, in May 1879.

abundant, there are many authentic records of over twenty lions having been seen together. In his article on "The Lion," published in the Badminton Library Series, Mr. F. J. Jackson, C.B., has noted the fact that on August 7, 1890, he and Dr. Mackinnon came across a troop of twenty-three lions near Machakos in East Africa. This troop consisted of three male lions with splendid dark manes, five or six lionesses, and the rest cubs. I have come to the conclusion that such large assemblages of lions as this, in which there are several full-grown males, are, in all probability, only of a very temporary nature, the chance meeting and fraternisation of several families which, as a rule, live and hunt apart; since I believe that the passions of love and jealousy would not allow two or more males to live permanently in the company of lionesses without fighting. When a troop of lions is met with, in which, besides a full-grown male and some females and small cubs, there are also one or two good-sized young males with small manes, I believe that they are the offspring of the old male and one or other of the adult females, and that they have lived and hunted with the troop since cubhood. Such young males are probably not driven away to hunt by themselves until they commence to aspire to the affections of one of the females of the party. In 1879 I encountered two pairs of male lions hunting in company in the Mababi country to the north of Lake N'gami. I shot the first pair, and should certainly have killed both the others had I only had a rifle and a few cartridges with me when I first saw them, as they were right out on an open plain from which the grass had been burnt, far away from the nearest bush, and I was riding the best hunting horse I ever possessed. The two lions which I shot were large and heavy, apparently just in their prime, and the other pair also appeared to be full-grown animals. Now the Masarwa Bushmen living near the Mababi plain—and these wild people are extraordinarily acute observers—declared that they knew both these pairs of lions well, and said that each pair were the cubs of one mother, and had been hunting together since cub-hood. Curiously enough, in the case of both these pairs of lions the two animals living and hunting together differed from one another very much. In each case one was of a very dark colour all over, with a dark mane, whilst the body of the other was of a pale yellow, and it had scarcely any mane at all. A few days after encountering the second pair of lions, a friend and myself came upon two lionesses on the same open plain, both of which we shot. One of these lionesses was on the point of giving birth to three cubs, which we cut out of her womb. Two of these cubs were males, and they differed very much one from another in colour even before birth. One was very dark indeed, owing to the blackish tint of the tips of the hairs of its little fluffy coat. The other was of a reddish yellow. The fur of the female cub was also of a much lighter colour than in the dark male. Now I cannot but adhere to the opinion which I wrote down in my diary at the time, that these two male lion cubs would, had they lived, have grown up into animals differing very much in appearance one from the other. The dark cub would have become a dark-skinned, dark-maned lion, the lighter coloured one a yellow lion with probably very little mane.

Commenting upon such a case as the above, Mr. R. Lydekker, in one of his recently published zoological essays, says that when light- and dark-maned cubs are met with in the same litter it is due to crossing between lions of different races. Mr. Lydekker has also stated that "with regard to the lion, it has now been ascertained that the black-maned and tawny-maned specimens belong, in most cases at any rate, to distinct local races."

The objection to this theory is that you cannot classify all African lions under two heads, the black-maned and the tawny-maned. Dealing with this subject in 1881, and referring only to the skins of lions I had seen which had been killed in the country between the Limpopo and the Zambesi, I wrote as follows: "I cannot see that there is any reason for supposing that more than one species (of lion) exists, and as out of fifty lion skins scarcely two will be found exactly alike in the colour and length of the mane, I think it would be as reasonable to suppose that there are twenty species as two. The fact is, that between the animal with hardly a vestige of mane and the far handsomer but much less common beast with a long flowing black mane every possible intermediate variety may be found." Since that time I have seen a great many more skins of lions shot in the country to the south of the Zambesi, as well as a number from limited areas of country in East Africa and in Somaliland, and it appears to me that the lions of these two latter very limited areas show exactly the same variations as regards colour and profuseness of mane as their congeners in the more southerly parts of the continent.

I have seen the skins of many lions and lionesses in South Africa, which seemed to be those of full-sized animals though they may have been young in years, showing very well-defined red-brown spots on the legs, flanks, and belly. The old Boer hunters, indeed, had a name for such lions, "bont pod leeuws" (spotted-footed lions), which some of them maintained belonged to a distinct species. I once, however, showed the skins of five lions, which I had recently shot in Mashunaland, to a well-known Boer hunter. One was that of a large male with a fine dark mane. This he declared to be the skin of a "swart voer-leif leeuw" (lion with the front part of the body black); whilst the skin of a lioness which showed a good many spots on the legs and belly, he declared to be that of a "bont pod leeuw, de kwai sort" (spotted-footed lion, the vicious kind). As, however, these two animals were consorting together when I shot them, I do not believe that they belonged to different species or even races. I am inclined to think that lions showing spots on the legs and belly, when adult but still not old, might very likely lose them in later life.

In regard to wild lions, it may be said, as a general proposition, that the mane usually grows round the neck and on the chest only, with a prolongation from the back of the neck to behind the shoulder-blades. Sometimes large full-grown male lions will be practically maneless. Occasionally specimens will be met with in which the entire shoulders as well as the neck will be covered with mane. When writing of lions in 1881, I stated that I had never seen the skin of a wild lion in which the whole belly was covered with long hair, as is so often the case with lions in captivity in this country, though I had seen full-maned wild lions with large tufts of long dark hair on the elbows and in the flanks. A few years later, however, Lo Bengula, the last chief of the Matabele, gave me the skin of a lion which had been killed near the upper course of the Umzingwani river, not far from Bulawayo, with a very fine mane. In this specimen the tufts of hair in the flanks were very profuse, almost meeting across the belly, and there were a few long hairs all over the under parts of the skin. There is also, I think, good evidence to show that in the more southerly portions of South Africa lions not infrequently developed a growth of long hair all over their bellies; for not only are all the lions figured by Captain (afterwards Sir Cornwallis) Harris so adorned, but there is now in the Junior United Service Club in London a mounted specimen of a South African lion with not only an extraordinary wealth of mane covering the whole of the fore-part of the body, but also with a thick growth of long hair all over its belly. This lion is said to have been killed near the Orange river about 1830, probably, I should think, on the bontebok flats, near Colesberg, in the Cape Colony, though possibly on the plains to the north of the river. Now, personally I believe that cold has more to do with the development of a lion's mane than anything else. The winter cold of the high plateaus of the Cape Colony, the Orange Colony, and the Southern Transvaal is much more severe than in any part of Africa where lions exist to-day, and Harris's drawings and the mounted specimen of the lion I have above referred to, which was killed near the Orange river long ago, show that wild lions sometimes attained very profuse manes and had their bellies covered with long hair in that part of Africa. To-day, lions with really fine manes are never found except in countries where the nights are cold during the winter months, such as the Athi plains, the Uas N'gishu plateau, the high downs of Matabeleland and Mashunaland, and the Haud of Somaliland, as well as other elevated regions. In the Pungwe river district some few lions attain fairly good, but never, I believe, extraordinarily profuse manes. Only a certain proportion of the lions found on high and cold plateaus have, however, fine long dark manes. Many have very poor manes, but it seems to me impossible that there can be more than one species of lion in so confined an area. In the hotter parts of Africa, lying below the level of the more elevated plateaus, I think I am correct in saying that lions never get fine manes, and the hotter the climate, the poorer on the average the manes will be. The fact that the high, cold plateaus are always open grasslands free from thorn-bush, whilst the lower parts of the country are usually covered with scrubby bush and thorny thickets, has led many people to think that lions have poor manes in bush-covered countries because the thorns tear out the hair; but I think that this is quite a mistaken idea, for in the western part of Matabeleland, in the neighbourhood of the Ramokwebani and Tati rivers, where the winter nights are very cold, although the whole country is covered with forest, much of it dense thorn-bush, the lions used sometimes to grow very fine long manes. Personally, therefore, I am convinced that climate is the main factor in the production of a lion's mane, and possibly very high feeding may help to produce certain exceptionally fine animals. As the high plateaus of Southern and Eastern Africa have, before the advent of Europeans, always teemed with great multitudes of zebras and antelopes, and in some cases buffaloes as well, the lions of the high and cold plateaus have most certainly always been well fed. The lions living in the Pungwe river district too must, before the advent of Europeans, have been exceptionally well fed.

It has always seemed to me that in Africa and India, where, although the nights may be cold, the sun is always hot, a heavy mane must be more or less of a nuisance and encumbrance to a lion; and I believe that such a wonderful growth of hair must be a reversion to an ancestral adornment first evolved in a cold climate.

The fossil remains of the so-called cave lion (*Felis spelaea*), which have been discovered in great abundance in the cave deposits of Pleistocene times in Western Europe, are said by Professor Boyd

Dawkins to present absolutely no osteological or dental character by which they can be distinguished from those of existing lions, and I think that we are therefore justified in believing that the lion was first evolved in a cold climate, and that in the course of ages it gradually spread south and east, following the migrations of the game on which it preyed. It probably entered Africa before that continent was separated from Europe by the Mediterranean Sea, at the same time as the ancestors of the giraffes, antelopes, buffaloes, elephants, and rhinoceroses of to-day, and accompanied them through Eastern Africa right down to Cape Agulhas. Some lions remained in Europe long after the separation of Africa from that continent, and even in the time of Herodotus these animals appear to have been still common throughout South-Eastern Europe.

As the ancient cave lions which roamed the woods and plains of Western Europe co-existed with bears, mammoths, reindeer, elk, wild cattle, and other denizens of a cold country, there can be little doubt that their coats were thick and furry in both sexes, whilst a heavy mane would have been an adornment to the males without being an encumbrance.

That the flowing mane and shaggy hair on the belly of the male lion were first evolved in a cold climate is, I think, proved by the undoubted fact that there is an inherited tendency in all lions to grow a mane, which is crippled and dwarfed by a hot climate but encouraged by exposure to cold. Quite recently there was a fine lion in the Zoological Society's Gardens at Regent's Park which was presented by Messrs. Grogan and Sharpe. This animal was caught near the Pungwe river, in South-East Africa, and brought to England by these gentlemen when quite a small cub. When full-grown it developed a very much finer mane than I believe has ever been seen in a wild lion that has come to maturity in the part of Africa from which it was brought. Similarly, some thirty years ago there was a very fine lion in the Society's Gardens which was brought by Colonel Knox from the Soudan. Colonel Knox took me to the Gardens to see this animal, and pointed out to me the fact that it had developed a far finer mane (extending much farther back over the shoulders and under the belly) than any man had ever seen in a wild lion in the country from which it came. Lion cubs brought to this country from India also grow fine manes, though I do not think that there is any record of a lion ever having been shot in India with anything more than a fairly good mane. The fact that lion cubs captured in any part of Africa or Asia, and brought up in the comparatively cool and damp climate of Western Europe, always—or nearly always—grow fine manes, which usually cover the whole shoulders and often extend all over the under-surface of the body, and the further fact that in the hotter parts of Africa lions always have very scanty manes, but on the high, cold plateaus often develop good, and occasionally very luxuriant manes, appears to me to show that a heavily maned lion is a reversion to an ancient ancestral type, first evolved in Pleistocene times in a cold and inclement climate.

CHAPTER V

NOTES ON THE LION (*concluded*)

Method of opening a carcase—Removal of paunch and entrails—Lions skilful butchers—Paunch and entrails not usually eaten—Lions not bone-eaters—Will eat putrid meat—Will sometimes devour their own kind—Number of cubs at birth—Check on inordinate increase of carnivorous animals—The lion's roar—Diversity of opinion concerning its power—Probable explanation—Volume of sound when several lions roar in unison—A nerve-shaking experience—Lions silent when approaching their prey—Roar after killing—And in answer to one another—Lions only roar freely in undisturbed districts—Lions essentially game-killers—But change their habits with circumstances—Killing lions with spear and shield — Bambaleli's splendid courage—Lions killed by Bushmen with poisoned arrows—Behaviour of domestic animals in the presence of lions—Cattle sometimes terrified, at other times show no fear.

WHEN once a lion or lions have killed an animal they almost always open the carcase at the point where the skin is thinnest, that is, in the flank just in front of where the thigh joins the belly. They then at once tear off and eat this thin skin and the flesh attached to it, and all the skin and flesh covering the paunch and entrails, which latter they then proceed to remove from the carcase. The neatness and cleanliness with which lions can take the inside out of an animal they have just killed has always struck me as little short of marvellous. Every one who has had to do much cutting up of large animals knows how easy it is to tear the skin of the paunch and get some of its contents on the meat, and African natives are nearly always very clumsy and dirty in this respect. Lions, however, are able to remove the paunch and entrails from the carcase of a large animal as skilfully as a trained butcher. The offal itself is dragged away to a distance of ten yards or so, and then covered with earth or grass, which is scratched up and thrown over it. As a rule, lions certainly do not eat the paunch and entrails of any animals which they may kill, but I once had occasion to search through a refuse-heap left by a party of lions near the carcase of a buffalo they had killed, in the hope of finding some scavenger beetles of a rare species, and I found that it contained nothing but vegetable matter —the contents of the buffalo's stomach. If the lions had not eaten the entrails and the covering of the paunch, I do not know what had become of them. This refuse-heap as usual had been thickly covered with earth and grass, which had been scratched up from all around it. Once the inside of a carcase has been removed, the liver, kidneys, heart, and lungs are eaten, with all the fat adhering to them. Then the carcase is again torn open at the anus, and the soft meat of the buttocks is devoured in great lumps, which are swallowed whole with the skin attached. No lion will ever scrunch up heavy bones like a hyæna, but should he kill an animal in good condition, he will swallow all the comparatively soft bones of the brisket, and also gnaw off the ends of all the rib-bones. The idea that lions will not eat the flesh of any animal which they have not killed themselves is quite erroneous. It would, indeed, be more correct to say that as long as lions can find dead animals to eat, they will not take the trouble to hunt. Nor are they at all particular as to the condition of any carcase they may chance to come across. As long as there is any meat left on it, they will eat it, and I have known lions to remain for days in the neighbourhood of the putrid carcases of elephants, on which they fed nightly, in preference to hunting for fresh meat, although game of all kinds was plentiful in the neighbourhood. Two instances of lions eating the flesh of one of their own kind have come under my personal observation, and although such a practice is undoubtedly of unusual occurrence, yet I should imagine that, provided hunger and opportunity were both present, there are few lions that would disdain a meal off the carcase of an individual of their own species.

Although I am informed that lionesses in captivity often give birth to four, and sometimes to as many as five or six cubs, in the wild state the usual number is certainly three, and of these a large number, for some reason which has never been ascertained, never reach maturity, for it is seldom that lionesses are met with accompanied by more than two large cubs, and they often only rear one.

It is an axiom that all birds and mammals living in countries where the climatic conditions are favourable, and where they have no enemies, will increase in numbers up to the limit of the food-supply available for them. When the ground becomes overstocked, diseases break out, which only the strongest and healthiest animals are able to resist, and these survivors perpetuate the race, which will once more increase and multiply up to a certain point. But what is it that checks the inordinate increase of carnivorous animals? They certainly do not go on increasing in numbers up to the limit of their food-supply, otherwise there are many parts of Africa in which, before the advent of the white man, lions, leopards, cheetahs, hyænas, and wild dogs, not to mention all the smaller carnivora, would have increased to such an extent that they would gradually have denuded the country of all herbivorous animals, and would then have died in large numbers themselves, till in the end there would have been few animals of any kind left. But such catastrophes never occur. Wherever, before the advent of the white man, game was very plentiful in Africa, lions and all other carnivorous animals were also numerous, but the meat-eaters never increased to such an extent as to reduce the numbers of the grass-eaters on which they preyed. Let us take the Pungwe district in South-East Africa for example. In 1891 I found the country both east and west of the Pungwe river teeming with game, particularly buffaloes and zebras, the favourite food of the lion. Up to that time no Europeans had ever hunted or in any way disturbed the wild beasts in that country, and the few scattered natives living there were timid and ill armed, and certainly never killed or interfered with lions, which animals therefore were absolutely without enemies. As this state of things must have endured for centuries, or more probably for untold thousands, of years, why had not the lions and other carnivorous animals, living as they had been doing in such a well-stocked preserve, increased up to the limit of their food-supply? They certainly had not done so up to 1891, the year the white man first entered the country, and at once of course changed all the natural conditions. Many lions certainly seem to die in early cubhood, and this may be a provision of nature to check their inordinate increase; but that neither they nor any other species of carnivorous animal in Africa ever become so numerous, under the most favourable conditions, as to seriously diminish the numbers of the animals on which they prey is a well-ascertained fact.

Lionesses, I believe, only give birth to cubs at long intervals, for although I have often seen young lions and lionesses with their mothers which must have been at least two years old, I have never seen a lioness accompanied by cubs of different ages.

One of the most distinguishing characteristics of the lion, and the one which perhaps differentiates it more than anything else from all other members of the cat tribe, is its roar. During more than twenty years spent in hunting and pioneering in the African wilderness, I have heard lions roaring under all sorts of conditions: in the stillness of frosty winter nights, when the camp fire blazed merrily, and as each fresh log was thrown upon it sent up showers of sparks towards the cloudless, star-decked sky; or amidst the crashing thunder-peals and blinding flashes of lightning of a stormy night during the rainy season, when it was sometimes quite impossible to keep a fire alight at all. On such a night, when sitting wet and cold amongst one's Kafir boys, huddled up beneath the scanty shelter of a few boughs (for I never carried a tent with me in South Africa), the roaring of lions is not altogether a reassuring sound.

On a still night the roaring of lions can be heard at a very great distance, and should a party of these animals roar loudly quite a mile away, I think most people would imagine that they were within one hundred yards. One reason, I think, for the diversity of opinion as to the power and volume of the lion's roar is, that very few people have ever really heard several lions roaring together quite close to them, although they may believe they have done so. In 1891, and again in 1892, I spent some weeks travelling and hunting in the country between Lake Sungwe and the Pungwe river, in South-East Africa, and there was scarcely a night on both those trips when lions were not heard roaring, often as many as three, and once four, different troops of these animals appearing to be answering one another from different points of the compass; but although on the second trip—I was alone in 1891—my companions, who had not had much experience in the veld, often thought the lions were very near us, I am sure they were never within a mile of our camp.

When a party of lions are together, perhaps on their way to drink after a meal, one of them will halt and breathe out from its expanded lungs a full-toned note, which rolls afar across the silent wilderness. As it draws in its breath for another effort, a second member of the party emulates the leader, and then a third, a fourth, and a fifth perhaps will join in, and all of them then seem to vie with one another as to which can produce the greatest volume of sound, and it is a fact that at the climax of the roaring of a troop of lions the whole air seems to vibrate and tremble. Of a sudden the grand booming, vibrating notes cease, and are immediately succeeded by a series of short, deep-toned, coughing grunts, which gradually die away to a mere hissing expulsion of the breath. Then not a sound is heard until, after an interval of a few minutes, the grand competitive roaring peals across the lonely veld once more. During some few out of the thousands of nights I have lain on the ground, beneath the stars, in the interior of South Africa, I have heard lions roaring pretty near my camp; but never quite so near as one dark night in 1879. I was returning from the Chobi river to where I had left my waggons in the Mababi country, and was alone with five Kafirs. One evening just at dusk we reached the last water-hole in the Sunta river. We had made a long march in intense heat, as it was the month of November, and were all so tired that we made no camp nor collected much firewood, but just lay down on the sandy ground round a very small fire. Not long after dark we heard a troop of lions roaring in the distance; presently they roared again evidently nearer, and roaring magnificently at intervals, they continued to approach until there could be no doubt that they were coming down to drink at the water-hole close to our bivouac. This water-hole was situated in the bed of the river at the foot of a steep high bank on the top of which we were lying. A game-path led down into the river-bed some fifteen yards away, and the lions were coming down this path. The night was inky black, as the sky was overcast with heavy clouds, for the rainy season was close at hand. Our fire had died down to a few embers, and it was useless looking for wood in such darkness. I don't think the lions ever noticed our dying fire, or ever had any idea of our close proximity to the water-hole, as, after having roared about a quarter of a mile away, they walked noiselessly past us along the game-path, and descending to the river-bed, commenced to slake their thirst. We could hear them lapping the water when they were drinking. They roared three times in the river-bed just below us, and the volume of sound they emitted when all roaring in unison was nerve-shaking. My Kafirs sat motionless and silent, holding their hands over their mouths. There were no trees of any size near us, only small bushes, so they could not make a run for it to any place of safety. They confessed to me the next morning that when they heard the lions roaring so near them "their hearts died," meaning that they were terrified; and although I myself was not then of a very nervous disposition, and moreover believed that when lions roared loudly they were not hungry, and would therefore be unlikely to attack a human being, I was very glad when they at last left the water and we heard them go roaring back to where they had probably been feeding on the carcase of a buffalo or some other animal before they came to drink.

I certainly do not believe that lions roar when

approaching their prey, for surely such a proceeding would be as foolish as it would be for a burglar to whistle and sing whilst committing a robbery, but they will sometimes roar loudly in the late evening or early night, just as they leave their lairs and set out to look for prey. When moving about at night, lions sometimes give vent to a low purring growl—very different in sound to a roar—which may be a call-note to others of their party, and if driven off by shots from a horse or an ox they have killed in the night, they will growl loudly. In approaching a camp with the intention of killing oxen, horses, donkeys, or human beings, lions are absolutely silent, as I believe they always are when approaching any kind of wild game. I believe that lions often roar after they have killed an animal and before commencing to feed, and at intervals during the night, as they lie round the carcase, and they certainly often roar when on their way to drink in the early hours of the night, but probably after they have killed some large animal and made a meal. The roaring of one lion or party of lions undoubtedly excites other lions within hearing to roar in answer. I once heard several lions roaring loudly throughout the night, and even after the sun had risen the next morning, and I found that a solitary male lion had approached a party consisting of another male, two females, and two large cubs, standing as high at the shoulder as the full-grown females. The single male was, I imagine, jealous of his married kinsman, but feared to engage in deadly combat with him, and so contented himself by roaring defiance at his rival, who answered with counter roars, in which his whole family joined. The next morning I just missed getting a shot at the unattached lion, but killed the other, a very fine but hasty tempered animal, as he charged me at sight without any provocation.

"A PICKED MAN OF DAUNTLESS HEART . . . WOULD RUSH FORWARD ALONE . . ."

In countries where lions have long lived undisturbed by human beings, and where they have really been the undisputed lords of the wilderness, they roar very freely, and may often be heard even after the sun has risen. But when white men suddenly invade a well-stocked game-country and disturb its peace by continual shooting, lions gradually grow more and more silent, till it becomes rare to hear one roar at all, though there may still be a good many of them about. The African lion is essentially a wilderness hunter and a game-killer, but when man, whether savage or civilised, encroaches upon his preserves, killing or driving off the game, and bringing in cattle, sheep, and goats in their place, then he preys upon these newly introduced animals and wars with their guardians to the death.

Before the introduction of firearms amongst the Matabele, these courageous savages, though only armed with shield and spear, were accustomed to join battle without a moment's hesitation with any lion or lions that interfered with the cattle given over to their charge by their king. Full and drowsy after his feed of beef, the marauding lion would not usually go far from the carcase of the ox or cow he had killed before lying down to sleep. Soon after break of day the swarthy cattle guards would track him to his lair and silently surround and then close in on him, heaping every term of abuse upon his head as they did so. The lion thus roused, and seeing all retreat cut off, would stand at bay, and growling savagely, with head held low, ears laid flat, lashing tail, and mouth held slightly open, would glance from side to side with blazing eyes upon its foes. Then a picked man of dauntless heart, armed with a single stabbing spear and a very large ox-hide shield, would rush forward alone towards the lion, cursing and abusing it in true

Homeric fashion. The lion, seeing its retreat cut off, almost invariably accepted the challenge and rushed upon the advancing savage, whose endeavour it was to strike one blow at his assailant and then fall to the ground beneath his broad shield. At the same time, his friends would rush in from both sides and quickly spear the lion to death, but often not before one or two of them had paid the penalty for their daring with their lives. Many lions used to be killed annually in the olden time round the outlying cattle posts in Matabeleland, and many of Umziligazi's[1] bravest warriors died of wounds received in these gladiatorial games. Many years ago I used to be very friendly with the second Enduna of Bulawayo, one Bambaleli, a splendid specimen of a good, brave, honest, heathen gentleman. He told me that on five occasions he had been chosen to rush in on a lion that had been surrounded and brought to bay. Twice he escaped without a wound, thanks to the protection afforded by his great shield and the quickness with which his comrades had rushed in to his assistance; but in the other three encounters he had been severely bitten, once in the right shoulder and twice through the muscles of his thigh, and he bore the scars of all these honourable wounds to his grave. The fact that, on each of the occasions when he was hurt, his formidable assailant had only been able to get in one savage bite, shows, I think, the quickness with which his friends had come to his rescue.

Before they were supplied with firearms by their Bechwana masters, the Bushmen of the Kalahari sometimes killed lions with poisoned arrows. Old Bushmen have assured me that they had themselves killed lions by this means. Their plan, they said, was to creep close up to a lion lying asleep after

[1] The father of Lo Bengula.

a heavy meal, and then to shoot one of their little reed arrows into some part of its body from behind the shelter of a bush or tree. The sharp prick would awake the lion but not greatly alarm it, and as it would see nothing to account for the disturbance of its slumbers, it would probably think it had been stung by some fly. It would probably, however, get up and walk away. The shaft of the arrow would soon fall to the ground, but the bone head, barbed and thickly smeared with poison, would remain fixed in its victim's hide, and the deadly compound would gradually permeate its blood and sap its strength. The Bushmen averred that a lion once struck by a poisoned arrow never recovered, though it would not die till the third day.

Domestic animals such as horses and oxen sometimes show great alarm at the near proximity of lions, at others they only seem slightly scared, and sometimes they do not seem to be frightened at all. If a horse has once been bitten by a lion, or if another horse tied up close to it has been attacked, it will probably ever afterwards evince great fear at the smell of a lion. But, on the other hand, I have had several horses in my possession, which I bought in the Cape Colony or the Orange Free State, which, when I had trained them to carry the meat of antelopes, never showed the slightest sign of fear when a reeking lion skin was put on their backs, although they could never possibly have seen or smelt a lion before I took them up country. I had some trouble at first to train some of these horses to carry the meat of any kind of fresh-killed game, and they always began by smelling it and then snorting; but once they became accustomed to the smell of antelope meat, they showed no further alarm when the skin of a freshly killed lion was thrown over the saddle.

I have known a herd of cattle, after one of their

number had been killed by a lion, travel more than twenty miles without feeding, evidently in a state of terror all the time. On the other hand, I was lying in my blankets at my camp on the Hanyani river, in Mashunaland, one day early in 1885, just in the throes of a sharp attack of fever and ague, when my cattle-herd came rushing in, saying that there was a lion amongst my cattle, and that it was killing a heifer. This was about two o'clock in the afternoon. Pulling myself together, I had one of my horses saddled up, and calling my dogs, rode out to see what had happened. I found my cattle, over fifty altogether in number, all feeding quietly not 400 yards away from my camp, just where they were, my herd-boy said, when the lion came amongst them. As it turned out, it was a lioness. She had clawed a three-year-old heifer in the flanks and on the hind-quarters, but had either been kicked off by the heifer itself or driven off by the rest of the herd. At any rate, the sudden appearance of this lioness in their midst had created no panic amongst the cattle. I had a chase after this lioness with my dogs, but she crossed the river and got into some very thick bush, and as I could not get a sight of her and was feeling very unwell, I returned to camp.

In 1887, one day about noon, four lions—two males and two females—attacked my oxen and killed two of them, but without apparently alarming the others in the slightest degree, as they never ran away nor showed any sign of having been frightened. One dark night early in 1892, I was camped near the Revue river, in South-East Africa, and my oxen were lying loose round the waggon, as I thought there were no lions in the neighbourhood. About midnight five lions came up to reconnoitre, and my oxen no doubt smelt them, for they jumped up and stampeded in a body. As they ran, the lions caught and pulled down one of them. The next morning I thought I might possibly have to follow my frightened oxen a long way before overtaking them, but I found them feeding quietly, and showing no signs of having been terrified, only a few hundred yards away. On the whole, I do not think that domestic animals have that ingrained and instinctive fear of lions with which they are usually credited, though the smell of these animals is doubtless disagreeable to them.

CHAPTER VI

NOTES ON THE SPOTTED HYÆNA

Character of hyænas—Contrasted with that of wolves—Story illustrating the strength and audacity of a spotted hyæna—How a goat was seized and carried off—A mean trick—Boldness of hyænas near native villages — More suspicious in the wilderness—Very destructive to native live stock—Will sometimes enter native huts—Giving an old woman to the hyænas—How the smelling out of witches benefited the hyænas—"Come out, missionary, and give us the witch"—Number of hyænas infesting Matabeleland in olden times — Trials for witchcraft in Matabeleland — Food of hyænas — Strength of jaws—Charged by a wounded hyæna—Heavy trap broken up—Killing hyænas with set guns—Hyæna held by dogs—Hyæna attacked by wild dogs—Pace of hyænas—Curious experience on the Mababi plain — The hyæna's howl—Rhinoceros calf killed by hyænas—Smell of hyænas—Hyæna meat a delicacy—Small cows and donkeys easily killed by hyænas—Size and weight of the spotted hyæna—Number of whelps.

It has always appeared to me that the qualities and characteristics of the African spotted hyæna have met with somewhat scant recognition at the hands of writers on sport, travel, and natural history, for this animal is usually tersely described as a cowardly, skulking brute, and then dismissed with a few contemptuous words.

Yet I think that the spotted hyæna of Africa is quite as dangerous and destructive an animal as the wolf of North America, which is usually treated with respect, sometimes with sympathy, by its biographers, though I cannot see that wolves are in any way nobler in character than hyænas. Both breeds roam abroad by night, ever crafty, fierce, and hungry, and both will be equally ready to tear open the graves and devour the flesh of human beings, should the opportunity present itself, whether on the shores of the Arctic Sea, where men's skins are yellowy brown, or beneath the shadow of the Southern Cross, where they are sooty black. There is nothing really noble, though much that is interesting, in the nature of either wolves or hyænas, but neither of these animals ought to be despised. Hyænas are big, powerful, dangerous brutes, and at night often show great determination and courage in their attempts to obtain food at the expense of human beings. The following story will illustrate, I think, both the strength and the audacity of a spotted hyæna.

I was once camped many years ago near a small native village on the high veld of Mashunaland to the south-east of the present town of Salisbury. A piece of ground some fifty yards long by twenty in breadth had been enclosed by a small light hedge made of thornless boughs, as it was supposed that there were no lions in this part of the country. In the midst of this enclosure my waggon was standing one night with the oxen tied to the yokes, and my two shooting horses fastened to the wheels. On the previous day I had shot three eland bulls, and had had every scrap of the meat as well as the skins and heads carried to my waggon, and on the evening of the following day there were a large number of natives in my camp from the surrounding villages. These men had brought me an abundant supply of native beer, ground nuts, pumpkins, sweet potatoes, maize, etc., and as I, on my side, had given them several hundredweights of meat, both they and my own boys were preparing to make a night of it in my encampment.

About an hour after dark, the boy who looked after my horses stretched one of the eland hides on the ground behind the waggon, and then pouring a large pot full of half-boiled maize upon it, spread it out to cool before putting it into the horses' nosebags for their evening feed. At this time my whole camp was lighted up by the blazing fires the natives had lit all along one side of the enclosure, and of course within the hedge. Every one was happy, with plenty of fat meat to eat and beer to drink, and the whole crowd kept up an incessant babble of talk and laughter, as only happy Africans can.

I was quite alone, as I had been for months, with these good-tempered primitive people, and I may here say that I went to sleep every night in their midst, and always completely in their power (as I had not a single armed follower with me), feeling as absolutely safe, as indeed I was, as if I had been in an hotel in London.

I had just finished my evening meal, and was sitting by the fire that had been lighted at the foot of my bed of dry grass, when I saw a big hyæna burst through the lightly made hedge of boughs on the other side of the waggon and advance boldly into the centre of the enclosure, where he stood for a moment looking about him, plainly visible to every one in the bright light cast by twenty fires. The next moment he advanced to where the eland skin lay spread upon the ground behind the waggon, and seizing it, dashed back with it through the fence and disappeared into the darkness of the night.

I had several large dogs with me on this trip, which were all lying near the fires when the hyæna entered the encampment from the other side, but as the latter had come up against the wind, they had not smelt him. When, however, he appeared within a few yards of them, and in the full light of the fires, they of course saw him, and as he seized the eland skin and dashed off with it, scattering my horses' feed to the winds as he did so, the dogs rushed after him, barking loudly. I do not know exactly what the green hide of a big eland bull may weigh, but it is certainly very much heavier than the skin of a bullock, and of course a very awkward thing to carry off, as the weight would be distributed over so much ground. Yet, although this hyæna had only a start of a few yards, my dogs did not overtake him, or at any rate did not force him to drop the skin, until he had reached the little stream of water that ran through the valley more than a hundred yards below my camp. Here we found the dogs guarding it a few minutes later, and again dragged it back to the waggon.

I knew the hyæna would follow, so I went and sat outside the camp behind a little bush on the trail of the skin, and very soon he walked close up to me. I could only just make out a something darker than the night, but as it moved, I knew it could be nothing but the animal I was waiting for, and when it was very near me I fired and wounded it, and we killed it in the little creek below the camp. It proved to be a very large old male hyæna, which the Mashunas said had lately killed several head of cattle, besides many sheep and goats.

I cannot help thinking that this hyæna must have thrown part of the heavy hide over his shoulders as he seized it, though I cannot say that I saw him do this, but if he did not half carry it, I don't believe he could possibly have gone off with it at the pace he did, for the dogs did not overtake him until he had nearly reached the stream, more than a hundred yards distant from my camp. I am inclined to the view that this hyæna must have half carried, half dragged this heavy hide, as I once saw one of these animals seize a goat by the back of the neck, and throwing it over its shoulders, gallop off with it. This was just outside a native kraal in Western Matabeleland near the river Gwai. I had outspanned my waggon there one evening, and having bought a large fat goat, which must have weighed fifty pounds as it stood, I fastened it by one of its forelegs to one of the front wheels of the waggon. I then had some dry grass cut, and made my bed on the ground alongside of the other front wheel, not six feet distant from where the goat was fastened.

It was a brilliant moonlight night and very cold, and I had not long turned in, and was lying wide awake, when I heard the goat give a loud "baa," and instantly turning my head, saw a hyæna seize it by the back of the neck, break the thong with which it was tied to the waggon wheel with a jerk, and go off at a gallop with, as well as I could see, the body of the goat thrown over his shoulders. All my dogs were lying round the fires where the Kafirs were sleeping when the hyæna seized the goat, and as he had come up against the wind, had not smelt him. But when the goat "baaed" they all sprang up and dashed after the marauder, closely followed by my Kafirs. The dogs caught up to the hyæna after a short chase and made him drop the goat, which the Kafirs brought back to the waggon. It was quite alive, but as it had been badly bitten behind the ears I had it killed at once.

A hyæna once played me a particularly mean trick. I was outspanned one night towards the close of the year 1891 in Mashunaland near the Hanyani river, not many miles from the town of Salisbury. It was either the night of the full moon or within a day or two of it. At any rate, it was a gloriously bright moonlight night. I had shot a reedbuck that day, and in the evening placed its

"ON THE SECOND NIGHT THEY ONCE MORE LEFT IT ALONE, BUT ON THE THIRD THEY DEVOURED IT."

hind-quarters on a flat granite rock, close to where my cart was standing. I then made my bed on the ground close to the flat rock, and, as the moonlight was so bright, never troubled to surround my camp with any kind of fence. Pulling the blanket over my head, I soon went fast asleep. During the night I woke up, and was astonished to find that it was dark. This I soon saw was owing to a complete eclipse of the moon. When the shadow had passed, and it once more became light, I found that the choice piece of antelope meat which I had placed on the stone close behind my head was gone, and I have no doubt that it had been carried off by a hyæna during the eclipse of the moon.

Hyænas are always far bolder and more dangerous in the neighbourhood of native villages than they are in the uninhabited wilderness.

In the year 1872 a Bushman Hottentot who had shot a Kafir in cold blood, was beaten to death with clubs by friends of the murdered man close to where my waggon was standing near the Jomani river, in a wild, uninhabited part of Eastern Matabeleland. I did not know anything about this summary administration of justice until it was over, as it took place at the waggons of some Griqua hunters who were camped near me. The body of the Hottentot was then dragged to a spot less than three hundred yards from my waggon, and quite close to the Griqua encampment. That night several hyænas laughed and cackled and howled round the corpse from dark to daylight, but they never touched it. On the second night they once more left it alone, but on the third they devoured it. I do not know why these hyænas waited until the third night before making a meal off the body of this dead Hottentot, but I imagine that it was because they were hyænas of the wilderness, unaccustomed to, and therefore suspicious of the smell of a human being. I have noticed, too, that in the wilds hyænas will often, though not always, pass the carcase of a freshly killed lion without touching it.

In any part of the country, however, where there is a considerable native population, and where consequently there is little or no game, hyænas have no fear or suspicion of a dead man. They make their living out of the natives round whose villages they patrol nightly. They soon discover any weak spot in the pens where the goats, sheep, or calves are kept, and kill and carry off numbers of these animals. They often, too, kill full-grown cows by tearing their udders open and then disembowelling them, and will sometimes enter a hut, the door of which has been left open, and make a snap at the head of a sleeping man or woman, or carry off a child. When lying once very weak and ill with fever in a hut in a small Banyai village near the Zambesi, I awoke suddenly and saw a hyæna standing in the open doorway, through which the moon was shining brightly. I lay quite still and he came right inside, but he heard me moving as I caught hold of my rifle, and bolted out, carrying with him a bundle tied up with raw hide thongs. The latter he afterwards ate, but we recovered the contents of the bundle the next morning.

Besides being able to dig up the carelessly buried bodies of natives who have died a natural death, the customs of some of the warlike tribes used to provide hyænas with many a dainty meal. In 1873 my old friend the late Mr. Frank Mandy—afterwards for so many years the manager of De Beers Compound at Kimberley—saw some natives dragging, with thongs attached to the wrists, what he thought was a dead body across the stony ground outside the native town of Bulawayo.[1] On going

[1] The original native town built by Lo Bengula in 1870, about twelve miles from the present European city.

nearer he was horrified to find that the body was that of an old woman, and that she was alive. On remonstrating with the men who were dragging the poor creature along, and taxing them with their inhumanity, they seemed quite hurt, and said, "Why, what use is she? She's an old slave, and altogether past work, and we are going to give her to the hyænas." They accordingly dragged her down to the valley below Bulawayo and tied her to a tree. My friend had followed and watched them, and that evening, as soon as it was dusk, he and a trader named Grant—who was murdered in Mashunaland by the natives during the rising of 1896—went down to her with a stretcher, and cutting the thongs that bound her to the tree, carried her up to Mandy's hut, where, however, she died during the night.

I do not wish it to be understood that the custom of tying old and worn-out slaves to trees, whilst still alive, to be devoured by hyænas, was very common, but it cannot have been very unusual either, as Mandy told me that many natives looked on with absolute indifference whilst the old woman whose fate I have described was dragged past them; so the hyænas must have got many a good feed in this way, especially round the larger towns. But the native custom which was most advantageous to these animals was the practice of smelling out witches. In Matabeleland, in the time of Umziligazi and his son Lo Bengula, people were continually being tried and convicted of witchcraft, and very often not only was the actual witch, man or woman, killed, but their families as well, sometimes even all their relations, as in the case of Lotchi, head Enduna of the town of Induba, who was put to death in 1888, and the number of whose wives, children, and other relations who were killed with him amounted to seventy. When the evidence had been heard the king pronounced the sentence, which was often conveyed by the two words "niga impisi" (give him, her, or them to the hyænas). The wretches were then taken just outside the kraal fence and clubbed to death. Their huts were also pulled down and thrown out. I remember I was once sleeping at the house of Mr. C——, a missionary in Matabeleland, when a lot of natives came to the door very early in the morning, and kept shouting out in a very excited manner, "Come out, missionary, and give us the witch; we want to take him to his mother, who is a witch also, and kill them both together." It appeared that the man they said was a witch was a native, who had been left in charge of another missionary's house during his master's absence in the Cape Colony, and who by steady work had accumulated enough money to buy a few head of cattle. This man had been accused of bewitching some of the king's cattle, and Lo Bengula had pronounced sentence of death upon him. Directly I saw the men outside Mr. C——'s house I thought from their manner that they had already killed the falsely accused man, although they denied having done so; but when Mr. C—— and I went across the valley towards the poor fellow's kraal on the other side, they all left us.

It was as I had surmised; for we found Mr. H——'s faithful servant lying on his face just outside the fence of his kraal, with his elbows tied behind his back and his head in much the same condition as that of Banquo's ghost, as represented on the London stage. On the evening of that day the sun had not been long down when we heard the hyænas howling, and that night they held high carnival over the murdered man's remains.

Some idea of the number of hyænas that used to infest Matabeleland in the old savage times may be gathered from the fact that my old friend the late Mr. G. A. Philips once poisoned with strychnine twenty-one of these animals round the old town of Bulawayo in one night.

I was never able to get a full account of the proceedings at a trial for witchcraft in Matabeleland, but from all I have heard they must have been strangely similar to those trials for the same alleged crime which were so common a few centuries ago in England and Scotland. In recent times in Matabeleland, just as in mediæval times in England, everybody, almost without exception, believed in witchcraft, and there can be no doubt that in both countries men and women existed who firmly believed themselves to be possessed of the powers ascribed to witches. One of the commonest accusations against men accused of witchcraft in Matabeleland was that they had been seen riding a hyæna at night, and on this account when one of these animals was killed, it was looked upon as an unfeeling joke to point to it and say to any native, "Nansi ibeza yako" ("There lies your horse").

Although hyænas eat large quantities of soft meat when they get the chance, they can do very well on a diet of little else than bones. When a large animal is killed by lions, these purely carnivorous animals eat the greater part of the soft meat, and then leave the carcase to the hyænas, which are pretty sure to be at hand. These latter then scrunch up and swallow many of the bones. So powerful are their jaws that they can break the leg-bones of buffaloes and giraffes, the ends of which they gnaw off after extracting the marrow.

I once wounded a large hyæna as he ran out of a patch of long grass, where he had been lying asleep. After following on his blood spoor for a few hundred yards, I came upon him lying under a bush, evidently badly wounded. On the previous day I had bought a very large-bladed assegai from a Mashuna blacksmith, and so, dismounting, I took this assegai from the Kafir who was carrying it, and advanced on the wounded hyæna to give him the *coup de grace*. When I was still about ten yards away from him, he jumped up and came towards me, not with a rush certainly, but still pretty quickly, and with the evident intent to do grievous bodily harm. As he advanced he repeatedly clacked his jaws together, making a loud noise. I stood my ground with my heavy assegai poised to strike, and when the hyæna was close to me I drove it with all my force into his mouth. His jaws closed instantly on the heavy iron blade, nor was I able to again withdraw it, for although the wounded animal bit it all over from one end to the other, he opened and shut his jaws with such surprising quickness that he never lost possession of it. Finally, he pulled the iron blade of the assegai out of its wooden shaft, and then, weakening from loss of blood, fell to the ground, still clashing his jaws on it. He was not able to rise to his feet again, and the Kafirs speared him to death as he lay. I found that the heavy assegai blade had been twisted and bent and bitten in a most extraordinary manner. I kept it for a long time, and wish I still had it in my possession, as it was a veritable curiosity.

I once caught a hyæna in a very large heavy iron trap, which it required the strength of two ordinary men to set. To this trap I had attached a heavy iron waggon chain, but the other end of this chain was not made fast to anything. I caught this hyæna by hanging up the hind-leg of a sable antelope in a tree by the roadside about a hundred yards from where my waggon was outspanned. The trap was set at the foot of the tree without any bait and carefully covered. The hyæna must have jumped up at the meat and sprung the trap as he came to the ground again. One of the large iron spikes which projected from the jaws of the trap must have gone right through the leg that had been caught, as it was broken off and there was a lot of blood on the trap. When the hyæna was caught he made no noise, at least no one heard anything, but just dragged the trap with the heavy chain attached for a distance of about a hundred yards away from the waggon road and then broke it up. One jaw of the trap had been wrenched off, and the solid iron tongue which supports the plate when such a trap is set, had been twisted right round. The trap, which would probably have held a lion, was of course destroyed and the hyæna gone.

I have killed many hyænas both near native villages and in wild uninhabited parts of the country by setting guns for them, usually baited with a lump of meat tied over the muzzle, and attached with a string to a lever rigged on to the trigger, so that a straight pull exploded the charge. Of course, one arranged the trap in such a way, with the help of a few thorn bushes, that the hyæna was obliged to take the meat from in front; but I never knew these animals show any hesitation in doing so, with the result that they received the charge full in the mouth and were killed instantly. I have no doubt, however, that if a constant practice were made of setting guns for hyænas in a certain district, they would become wary and suspicious after a few of their number had been killed.

On one occasion my own dogs held a large old bitch hyæna until the Kafirs came up and speared her, but this animal had, we afterwards discovered, been shot some time previously through the lower jaw, the end of which, with both the lower canine teeth, was gone, so that she could not bite. This hyæna was, however, very fat, and the wound she had received had long since healed up after all the broken pieces of bone had sloughed out. How she had managed to eat anything but soft food I cannot imagine, for what was left of her lower jaw, being in two separate pieces, must have been useless for scrunching up bones.

One moonlight night I wounded a large male hyæna, partially paralysing his hind-quarters, and my pack of dogs at once ran up to and attacked him. Several of these dogs were large, powerful animals, and holding the hyæna by the ears, throat, and neck, they certainly prevented him from using his teeth to their discomfort, but they seemed quite unable to pull him to the ground, and when I at last drove them off, I could not see that they had hurt him in any way, so I shot him.

My friend Mr. Percy Reid once, when hunting on the Chobi river, heard a great noise, a mixture of howls and yells going on near his camp during the night, and his Kafirs asserted that they could distinguish the cries both of wild dogs and spotted hyænas. The next morning the weird sounds were again heard, and appeared to be approaching the camp, so Mr. Reid went out to see what was going on. He had only walked a short distance when he saw a very interesting sight. An old hyæna was standing with its back to a large tree, surrounded by a double circle of some twelve to fifteen wild dogs. The inner circle of these, by turn, flew in on the hyæna and tried to bite him, falling back after they had done so, and fearing apparently to come to close quarters. At the end of some five or ten minutes the old hyæna, seizing an opportunity, bolted for an adjacent tree, and, standing with his back to this, again renewed the fight. Both the hyæna and his assailants were so intent on their own concerns that they paid no heed whatever to my friend's approach, and he walked up to within fifty yards of them and shot two of the wild dogs. The remainder of the pack then ran off, leaving the hyæna alone. Mr. Reid would not shoot him, because of the brave and determined fight he had made, and he presently lumbered off at a heavy gallop, apparently none the worse for his all-night encounter with the wild dogs.

Hyænas do not always lie up during the day in caves or in holes in the ground. I have often found them sleeping in patches of long grass, and have had many a good gallop after them. I always found they ran very fast, though I have galloped right up to several in good open ground, but it was just as much as my horse could do to overtake them. Once whilst riding across the Mababi plain in 1879, about two hours after sunrise I heard some hyænas howling; but they were so far off that I could not see them, though the plain was perfectly level and open, as all the long summer grass had been burnt off. As the noise they were making, however, was very great and quite unaccountable by broad daylight, I determined to see what was going on, and galloped in the direction of the strange sounds. After a time I sighted a regular pack of hyænas trotting along towards the belt of thorn bush at the top end of the plain, and beyond the hyænas I could see there were three animals which looked larger and of a different build, and which I thought must be lions. I then galloped as hard as I could in order to get up to these three animals before they entered the bush. As I galloped, I passed and counted fifteen hyænas, trotting along like great dogs, most of which stopped and stood looking at me without any sign of fear as I rode close past them. All the time some of them kept howling. I now saw that the three larger animals were lionesses, and that there were several more hyænas in front of them, so that there must have been more than twenty of these animals out on the plain with the lionesses, two of which latter I succeeded in shooting. After I had skinned them, I rode back over the plain, but could discover no sign of the carcase of a dead animal, as I should have done, had it been anywhere near, by the flight of the vultures. Why had all these hyænas collected round these three lionesses, and why were they escorting them back to the bush again over the open plain? I can only hazard the suggestion that they had followed the lionesses in the hope that they would kill some large animal, whose bones they would then have picked after the nobler animals had eaten their full. When I heard them howling, perhaps they were upbraiding the lionesses for their want of success. Hyænas do not live in packs, but when a large animal has been killed, they scent the blood from afar and collect together for the feast, separating and going off singly to their several lairs soon after daybreak. The rapidity with which hyænas sometimes collect round a carcase is truly astonishing, and shows how numerous these animals are in countries where game is still plentiful.

I remember arriving late one evening, in July 1873, at a small water-hole in the country to the west of the river Gwai, in Matabeleland. I had left my waggon at a permanent water called Linquasi two days previously, but being only armed with two four-bore muzzle-loading elephant guns, and not having met with either elephants, rhinoceroses, or buffaloes, was still without meat for myself and my Kafirs, as, although I had seen giraffes, elands, and other antelopes, I had not been able to get within shot of any of these animals with the archaic weapons which were the only firearms at that time in my possession.

The water-hole was situated on the edge of a large open pan, at the back of a small hollow half beneath a low ledge of rock, and must have been fed from an underground spring, as the Bushmen told me that it never dried up.

As, on the evening in question, the moon was almost at the full, I determined to watch the water during the early hours of the night, in the hope of getting a shot at some animal at close quarters as it came to drink, for there was a great deal of recent spoor in the pan of rhinoceroses, buffaloes, zebras, and antelopes.

As soon, therefore, as my Kafirs had made a "scherm"[1] amongst some mopani trees, just beyond the edge of the open ground, I took one of my blankets and both my heavy elephant guns, and established myself on the ledge just above the pool of water. Lying flat on my stomach, I was completely hidden from the view of any animal coming towards me across the open pan by the long coarse grass, which grew right up to the edge of the rock ledge beneath which lay the pool of water.

I had not long taken up my position when a small herd of buffaloes came feeding up the valley behind me. They, however, got my wind when still some distance away from the water, and ran off.

About half an hour later, I suddenly saw a rhinoceros coming towards me across the open pan, and as the wind was now right, I thought he would be sure to come to the water.

He was, however, very suspicious, and kept continually stopping and turning sideways, apparently listening. In the brilliant moonlight I had made him out to be a black rhinoceros almost as soon as I saw him, for he held his head well up, whilst as a white rhinoceros walks along its great square

[1] A semicircular hedge of thorn bushes within which we slept with fires at our feet.

muzzle almost touches the ground. At last the great beast seemed to make up its mind that no danger threatened it, for after having stood quite still for some little time about fifty yards away from me, it came on without any further hesitation and commenced to drink at the pool beneath the ledge on which I was lying. Its head was then hidden from me, but if I had held my old gun at arm's length I could have touched it on the shoulder. Raising myself on my elbows, I now lost no time in firing into the unsuspecting animal, the muzzle of my gun almost touching it at the junction of the neck and the chest as I pulled the trigger.

The loud report of my heavily charged elephant gun was answered by the puffing snorts of the rhinoceros, which, although mortally wounded, had strength enough to swing round and run about fifty yards across the open ground before falling dead.

As it was still quite early, and the night was so gloriously fine, I thought I would lie and watch for an hour or two longer to see if anything else came to drink at the water.

I don't think the rhinoceros had been dead five minutes when a hyæna came across the pan and went straight up to the carcase. This first arrival was soon followed by others, and in less than half an hour there were at least a dozen of these ravenous creatures assembled for the prospective feast. All the time I was watching them they neither howled nor laughed nor fought amongst themselves, but kept continually walking round the dead rhinoceros, or watching whilst one or other of their number attempted to tear the carcase open. This they always attempted to do at the same place—in the flank just where the thigh joins the belly. The soft, thick, spongy skin, however, resisted all their efforts as long as I left them undisturbed, though I could hear their teeth grating over its rough surface. Presently I heard a troop of lions roaring in the distance, and as I thought they might be coming to drink at the pool of water close to which I was lying all by myself and without any kind of shelter, I stood up and shouted to my Kafirs to come and cut up the rhinoceros, and bring some dry wood with them so that we could make a fire near the carcase.

As my hungry boys came running up, the hyænas hastily retired; but after we had opened the carcase of the rhinoceros and cut out the heart and liver and some of the choicest pieces of meat and carried them to our camp, they returned and feasted on what was left to their heart's content. The noise they made during the remainder of the night, howling, laughing, and cackling, was in strange contrast to their silence when they first came to the carcase, but found themselves unable to get at the meat, owing to the thickness of the hide by which it was covered. The lions which I had heard roaring in the distance did not come to drink at the pool near which we were encamped. They were probably on their way to a much larger pool of water some miles to the eastward.

Spotted hyænas are very noisy animals, and their eerie, mournful howling is the commonest sound to break the silence of an African night.

The ordinary howl of the spotted hyæna commences with a long-drawn-out, mournful moan, rising in cadence till it ends in a shriek, altogether one of the weirdest sounds in nature. It is only rarely that one hears hyænas laugh in the wilds of Africa, as these animals can be made to do in the Zoological Gardens by tantalising them with a piece of meat held just beyond their reach outside the bars of their cage. But when a lot of hyænas have gathered together round the carcase of a large animal, such as an elephant or a rhinoceros, and are feasting on it undisturbed, the noises they make are most interesting to listen to. They laugh, they shriek, they howl, and in addition they make all kinds of gurgling, grunting, cackling noises, impossible to describe accurately. Once, late one evening in 1873, I shot a white rhinoceros cow that had a smallish calf, which, however, I thought was large enough to fend for itself and get its own living. That night, after having cut off all the best and fattest meat of the rhinoceros, we camped some two hundred yards from the carcase, which lay in an open valley close to a pool of water. Soon after dark the hyænas began to collect for the feast, and whether the calf returned to its mother's remains and the hyænas forthwith attacked it, or whether it resented their presence and first attacked them, I do not know; but we first heard it snorting and then squealing like a pig, and for half the night it was rushing about, closely pursued by some of the hyænas, which, I fancy, must have been hanging on to its ears and any other part they could get hold of. Twice the young rhinoceros charged almost into our camp, squealing lustily. Finally, the hyænas killed it, and had left hardly anything of it the next morning. I shall never forget the extraordinary noises these animals made that night.

Contrary to generally accepted ideas, I have not found hyænas when killed to be more stinking animals than other carnivorous beasts. The carcase of a freshly killed hyæna certainly does not smell as strongly as that of a lion. I have often had the raw hide neck straps attached to the ox yokes of my South African waggon eaten by hyænas at night in Matabeleland, and to do this, these animals must have been right amongst the oxen, gnawing the raw hide thongs within a few feet of them, yet I never remember such a proceeding to have caused them any alarm. On three occasions, two of which were on bright moonlight nights, I actually saw hyænas right in amongst my oxen, and at first thought they were dogs, as they were sniffing about on the ground. Two of these hyænas I shot. On all these occasions my oxen did not pay the very slightest attention to the hyænas, and I cannot therefore believe that these animals have a more fetid or disagreeable smell than dogs. I remember once shooting a hyæna in the Mababi country, close to the permanent camp where my waggons stood all through the dry season of 1879. Several waggons belonging to Khama's people were standing close by, and when Tinkarn, the headman of the party, saw the dead hyæna he asked me if he and his people might have it. When I inquired what they wanted it for, they answered "To eat," and averred that no other meat obtainable in the African veld was equal to that of a fat hyæna. I gave them the coveted carcase, and they ate it with every appearance of satisfaction. These men were not low savages, but Christianised Bechwanas, all of whom could read and write. They had plenty of good antelope meat, too, at the time, so that they certainly ate the hyæna from choice. I have, however, never come across any other tribe of African natives who would willingly eat the flesh of a hyæna, their objection to it being that it is that of an animal which eats the bodies of human beings. This objection, however, would not apply to the vast majority of hyænas that live in the wilderness, far from any human habitations. Hyænas will attack and kill old and worn-out oxen after they have become very weak; but I have never heard of a case of an ox or a horse in good condition being interfered with by these animals. They often kill the small native cows of South-East Africa, however, always tearing open their udders, and then dragging out their entrails through the wound thus made. I once started on a journey down the northern bank of the central Zambesi in 1877, taking with me four fine strong donkeys. Three of these donkeys were killed near the mouth of the Kafukwe river by hyænas, and the fourth badly lacerated. These donkeys were so completely devoured by what, judging from the noise they made, must have been a regular pack of hyænas, that it was impossible to tell how they had been killed. In 1882, when travelling through the eastern part of Mashunaland beyond the Hanyani river, I had a very fine large stallion donkey killed one night close to my camp by a single hyæna. We heard the poor creature give a heart-rending screaming cry when it was first seized, and ran to its assistance at once, but when we got to it, it was already dead. Its powerful, strong-jawed assailant had seized it between the hind-legs, torn a great hole in its abdomen, and dragged out half its entrails in an incredibly short space of time.

I have never measured or weighed any of the hyænas I have shot, but Mr. Vaughan Kirby speaks of a very large one as having stood three feet high at the shoulder, and I believe that such an animal must have weighed more than 200 pounds.

Very little is known of the life-history of the spotted hyæna. Bushmen have told me that the females give birth only to two whelps at a time. These are usually born in one of the large holes excavated by the African ant-eaters (*Aardvarks*). Although I have seen a great number of hyænas on various moonlight nights, I have never seen a very young or even a half-grown one accompanying its mother, and I cannot help thinking, therefore, that young spotted hyænas remain in the burrows where they are born, and are there fed by their parents until they are at least eight or nine months old.

CHAPTER VII

NOTES ON WILD DOGS AND CHETAHS

Wild dogs not very numerous—Hunt in packs—Attack herd of buffaloes—First experience with wild dogs—Impala antelope killed—Koodoo cow driven into shed—Koodoo driven to waggon—Wild dogs not dangerous to human beings—Greatly feared by all antelopes—Wild dog pursuing sable antelope—Great pace displayed—Wild dogs capable of running down every kind of African antelope—General opinion as to the running powers of wild dogs—Curious incidents—Chasing wild dogs with tame ones—One wild dog galloped over and shot—Two others caught and worried by tame dogs—Wild dog shamming dead—Clever escape—Chetahs overtaken on horseback—Three chetahs seen—Two females passed—Male galloped down—A second chetah overtaken—Great speed of trained Indian chetahs—Three chetah cubs found—Brought up by bitch.

I do not think that the Cape hunting dog (*Lycaon pictus*) was ever very numerous in the interior of South Africa, as at the time when I was elephant-hunting, many years ago, and continually moving about, day after day and year after year, in countries where game was plentiful, I never encountered more than two or three packs of these animals in a year's wanderings, and there were several years—not consecutive—during which I did not meet with any at all. So far as my memory serves me, I think that the wild dogs I came across—with the exception of a single animal which was chasing a sable antelope bull—were in packs of from fifteen to thirty.

At times I have come across these animals lying

in the shade of scattered trees, on bare ground, from which all the grass had been burnt off, and they would then trot away, continually stopping and looking back, but making no sound. But I can remember distinctly two occasions on which I suddenly disturbed a pack of wild dogs in longish grass. On both these occasions they were very near to me, but could not very well make me out, owing to the length of the grass. They retreated very slowly, and kept jumping up, looking at me inquisitively, with their large ears cocked forward. At the same time they gave vent to a kind of bark, the sound being repeated twice. This double note might be represented by the syllables "hoo-hoo."

On one of these two occasions which I say I remember so well, I was hunting—in 1873—in the country about half-way between Bulawayo and the Victoria Falls, not very far, I fancy, from the present railway line. After a long march I had reached a swampy valley—then known by the name of Dett—where there was water, and where I intended to camp. Seeing some buffaloes drinking a little way down the valley, and wanting some fresh meat, I at once proceeded to stalk them. The stream at which the buffaloes were drinking ran down the centre of an open valley some 300 yards broad, in which there was no cover, except that afforded by coarse grass, some 2½ feet to 3 feet in length. Being armed with only an old muzzle-loading four-bore gun, I had to get pretty close to anything I wanted to shoot, and I had crawled half-way to the buffaloes when I saw them all suddenly raise their heads and look down the valley. I immediately looked in the same direction, and then heard a heavy trampling noise, which I knew must be caused by a herd of large animals running.

This noise came rapidly nearer, and on raising myself so that I could look over the grass, I saw a herd of perhaps forty or fifty buffaloes coming straight towards me at a lumbering gallop. At the same time I heard a noise which sounded like kak-kak-kak constantly repeated. The buffaloes came straight on towards me, and had I remained quiet would have run right over me, so when they were within twenty yards I jumped up and shouted. The leaders stopped for a moment, and then, swerving slightly, dashed close past me. I fired into one of them, and immediately afterwards saw some wild dogs—a pack of about twenty—jumping up in the long grass to look at me.

They had been hanging on to the rear of the herd of buffaloes, which they had undoubtedly first put to flight, and had they not been disturbed, would, I think, have probably succeeded in pulling down a young animal. Had I not witnessed this incident with my own eyes, I never should have thought it possible that a herd of buffaloes would have allowed themselves to be stampeded by a few wild dogs. These latter gave up the chase as soon as they saw me, and after hoo-hooing a little, trotted off. The barking hoo-hoo and the clacking kak-kak-kak are the only sounds that I have ever heard wild dogs make, but I cannot claim to have had much experience with these animals. Wild dogs sometimes hunt by day, but more usually at night, and in the latter case must be guided entirely by their acute sense of smell. As a rule, they certainly run mute.

On the first occasion on which I ever had anything to do with wild dogs, they ran into and killed an impala antelope quite close to my waggon on a dark night in 1872. We ran up with lights and drove them from the carcase, a good deal of which they had, however, already devoured. About a month later another pack of wild dogs drove a koodoo cow into a shed used as a stable, attached to a store near the Blue Jacket gold mine at Tati, in Matabeleland. I was there at the time, and on this occasion the wild dogs were driven off by some Kafir boys, who speared the koodoo inside the shed.

For some time during the year 1888 my waggon was standing at Leshuma, a water-hole which is situated just ten miles from the junction of the Chobi and Zambesi rivers. One morning I walked down to Kazungula, at the junction of the rivers, and on returning to my waggon the same evening, was surprised to see the meat of a freshly killed koodoo hanging up in my camp, as game of all kinds was very scarce in the district. On asking my old Griqua servant where he had shot the koodoo, he replied, "Master, the good Lord gave it us, for the wild dogs brought it right up to the waggon." On further inquiry, I found that soon after midday a pack of those animals had chased the koodoo to within less than a hundred yards of the waggon, and then run it in a circle completely round it. When my waggon-driver ran out with his rifle, both the wild dogs and the koodoo stopped and looked at him, the latter evidently very much distressed. Jantje at once shot the antelope, and its pursuers then ran off.

It has always struck me as somewhat remarkable that animals so confident in their powers of offence that they will sometimes attack a herd of buffaloes, and that a single one of them will occasionally try conclusions with so fierce and powerful an animal as a sable antelope bull, should never have turned their attention seriously to man as an article of diet; yet in all my experience I have never heard of wild dogs attacking human beings, nor have I ever heard either Kafirs or Bushmen express any fear of them. This is all the more remarkable because when they are met with they do not show any great fear of man, but retreat very leisurely, constantly halting and looking back curiously before finally trotting off.

All African antelopes probably live in deadly fear of wild dogs, for on the occasion when, with two companions, I saw a single wild dog overtake a sable antelope bull, the latter halted and looked round when its pursuer was about fifty yards behind it, and then, instead of showing fight, as I should have expected it to do, threw out its limbs convulsively and ran at its utmost speed; but the wild dog overhauled it with apparent ease, and twice jumped up and snapped at its flank, each time, I think, making good its bite. Now this wild dog must have been running very much faster than any South African hunting horse could do, for although it is easy enough to gallop up to sable and roan antelope cows in August and September, when these animals are heavy with calf, I have never been able to run into a bull of either of these species, though I have often attempted to do so, with very good horses, on the open downs of Mashunaland. Wild dogs, too, can run down koodoo cows and impala antelopes, as well as hartebeests and tsessebes, none of which animals can be overtaken on horseback, and I believe that the general concensus of opinion amongst African hunters would be that no horse could overtake a wild dog.

I will, however, relate an experience which shows that this is not always the case, and which will probably be read with great surprise, if not with incredulity. Early one morning in November 1885, I was travelling near the source of the Sebakwe river, in Mashunaland, in company with the late Mr. H. C. Collison, Mr. James Dawson, and Cornelis van Rooyen, a well-known Boer hunter. We were all riding together in very open country, just in front of our four bullock waggons, when we saw fifteen or twenty wild dogs emerge from a small watercourse that we had just crossed.

When we first saw them they were nearly abreast of us, and not more than 300 or 400 yards to our left. They trotted quietly along, stopping frequently to look at us, as is their wont. We possessed amongst us a large number of dogs, most of them big, rough, powerful mongrels, such as one sees on a Boer farm in the Transvaal. Calling to our dogs, we galloped towards their wild cousins, and twelve or fifteen of the former soon rushed past our horses and took up the chase at a great pace. The wild dogs now broke into a gallop, but, strange to say, instead of leaving their pursuers far behind them, they did not seem able to show any great turn of speed. We were soon right amongst them with our horses, and our dogs mobbed and pulled down two, which they held in such a way that they were quite unable to bite. Personally I picked out a fine large wild dog, in good coat, and rode at him. When my horse's forefeet were almost touching him he suddenly rolled on his back and my horse jumped over him. I galloped over this wild dog several times, and finally shot him.

During this time my companions had occupied themselves in encouraging our dogs to hold on to the two they had seized, and the rest of the wild pack had galloped off. As each of the two wild dogs that had been caught had been worried for some minutes by five or six assailants, all larger and heavier than itself, we thought they were dead and beat off our dogs. Their two badly used relatives lay quite still and limp, and we dragged them, together with the one I had shot, to a tree near a small stream, where we intended to skin them. All our dogs then went back to the waggons, which had not halted.

We had just commenced to skin the wild dog I had shot when, on looking round, I caught the eye of one of the other two that was lying dead, as we had thought, at the foot of the tree, and instantly saw that it was alive. It must have been shamming dead all the time in order to recover its strength, as immediately it caught my eye it sprang to its feet and dashed off. Two shots were fired at it as it ran, but it got clean away, apparently none the worse for the worrying it had endured. The other one which had been caught by our dogs was not quite full-grown, and as it had been held by the throat by one of our most powerful hounds, was quite dead.

I can offer no explanation as to why we were able to overtake this pack of wild dogs so easily, after chasing them for less than a mile, but the facts are as I have stated them. It is possible, I suppose, that we disturbed these wild dogs soon after they had killed some large antelope, and just after they had made a heavy meal. I cannot say, but I remember that the one I galloped over had its tongue lolling from its jaws, and showed every sign of distress.

I have, however, had two somewhat similar experiences with chetahs, which are generally credited with being the swiftest of all four-footed animals; yet upon two separate occasions, once in company with the Boer hunter Cornelis van Rooyen, and again with three English friends, I have galloped after and overtaken a large male chetah. On each occasion the chetahs squatted suddenly when the horses were close upon them, and lay flat on the ground, in which position they were both shot.

As I think that these somewhat remarkable experiences ought to be put on record, I will briefly relate the circumstances under which they took place.

One day during September 1885, when hunting in company with Cornelis van Rooyen near the Umfuli river, in Mashunaland, I rode out of a belt of forest-covered country into a broad open valley, from half a mile to a thousand yards in breadth, and bounded on the farther side again with a tract of open forest. Down the centre of this open valley ran a small watercourse, which was, however, no longer running, though several deep pools were still full of water.

My friend and I had only ridden out a short distance into the open when three chetahs, a big male and two smaller animals which were no doubt females, emerged from the creek, and after trotting a short distance away from us across the open ground, turned round and stood looking at us.

Van Rooyen and I at once rode towards them. They let us come close to the creek before running off, but when they did so, they broke into a light springing gallop and got over the ground at a great pace. The long summer grass had all been burnt off in this district, and the ground in the open valley, being firm and hard and quite free from holes, was in excellent condition for galloping.

When we commenced to race after the chetahs they had a start of at least fifty yards—I think considerably more—and the edge of the forest for which they were making could not have been more than five hundred yards distant.

Both our horses were pretty fast and in good hard condition, and we raced neck and neck as hard as we could go behind the chetahs. Whether these latter were running at their utmost speed I cannot say, but, at any rate, we slowly but steadily gained on them, and were only a few yards behind them when they reached the edge of the forest, which was very open and free from underbush. Suddenly the two female chetahs, which were a little behind the male, came to a halt, and we galloped past within a few yards of them, as we wanted to kill the largest of the three. These two female chetahs did not crouch down, but stood looking at us as we shot past them. We chased the big male another fifty yards through the open forest, and were quite close up to him, when he suddenly stopped and crouched, all in one motion as it were, and lay with his long thin body pressed flat to the ground. Van Rooyen and I were so near him that, going at the pace we were, we could not pull in our horses until we were thirty or forty yards beyond where he lay. The chetah, however, never moved again, but lay perfectly still watching us, and we dismounted and shot him where he lay. We never saw anything more of the two females, which must have run off as soon as we had passed them.

Two years later, in October 1887, I was riding one day with three English gentlemen (Messrs. J. A. Jameson, Frank Cooper, and A. Fountaine, all of whom are alive to-day and will be able to corroborate my story) through the country lying between the upper waters of the Sebakwe and Umniati rivers in Mashunaland. The ground was not quite open, as it was covered here and there with a growth of small trees, but as these grew very sparsely there was nothing to stop one from riding at full gallop in every direction. As we rode along I was on the left of our party. Suddenly my horse turned his head and snorted. I at once pulled him in, calling to my companions to stop, as I thought my horse must have smelt a lion lying somewhere near us.

I had scarcely spoken when up jumped a very large male chetah within twenty yards of my horse and bounded away across the open ground, holding his long, thick, furry tail straight out behind him.

This chetah did not get much of a start, as we galloped after him as soon as ever we could get our horses started. The chase may have lasted for a mile, though I think certainly not farther, and the chetah never seemed to be able to get away from us, and if he was capable of going at a greater pace, I cannot understand why he did not do so. At the end of a mile, however, Jameson, who was the light-weight of our party, and who was, moreover, mounted on a very fast Basuto pony, was close up to the chetah, and the rest of us were perhaps thirty yards behind him. Suddenly the hunted animal squatted flat on the ground, and Jameson's pony was then so close to it that it jumped clean over it. The action of this chetah was exactly the same as in the case of the one that Van Rooyen and I had chased and overtaken in 1885, and in both cases it was very remarkable how the hunted animals suddenly stopped when going at a great pace and lay flat on the ground in a single movement, as it seemed. This second chetah was shot by Jameson from his horse's back as soon as he could pull in, and it never moved again after first crouching down.

Now when we read of the wonderful speed of the tamed chetahs kept for hunting purposes in India, it certainly seems very remarkable that in South Africa these animals can be overtaken in a short distance by ordinary shooting horses.

In Jerdon's *Mammals of India* a very interesting description is given of hunting with trained chetahs, and I think there can be no doubt that in that country these animals are able to overtake in a fair course antelopes and gazelles which cannot be ridden down, and whose speed surpasses even that of greyhounds.

Whether the African chetah has lost the great speed of his Asiatic progenitors, and if so why, are questions which I cannot answer, but the two animals which were galloped after and overtaken by my friends and myself were both fine specimens of their kind, in good condition and apparently in the prime of life, and why they did not run away from our horses and so save their skins, if they were able to do so, is more than I can understand.

Personally, I know very little as to the life-history of chetahs, and I doubt if any one else does, as they are very rarely encountered. I once saw six of these animals together near the town of Salisbury, in Mashunaland. The teeth of the chetah are very small and weak compared with those of the leopard, hyæna, or wild dog, and its semi-retractile claws not very sharp, so I should imagine that its chief prey would be the smaller species of antelopes.

When the pioneer expedition to Mashunaland was crossing the high plateau near the source of the Sabi river, in 1890, one of the troopers of the British South Africa Police Force, who was riding along parallel with and not far from the line of waggons, came on three chetah cubs lying in the grass, and brought them to me. They could only have been a few days old, as their eyes were not yet open. I do not know what became of those chetah cubs, as my duties as guide and chief intelligence officer of the pioneer force made it impossible for me to attend to them; but I believe they were suckled by a bitch and lived for some time.

CHAPTER VIII

EXTINCTION AND DIMINUTION OF GAME IN SOUTH AFRICA—NOTES ON THE CAPE BUFFALO

Extinction of the blaauwbok and the true quagga—Threatened extermination of the black and white rhinoceros and the buffalo in South Africa—Former abundance of game—Scene in the valley of Dett witnessed by the author in 1873—Buffaloes protected by the Cape Government—But few survivors in other parts of South Africa—Abundance of buffaloes in former times—Extent of their range—Still plentiful in places up to 1896—The terrible epidemic of rinderpest—Character of the African buffalo—A matter of individual experience—Comparison of buffalo with the lion and elephant—Danger of following wounded buffaloes into thick cover—Personal experiences—Well-known sportsman killed by a buffalo—Usual action of buffaloes when wounded—Difficult to stop when actually charging—The moaning bellow of a dying buffalo—Probable reasons for some apparently unprovoked attacks by buffaloes—Speed of buffaloes—Colour, texture, and abundance of coat at different ages—Abundance of buffaloes along the Chobi river—Demeanour of old buffalo bulls—" God's cattle "—Elephants waiting for a herd of buffaloes to leave a pool of water before themselves coming down to drink.

SINCE the first settlement of Europeans at the Cape of Good Hope in the seventeenth century, two species of the indigenous fauna of South Africa have become absolutely extinct. These are the blaauwbok (*Hippotragus leucophaeus*) and the true quagga (*Equus quagga*). Both these animals, however, were nearly related to species which still exist in considerable numbers, for the blaauwbok must in appearance have looked very much like a small roan antelope in which the black face markings and conspicuous white tufts under the eyes were wanting; whilst the true quagga was nothing but the dullest coloured and most southerly form of Burchell's zebra. Deplorable, therefore, as is the loss of these two animals, it is not quite so distressing as it would be had they been the sole representatives of the genera to which they belonged, and personally I look upon the disappearance of the Cape buffalo and the black and white rhinoceros from almost every part of Southern Africa, over which these animals once wandered so plentifully, with far greater regret; for when these highly specialised and most interesting creatures have completely disappeared from the face of the South African veld, there will be no living species of animal left alive in that country which resembles them in the remotest degree.

Of course, neither the Cape buffalo nor either of the two species of rhinoceroses indigenous to Africa are yet absolutely extinct in the country to the south of the Zambesi river; but of the great white or square-mouthed, grass-eating rhinoceroses, the largest of all terrestrial mammals after the elephant, none are left alive to-day with the exception of some half-dozen which still survive in Zululand, and a very few which are believed to exist in the neighbourhood of the Angwa river, in Southern Rhodesia. A few of the black or prehensile-lipped species are, I should think, still to be found here and there throughout the great stretch of uninhabited country which lies between the high plateaus of Southern Rhodesia and the Zambesi river, but, like their congener the white rhinoceros, they are now entirely extinct throughout all but an infinitesimal proportion of the vast territories over which they ranged so plentifully only half a century ago.

By the enforcement of game laws, and the establishment of large sanctuaries in uninhabited parts of the country, it will be possible, I think, to preserve in considerable numbers all the many species of antelopes still inhabiting South Africa, as well as the handsome striped zebras, for a long time to come; but never again can such scenes be witnessed as were constantly presented to the eyes of the earlier travellers in the interior of that country.

Then not only were many species of richly coloured graceful antelopes and zebras everywhere to be seen, but in the early mornings and evenings great herds of rugged horned buffaloes on their way to or from their drinking-places almost rivalled the lesser game in numbers, whilst, scattered amongst all these denizens of the modern world, the numerous long-horned, heavy-headed white rhinoceroses, together with their more alert and active-looking cousins of the prehensile-lipped species, must have appeared like survivals from a far-distant epoch of the world's history.

Even in my own time all the great game of Southern Africa was in places still abundant, and a scene which I once witnessed in October 1873 will never fade from my memory. I was at that time hunting elephants in the country to the south-east of the Victoria Falls, and one afternoon, when approaching a swampy valley known to the Bushmen by the name of "Dett," I came unexpectedly on a herd of these animals. I had killed one young bull and severely wounded a second, when I was charged by a big cow with long white tusks. I stood my ground and fired into her chest as she came on, on which she at once stopped screaming and swerved off, giving me the opportunity to place another shot in her ribs with my second gun. At that time I was only armed with two old muzzle-loading four-bore elephant guns, of the clumsiest and most antiquated description, but they hit hard nevertheless. Having got rid of the vicious old cow, I again followed the wounded bull, which I presently laid low. When my Kafirs had all assembled round the carcase, one of them said that he had seen the cow after I had fired at her, and that he thought she would not go far, as she was only walking very slowly and throwing great quantities of blood from her trunk. I at once resolved to follow her, and soon found that she was heading straight for the valley of Dett, for which I was very thankful, since the day had been intensely hot, and my Kafirs and I were badly in want of water, as we had drunk all we had been able to carry in our calabashes before we came on the elephants.

The sun was low in the western sky, and, seen through the haze of many grass fires, had already turned from blazing yellow to a dull red, when the spoor of the wounded elephant led us suddenly out of the forest into the open grassy valley, some three or four hundred yards broad, through which the little stream of the Dett made its sluggish way, forming many fine pools of water along its course. Immediately we emerged from the forest we saw the carcase of the elephant we had been following lying in the open ground within fifty yards of the water for which the poor animal had been making, but had not quite been able to reach. It was too late to commence chopping out the tusks, but, leaving some of my Kafirs to cut bushes and grass and prepare a camping-place for the night on the edge of the forest, I went with the rest to cut open the dead elephant and get the heart out for my supper.

It was whilst I was so engaged that I saw appear along the valley of Dett the most interesting collection of wild animals that I think I have ever seen collected together in a small extent of ground.

First, a few hundred yards higher up the valley than where we were working, a herd of nine giraffes stalked slowly and majestically from the forest, and, making their way to a pool of water, commenced to drink. These giraffes remained in the open valley until dark, one or other of them from time to time straddling out its forelegs in a most extraordinary manner in order to get its mouth down to the water. No other animals came to drink in the pools between us and the giraffes. Possibly some got our wind before leaving the shelter of the forest, though the evening was very still. But below us, as far as one could see down the valley, the open ground was presently alive with game. One after another, great herds of buffaloes emerged from the forest on either side of the valley and fed slowly down to the water. One of these herds was preceded by about fifty zebras, and another by a large herd of sable antelopes. Presently two other herds of sable antelopes appeared upon the scene, a second herd of zebras, and five magnificently horned old koodoo bulls, whilst rhinoceroses both of the black and white species (the latter predominating in numbers) were scattered amongst the other game, singly or in twos and threes all down the valley. Of course all this great concourse of wild animals had been collected together in the neighbourhood of the valley of Dett owing to the drying up of all the vleys in the surrounding country, and during the rainy season would have been scattered over a wide area.

It is sad to think that of all those buffaloes and rhinoceroses I saw in the valley of Dett on that October evening, less than five and thirty years ago, not one single one nor any of their descendants are left alive to-day. They were all killed off years ago, almost all by the natives of Matabeleland after these people became possessed of firearms, purchased for the most part on the Diamond Fields.

As was to be expected, the rhinoceroses were the first to go, but the buffaloes, in spite of their prodigious numbers in many parts of South Africa only a generation ago, did not long survive them, for wherever the epidemic of rinderpest penetrated in 1896 it almost completely destroyed all the buffaloes which up till then had escaped the native hunters.

It is very difficult to say with any exactitude how many buffaloes still exist in South Africa to-day. There are a certain number of these animals in the Addo bush and the Knysna forest, in the Cape Colony, which are protected by the Cape Government, and there is also a small but increasing herd inhabiting the game-reserve which has recently been established in the Eastern Transvaal. Besides these, there may be a few in the Zululand reserve which survived the rinderpest, whilst a poor remnant of the great herds I saw in the Pungwe river district in 1891 and 1892 undoubtedly still survive in that part of the country. Farther north, it is quite possible that there may still be a considerable number of buffaloes to the north and north-east of the high plateau of Mashunaland in the neighbourhood of Mount Darwin, and also in the valleys of the Umsengaisi, Panyami, and Sanyati rivers. It all depends upon whether the rinderpest penetrated to these regions in 1896 and 1897.[1]

[1] I have lately learned that the route followed by cattle which are now frequently brought from N.E. Rhodesia to Salisbury, in Mashunaland, is down the valley of the Loangwa river to the Zambesi, and after that river has been crossed up the course of the Panyami to Salisbury. In 1882, and again in 1887, I found buffaloes very numerous all along the Panyami river from the Zambesi to a point only a few miles north of Lo Magondi's, and wherever the buffaloes were found, tse-tse flies were also very numerous. There can be no tse-tse flies along the Panyami to-day, if I have been correctly informed that cattle are brought to Mashunaland by this route, and there can be no buffaloes there either, or the tse-tse flies would not have disappeared. No doubt the buffaloes were destroyed by the epidemic of rinderpest in 1896-97,

To the west of the river Gwai, however, I believe that few, if any, buffaloes still survive in the interior of South Africa, though in my own personal experience I met with these animals in extraordinary numbers wherever I hunted between 1872 and 1880 in that part of the country, whether to the south-east of the Victoria Falls, or farther westwards along the Zambesi and as far as I went along the Chobi, or in the valleys of the Machabi (an overflow from the Okavango), the Mababi, or the Tamalakan.

In fact, speaking generally, the Cape buffalo was formerly very abundant everywhere throughout South Africa wherever there was a plentiful supply of water and grass in close proximity to shady forests; for these animals never appear to have frequented open country anywhere to the south of the Zambesi. They spread themselves all down the thickly wooded coast belt of East and South Africa as far as Mossel Bay, and along all the tributaries of the Zambesi and the Limpopo rivers, and it was probably from the headwaters of the Marico and Notwani rivers that they found their way to the Molopo, and thence through Bechwanaland to the Orange river.

Buffaloes were met with in that district, about 1783, by the French traveller Le Vaillant, and in Southern Bechwanaland some five and twenty years later by the missionary John Campbell, whilst in 1845 Mr. W. Cotton Oswell still found large herds of these animals living in the reed beds of the Molopo; but it is worthy of remark that, owing to the gradual desiccation of the country, which has been and still is constantly taking place in South-Western Africa, there is to-day not enough water to support a herd of buffaloes either in the Molopo

and their disappearance was quickly followed, as has been the case in so many other districts of South Africa, by the dying out of the tse-tse flies. I fear that very few buffaloes can now be left in any part of Northern Mashunaland, since the rinderpest appears to have swept through all that country.

river or anywhere to the south of it, throughout Bechwanaland.

During the quarter of a century succeeding the year 1871 (during which I first visited South Africa) the range of the buffalo had been very much curtailed, but up to 1896 these animals were still numerous in many of the uninhabited parts of the country, and especially so in the Pungwe river district of South-East Africa. In the early part of that most fatal year, however, the terrible epidemic of rinderpest crossed the Zambesi, and besides depleting nearly the whole of South Africa of cattle before a stop was put to its ravages by Dr. Koch, almost absolutely exterminated the buffaloes. The few that remain will probably be gradually killed off, I am afraid, and I think it quite likely that before many more years have passed the only buffaloes left in South Africa will be those living in the Addo bush in the Cape Colony.

There was always a considerable difference of opinion amongst South African hunters in the old pre-rinderpest times as to the character of the Cape buffalo, but there is no doubt that this animal was looked upon by all experienced men as a dangerous antagonist under certain conditions, whilst by some it was considered to be the most dangerous of all African game. It is all a matter of individual experience. A man who has shot two or three lions and a few buffaloes, and who, whilst having had no trouble with the former animals, has been charged and perhaps only narrowly escaped with his life from one or more of the latter, will naturally consider the buffalo to be a more dangerous animal than a lion, and *vice versa*.

Personally I consider that, speaking generally, the South African lion is a much more dangerous animal than the South African buffalo, for not only can a lion hide much more easily and rush on to its antagonist much more quickly than a buffalo, but the former is, I think, much more savage by nature, on the average, than the latter. As regards viciousness I should be inclined to put the buffalo third on the list of dangerous African game, without reckoning the leopard (of which animal I have not had sufficient experience to offer an opinion) and the black rhinoceros (whose true character it seems so difficult to understand); for, whilst putting the lion first, I think the elephant should come second, as I believe that of a hundred elephants shot, a greater proportion will charge than of the same number of buffaloes. However, a charging elephant can almost always be stopped with a bullet, and it is most difficult to stop a charging buffalo; therefore the latter is perhaps actually the more dangerous animal of the two.

To follow a wounded buffalo into a bed of reeds, or into long grass, where it is almost impossible to see it before getting to very close quarters, is a most dangerous, not to say foolhardy, proceeding. It is quite exciting enough to follow one of these animals when wounded into thick bush, but there you have a chance of seeing it as soon as, if not before, it sees you.

I have had a very considerable experience with South African buffaloes, having killed 175 of these animals to my own rifle, and helped to kill at least fifty others. When hunting on the Chobi river in 1877, and again in 1879, I had to shoot a great many buffaloes to supply my native followers with meat, as I did not come across many elephants in either of those years.

During 1877 I killed to my own rifle forty-seven buffaloes, and in 1879 fifty. All these buffaloes, with the exception of five, which I shot when hunting on horseback near the Mababi river in the latter year, were killed on foot, and a large number of them were followed, after having been wounded, into thick bush, and there finally despatched.

If the Cape buffalo was really such a ferocious and diabolically cunning beast as it has often been represented to have been, it seems to me that I have been very badly treated in the way of adventures with these animals. I have, of course, had a few more or less exciting experiences with buffaloes, but they only happened occasionally, and I never thought it necessary to make my will before attacking a herd of these animals. In 1874, when very young and inexperienced, and very badly armed with a clumsy muzzle-loading elephant gun, my horse was tossed and killed by an old bull which I had been chasing, and I afterwards received a blow from one of its horns on the shoulder as I lay on the ground. I was once knocked down, too, by another buffalo, which charged from behind a bush at very close quarters, but I escaped without serious injury. On another occasion an old bull which had been recently mauled by lions, and at which one of my Kafirs had thrown an assegai, put me into a tree, as I had not a gun in my hands, when it charged. I once dodged a charging buffalo by leaping aside when its outstretched nose was quite close to me, and then, swinging myself round a small tree, ran past its hind-quarters; but I was young then, in perfect training and full of confidence in myself. Following on the blood spoor of wounded buffaloes, very cautiously in soft shoes, and holding my rifle at the ready and on full cock, I believe I have often in thick bush just got a shot in, in time to prevent a good many of these animals from charging. I became used to this work, and my eyes, through constant practice, could see a buffalo standing in thick cover as soon as it was possible to do so, and as soon as it could see me. My only clothing, too, in those days used to be a cotton shirt, a soft felt hat, and a pair of shoes. Had I been short-sighted or dull-sighted, and gone blundering into thick jungle after wounded buffaloes, in heavy shooting boots and thick clothes, as inexperienced sportsmen sometimes used to do, I might have met with more adventures than I have done.

Of course, in the pursuit of any kind of big game which becomes dangerous when wounded, accidents will sometimes occur to the most experienced hunters. The Hon. Guy Dawnay, it will be remembered, was killed many years ago in East Africa by a buffalo which he had wounded. This gentleman, whom I met in Matabeleland in 1873, had had a great deal of experience in hunting all kinds of African game before meeting with the accident which cost him his life, and was an exceptionally athletic young Englishman.

In all my experience I can only remember one wounded buffalo, when being followed through open forest, charging from a distance of perhaps a hundred yards, but lions when chased on horseback will often, even before they have been fired at, turn and charge from even a greater distance.

When wounded in open country a buffalo will always make for thick cover. Before it reaches this, it will perhaps see you several times following on its tracks. It will then stop, turn, and, with head raised and outstretched nose, stand looking at you for a few seconds, but if able to do so will almost invariably gallop off again. When it has reached the retreat for which it is making, it will presently halt, but unless very badly wounded will not lie down for some time. Personally, I have never known a wounded buffalo to circle round and then stand watching near its own tracks for its approaching enemies ; but I can imagine that one of these animals when wounded might go zigzagging about in a thick piece of jungle, and, without any fixed intention of waylaying its pursuers, might be just about to cross its own tracks at the very point these latter had reached when following on its spoor. Then it would almost certainly charge, with a good chance of scoring a success.

My own experience has been that in thick cover wounded buffaloes usually stood behind a bush at right angles to their tracks. In such a position, standing quite motionless, they were very difficult to see, whilst they had every chance of hearing or seeing anything approaching on their spoor before being themselves observed. In such cases they would nearly always be broadside on to the hunter, and if one's eyes were trained to pick up game quickly in all kinds of surroundings, there would be time to get a shot in before the wounded animals swung round and started on their charge. Struck in this way with a heavy bullet somewhere near the junction of the neck and the shoulder before the charge had actually commenced, a wounded buffalo would run off again. Once, however, a buffalo is actually charging, no bullet will turn or stop it, unless its brain is pierced or its neck or one of its legs broken. A charging buffalo comes on grunting loudly, with outstretched nose and horns laid back on its neck, and does not lower its head to strike until close up to its enemy. The outstretched nose of the buffalo which killed my horse was within a few inches of my leg before it dipped its head, and, with a sweeping blow, inflicted a fearful wound in the poor animal's flank.

I once hit a charging buffalo at a distance of perhaps thirty yards, right in the chest, with a round bullet fired from an old four-bore elephant gun. This bullet just grazed this old bull's heart, cutting a groove through one side of it, and then, after traversing the whole length of its body, lodged under the skin of one of its hind-legs; yet this brave and determined animal still came on, and struck a blow at a Kafir who was trying to climb a tree close beside me. It then, after running only a short distance farther, lay down and died. Almost always when a buffalo is dying it gives vent to a moaning bellow, which can be heard at a considerable distance. It is a sound which, once heard, can never be forgotten.

On June 24, 1877, I had a somewhat curious experience with a buffalo on the banks of the Chobi river. Some natives came to my camp on the morning of that day and informed me that there were three old buffalo bulls in the thick bush along the river's edge only a few hundred yards away, and at the same time begged me to try and shoot them, as they and their people were very badly off for food. Yielding to their entreaties, I at once went after the buffaloes, and, putting my Bushmen spoorers on their fresh tracks, soon came up with them in some thickish bush, and killed two of them with consecutive shots from a single-barrelled ten-bore rifle. The third ran off towards the river, and I dashed after him in hot pursuit. Just along the edge of the bush, and fringing the open ground which skirted the reedy swamp, through which the river ran at this point, there grew a fringe of palmetto scrub, the large leaves of which hung over to the ground. Into this the buffalo dashed, and I followed close behind him. I thought he had gone through the palmetto scrub, into which one could not see a yard, into the open ground beyond, and so never slackened my pace, but went at it at full speed; but the old bull had halted suddenly, and was standing still behind the screen formed by the overhanging leaves of one of the palmetto bushes. He could only just have turned himself broadside to listen when I ran full tilt into him, and was thrown on the ground flat on my back by the violence of the impact. Probably the buffalo was as much surprised as I was. At any rate, he never stopped to see what had happened, but galloped off again across the open ground on the other side of the palmetto scrub and plunged into the reeds.

Men who hunted big game in South Africa at a time when that country was worth living in, are often charged with wastefully slaughtering large numbers of wild animals. Every one must answer this charge for himself. Personally I do not plead guilty. I never killed any animal for mere sport; but it was often necessary to shoot what may seem to any one who does not realise the circumstances an extravagant amount of game in order not only to supply one's own followers with food, but also to gain the goodwill of the natives of the country in which one was travelling. I find an entry in my diary for August 20, 1879: "Shot six buffalo bulls." That without explanation seems a big order. But, as it happened, on the previous evening I had met my friends Collison and Miller on the banks of the Chobi, and found them both down with fever, and their native followers without food. The next day it was necessary for me to shoot enough meat not only to supply the immediate wants of more than fifty men, but to take them to the waggons on the Mababi river, which was several days' journey distant.

Taking up the spoor of a big herd of buffaloes, I killed six fine bulls, not one ounce of meat of any one of which was wasted. Incidentally I may say that I killed these six buffalo bulls with ten shots from a single-barrelled ten-bore rifle, using round bullets and six drachms of powder. I had no kind of adventure with any one of these animals. Another entry for December 6 in the same year stands: "Nine Burchell's zebras; two eland bulls." These animals were killed soon after leaving the Mababi for Bamangwato, and without the supply of meat thus obtained it would have gone very hard with the large number of Khama's people who were travelling with me, and who were almost entirely dependent upon me for food. Khama thanked me very heartily on my return to Bamangwato for the assistance I had given to his people.

To return to buffaloes, old bulls are often said to be very bad tempered and liable to charge without the slightest provocation. Many instances can, no doubt, be cited of men having suddenly been charged and either killed or badly maimed by one of these animals. If all these cases, however, had been thoroughly investigated, I believe it would have been found that such unprovoked attacks had for the most part been made by wounded animals lying in thick cover or long grass, which were suffering from injuries inflicted either by lions or by human hunters. Such animals would naturally be morose and dangerous to approach.

I have not shot many buffaloes when hunting on horseback, as in my time these animals were seldom found except in countries infested by the tse-tse fly, which fatally affects horses and cattle. However, I have galloped after at least a dozen herds of buffaloes, riding alongside of them and continually dismounting and firing at one or other of their number. Only on one occasion did an unwounded buffalo leave the herd and charge me. This was a cow which gave me a smart chase for perhaps a hundred yards. It is astonishing at what a speed a buffalo can run when charging. It certainly takes a good horse to get away from one, although when following a herd of buffaloes on horseback one can easily keep alongside of them at a hand-gallop. Even on foot I never found any difficulty in keeping up with a herd of buffaloes and shooting as many as I required to supply my native followers with food. But, of course, the life I led at that time, and the continual hard walking and running necessary to earn my living, kept me in perfect training.

In the interior of South Africa, where the nights are very cold in the winter-time, buffaloes used to get fairly abundant but never thick coats when in their prime. The calves, which were born during January, February, and March, were, when very young, covered with soft hair of a reddish brown colour, but as they grew, the reddish tinge gradually disappeared and they became dun coloured. They did not turn black until they were fully three years of age. The hair of the Cape buffalo when full-grown was always quite black and very coarse. The large ears were bordered with long fringes of soft black hair, and the end of the tail carried a good-sized tassel. When old, both bull and cow buffaloes lost most of their hair, first on the middle of the back; but the baldness gradually increased until very old animals of this species became almost as hairless as a rhinoceros.

In the early 'seventies buffaloes were everywhere very plentiful along the Zambesi and its tributaries, but nowhere so abundant as along the Chobi river. So numerous were they along both banks of this river, that one would have thought that they had reached the very limits of their food-supply. They were usually found consorting together in herds of from fifty or sixty to two or three hundred individuals. Once I saw what I think must have been several large herds collected together, as the total number of the troop could not have been less than a thousand. A grass fire had probably destroyed the pasture on the ground where several herds had lately been living, and they were all moving up the river together in search of food. In districts where buffaloes were plentiful, old bulls, which had either been driven from the herds by younger animals or had voluntarily retired from a society which bored them, would often be encountered either alone or two or three together. But along the Chobi I have often seen from five to ten old buffalo bulls consorting together, and I once saw as many as fifteen very old males in one troop.

Where the country had not been much disturbed, such old buffalo bulls were very slow about getting out of one's way, and would stand calmly watching the approach of so unaccustomed a visitor to their haunts as a human being without showing any sign of fear. Their demeanour was indeed apparently aggressive and truculent; still, although I have walked up to or close past a very large number in the aggregate of old buffalo bulls, I have never known one to charge before being interfered with. With outstretched noses these formidable-looking creatures would stand gazing at one with sullen eyes from under their massive rugged horns, and would not sometimes run off before sticks and stones were thrown at them; but in my experience they always did run off sooner or later. African buffaloes are, after all, nothing but wild cattle. My Matabele boys used frequently to speak of them as "Izinkomo ka M'limo" ("God's cattle"). I have walked past thousands and thousands of them, and have never known one to charge when unprovoked. But when a buffalo which has been mauled by lions or wounded by some hunter, and is lying sick and sore in long grass or thick bush, suddenly sees a number of human beings advancing towards its retreat, it will very likely jump up and charge through them, inflicting perhaps a deadly blow with one of its massive crooked horns as it passes. Once a buffalo has been wounded and gets into thick jungle or reeds or long grass, it becomes a most dangerous animal, especially to an inexperienced sportsman who has not yet acquired the art of

"SUCH OLD BUFFALO BULLS WERE VERY SLOW ABOUT GETTING OUT OF ONE'S WAY."

seeing an animal standing motionless in the shade of dense bush as soon as it is physically possible to do so, and who cannot walk noiselessly on the tracks of wounded game.

It has often been stated that on the approach of a herd of elephants to drink at a pool of water, all other animals will at once retire and make way for them. Very likely this may be true as a general rule, but I remember one occasion upon which a herd of some thirty elephants coming down to drink at a vley early in the night, and finding a large herd of buffaloes at the water before them, waited until these latter animals had quenched their thirst and fed slowly off into the forest before themselves going down to the pool.

This happened on a night in November 1873, when the moon, nearly at the full, was shining in a cloudless sky.

I was camped near a fine vley of fresh rain-water in the country to the west of the river Gwai, in Matabeleland, and had just finished my evening meal, when a large herd of buffaloes came to drink, and had hardly reached the water when we saw a troop of elephants approaching. These latter passed very near to my encampment, and must have seen our fires, as one after another they faced towards us, and stood looking in our direction with outspread ears. They did not, however, get our wind, and though they must have been suspicious, they were, I suppose, very thirsty. But as long as the buffaloes remained on the open ground round the pool of water, the elephants did not advance, remaining about a hundred yards away, just within the edge of a thin forest of mopani trees. Directly, however, the buffaloes had fed away into the forest on the other side of the vley, the greater beasts advanced very quickly to the water's edge, and, arranging themselves in a row, stood for a long time sucking up the grateful fluid through their trunks. As they were all cows and young animals, and there were some fine bulls in the district, I did not disturb them. Of course, I cannot say whether or no the buffaloes were aware of the proximity of the elephants, but I am quite certain that the latter not only saw and smelt the wild cattle, but waited until they had retired before themselves advancing to the water.

CHAPTER IX

NOTES ON THE TSE-TSE FLY

Connection between buffaloes and tse-tse flies—Sir Alfred Sharpe's views—Buffaloes and tse-tse flies both once abundant in the valley of the Limpopo and many other districts south of the Zambesi, in which both have now become extinct—Permanence of all kinds of game other than buffaloes in districts from which the tse-tse fly has disappeared—Experience of Mr. Percy Reid — Sudden increase of tse-tse flies between Leshuma and Kazungula during 1888—Disappearance of the tse-tse fly from the country to the north of Lake N'gami after the extermination of the buffalo—History of the country between the Gwai and Daka rivers—And of the country between the Chobi and the Zambesi—Climatic and other conditions necessary to the existence of the tse-tse fly—Never found at a high altitude above the sea—Nor on open plains or in large reed beds—"Fly" areas usually but not always well defined—Tse-tse flies most numerous in hot weather—Bite of the tse-tse fly fatal to all domestic animals, except native goats and perhaps pigs—Donkeys more resistant to tse-tse fly poison than horses or cattle—Tse-tse flies active on warm nights—Effect of tse-tse fly bites on human beings.

As it is impossible for any one who had much experience with buffaloes in the interior of South Africa in the days when these animals were excessively plentiful not to have a very lively remembrance also of the tse-tse flies by which they were almost invariably accompanied, I think a few words concerning these insects will not be out of place. My remarks must, however, be understood to apply not to all tse-tse flies—for there are several distinct species of the genus inhabiting different parts of Africa—but to *Glossina morsitans* alone, which, so far as I am aware, is the only species of tse-tse fly as yet known to occur in Africa to the south of the Zambesi river.

In the countries farther north, men of great experience have expressed the opinion that there is no connection between tse-tse flies and buffaloes or any other kind of wild animals. Writing on this subject, Sir Alfred Sharpe has recently stated, in the course of an article published in the *Field* newspaper for November 2, 1907:

> So far as Africa north of the Zambesi is concerned (*i.e.* British Central Africa, North-Eastern Rhodesia, Portuguese East Africa, the south-west portion of German East Africa, and the south-east corner of the Congo State), I am able to speak with some experience, having spent twenty years in those regions. The results of the last few years' careful observation have led me to a decided opinion that the existence of tse-tse is not dependent on wild game of any description. Tse-tse (mostly *Glossina morsitans* in British Central Africa), when it has the opportunity, sucks the blood of all such animals as it can get at in tracts of country in which it exists, but I think that blood is an exceptional diet (as in the case of the mosquito).

The great experience which Sir Alfred Sharpe has enjoyed in British Central Africa — which territory he has so ably administered for many years—entitles any views he may express on any subject concerning that country to the very greatest respect; but it must, nevertheless, be said that the conclusions he has arrived at concerning the requirements and life-history of the tse-tse fly (of the species *Glossina morsitans*), in the countries lying to the north of the Zambesi river, in which his observations have been made, are diametrically opposed to the teachings of history throughout the whole of Africa to the south of the Zambesi, where not only would it seem that these insects live entirely upon mammalian blood, but that they have become so highly specialised that they can only maintain their vitality on the blood of buffaloes; for it can be shown that wherever tse-tse flies were first encountered by the earliest European travellers in South Africa, there also buffaloes were either constantly present or visited such districts during certain months of every year; and that as soon as the buffaloes were either exterminated or driven out of any such territories, a remarkable diminution in the numbers of the tse-tse flies was at once observed; whilst in a very few years after the complete extinction of the buffaloes these insects entirely ceased to exist, even though other kinds of game remained in the country for years afterwards. A few facts bearing on this subject, which, being historical, can neither be questioned nor, I think, explained away as coincidences, are well worth enumerating.

In 1845 Mr. William Cotton Oswell—the well-known traveller and hunter—encountered tse-tse fly on the Maghaliquain river, a tributary of the Limpopo running through the Northern Transvaal, and it is an historical fact that at that time the whole of the Northern Transvaal lying between the Waterberg and Zoutpansberg ranges and the Limpopo, as well as a large area of country lying to the north of that river, was the haunt of great herds of buffaloes, and that the banks of every river draining this large territory, as well as many tracts of forest lying between these rivers, were at the same time infested with tse-tse flies.

In 1871 the well-known traveller Mr. Thomas Baines, as he has recorded in his book *The Gold Regions of South-East Africa*, still found the tse-tse fly numerous on the Maghaliquain river, as well as in the neighbourhood of the Macloutsie and Shashi rivers, and in many other places throughout the valley of the Limpopo.

In the following year, 1872, I visited Matabeleland for the first time, and it is within my own knowledge that at that time buffaloes were still plentiful in many parts of the valley of the central Limpopo.

About this time the natives of every tribe in South Africa were acquiring guns and ammunition in immense quantities in payment for work in the recently discovered diamond mines. The first result of the acquisition of firearms by the natives of the Northern Transvaal and the countries farther north was the destruction of all the buffaloes throughout the valley of the Limpopo to the west of the Tuli river, and it is a well-known fact that in a very few years after the disappearance of the buffaloes from this large area of country the tse-tse fly had also absolutely ceased to exist.

Yet for years after the disappearance of both buffaloes and tse-tse flies from the valley of the central Limpopo and its tributaries, other game, such as zebras, koodoos, wildebeests, waterbucks, impalas, and bushbucks, continued to exist in considerable numbers. I myself found all these animals still fairly numerous in 1886 along the Maghaliquain river, as well as on the Limpopo itself and along the lower course of the Macloutsie and Shashi rivers, and it seems to me that there can be no doubt that after the buffaloes had been exterminated the tse-tse flies gradually died out, because they could not maintain themselves on the blood of other kinds of game.

Again, it is an historical fact that when gold was first discovered in the Lydenburg district of the Transvaal, in the early 'seventies of the last century, the whole of the low-lying belt of country near Delagoa Bay was infested with tse-tse fly, and that buffaloes were also very plentiful in the same district.

Very heavy losses in cattle were the result of the first attempts to carry goods by ox waggon from Lourenço Marquez to the Transvaal goldfields. Ox-waggon transport was then abandoned and a service of donkey waggons established by, I think, a Mr. Abbot. Donkeys, however, though far more resistant to tse-tse fly poison than cattle, were found to soon grow weak from, and sooner or later to succumb to, its effects. Gradually, however, the buffaloes got killed off throughout the low country lying between the Lebombo range and the sea, and the tse-tse fly then gradually diminished in numbers, until, though many other kinds of game remained in the country, the waggon road leading from Barberton to Delagoa Bay at last became quite free from these insects.

It is a well-known fact, too, that up to the year 1878 buffaloes were plentiful on the Botletlie river to the south of Lake N'gami in the neighbourhood of the Tamalakan, where Livingstone and Oswell lost so many of their oxen from tse-tse fly bites in 1853.

Up to the year 1878, too, there were still two "fly"-infested tracts of forest to the west of the Botletlie, through which the waggon road to Lake N'gami from Bamangwato passed. These "fly" belts were always crossed during the coldest hours of the night by traders and hunters travelling to or from Lake N'gami with cattle and horses. During the year 1878 a number of emigrant Boer families, on their way from the Transvaal to Portuguese West Africa, spent several months camped along the Botletlie river. The men belonging to these families were all hunters, and they killed a great many buffaloes, and drove those they did not kill far up the Tamalakan. After 1878 no buffalo was ever seen again on the Botletlie river, and soon after the disappearance of the buffaloes the tse-tse flies, which had up to that time constantly infested two belts of forest near the western bank of the river, ceased to exist. There are neither tse-tse flies nor buffaloes along the Botletlie river to-day, though several species of antelopes as well as zebras were a few years ago, and are probably still, existent there.

Again, in the early 'seventies of the last century there were two "fly" belts lying across the road from Bamangwato to the Zambesi, the first a tract of forested country some twelve miles broad, situated to the south of Daka, and the second occupying a lesser extent of ground of similar character between Pandamatenka and the Zambesi. At the same date, all along the southern bank of the Zambesi and Chobi rivers to the westward of the Victoria Falls, tse-tse flies were present in such numbers that it was no exaggeration to speak of them as swarming, or as resembling a swarm of bees, whilst prodigious numbers of buffaloes were likewise to be found all the year round in the same locality. The buffaloes seldom went more than a mile or so away from the river, and it was my experience that where the buffaloes did not penetrate, the country was entirely free from "fly." Both the one and the other were confined in this part of the country to the near vicinity of the river, where, however, both literally swarmed. In the "fly" belts aforementioned, crossed by the waggon road to the Zambesi, buffaloes were only present during the wet season and the early part of the dry season, retiring eastwards as the vleys dried up. In these "fly" belts, however, tse-tse were not nearly so numerous as along the Zambesi and Chobi, where the buffaloes were present all the year round. Constant persecution from about 1876 onwards, chiefly by natives armed with guns, soon stopped the buffaloes from coming into the "fly" belts crossed by the waggon road to the Zambesi, and a few years later these animals had also entirely ceased to visit the southern bank of the Zambesi between the Victoria Falls and the mouth of the Chobi. After the buffaloes ceased to visit the tracts of forests infested by "fly" on the road to the Zambesi, these insects very soon entirely died out, though other kinds of game still remained in both those districts. Along the southern bank of the Zambesi to the west of the Victoria Falls the tse-tse flies began to diminish in numbers as soon as the buffaloes ceased to frequent this part of the country. It took some years certainly before the tse-tse had quite died out in this strip of country, but for many years past now neither buffaloes nor tse-tse flies have been seen in that district, where, however, game of various kinds other than buffaloes continued to exist long after the tse-tse flies had completely disappeared.

When exactly the buffaloes ceased to visit the neighbourhood of the Victoria Falls and the two tracts of country that were once known as "fly" belts on the road to the Zambesi, and how long it was after the disappearance of these animals that the tse-tse flies entirely died out in these same districts, I have been unable to ascertain. In 1874 I found both buffaloes and tse-tse flies in all these districts, and in 1877, on my second visit to the Zambesi, although I did not see any buffaloes or their fresh tracks in the two "fly" belts crossed by the waggon road, tse-tse flies still haunted both these localities, as I myself observed, and as has also been recorded by the late Dr. B. F. Bradshaw. I believe, however, that these insects were at that time rapidly diminishing in numbers in both those districts, owing to the fact that the buffaloes had almost ceased to come amongst them. In October 1877 I accompanied Dr. Bradshaw from Kazungula—where the Chobi joins the Zambesi—to the Victoria Falls. We walked the whole way along the bank of the Zambesi and found tse-tse fly very numerous everywhere, especially near the Falls. At this time buffaloes were already becoming scarce to the eastward of the junction of the Chobi with the Zambesi, most of them having already moved westwards up the course of the former river.

Eleven years later, in 1888, I travelled over the old waggon road to the Zambesi for the last time. Both buffaloes and tse-tse flies had then long since disappeared from the stretch of country to the south of Daka as well as from the "fly" belt to the north of Pandamatenka, whilst they were also entirely absent from the southern bank of the Zambesi near the Victoria Falls. There was still, however, a certain amount of game—zebras and several species of antelopes—left in all these districts.

In December 1888 I took two horses to the Falls, and rode one of them all along the narrow strip of open ground between the Rain Forest and the edge of the chasm into which the river falls. It seemed strange not to see a single "fly" in this district, where these death-dealing insects had literally swarmed only eleven years earlier.

Farther westwards, however, tse-tse flies continued to haunt the southern bank of the lower Chobi river in great numbers long after the buffaloes had ceased to live there constantly, though these animals still visited the district during the rainy seasons. At such times they probably grazed down the river in great numbers to within a few miles of its junction with the Zambesi.

A letter I have lately received from my old friend Mr. Percy Reid, who has made many hunting trips to the Chobi and Zambesi rivers, the last two of which were undertaken, the one the year before and the other three years after the epidemic of rinderpest had killed off all the buffaloes on the lower course of the Chobi river, throws a great deal of light on the disputed question as to whether or no there is or has ever been any connection between the buffalo and the tse-tse fly in South Africa.

In the course of his letter Mr. Reid says:

I was at Kazungula (the junction of the Chobi and Zambesi rivers) in 1885, 1888, 1895, and 1899. In 1885 I did not take my oxen beyond Pandamatenka, as it was not considered safe to take them to Kazungula; but even in that year I saw no "fly" between Leshuma[1] and the junction of the rivers, though I remember that a few were said to still exist there at that time. There were no buffalo there then, and the fact that the "fly" still lingered in this district was put down, though I do not know with how much truth, to the great number of baboons which, as you will remember, always frequented the bush near Kazungula.

In 1888 and subsequent years I sent oxen and horses backwards and forwards from the river to Leshuma at all hours of the day, and never lost any from "fly" bites.

In 1895 there were plenty of both fly and buffalo up the Majili,[2] and *swarms of fly* up the Chobi, but I did not go very far, and saw no buffalo there.

In 1899, only three years after the rinderpest had swept off all the buffaloes, I went along the north bank of the Chobi right past Linyanti, and, crossing above the swamps, came back along the south bank. *There was not a fly to be seen* where, only four years before, I had counted thirty or forty on a native's back at one time, and we had actually to light fires and sit in the smoke to

[1] Leshuma is ten miles south of Kazungula.

[2] A river running into the Zambesi from the north, not far above its junction with the Chobi.

protect ourselves from them. On the whole trip we saw no buffalo, and only got fairly old spoor of one very small lot on the north bank. I certainly always understood that in a very few years after the buffalo disappeared from any district the "fly" followed suit. All the old hunters up on the Zambesi were agreed on that point, and I recollect George Westbeech[1] saying the same thing.

This letter conclusively proves that although tse-tse flies continued to swarm along the southern bank of the Chobi to within a short distance above Kazungula for some years after the buffaloes had ceased to live all the year round in this district (as they used to do up to the early 'eighties of the last century), and only spent the rainy season there, these insects absolutely disappeared within three years after the final destruction of the buffaloes by rinderpest in 1896.

Mr. Reid's letter also seems to show that if buffaloes live in great numbers all along the bank of a certain river where tse-tse flies also swarm, and that if through persecution the buffaloes should be driven far up the river at certain times of year, only returning to their old haunts during the rains, when all hunters have left the country, a large proportion of the tse-tse flies do not migrate backwards and forwards with the buffaloes, but remain constantly on the section of the river where they first appeared as perfect insects, not appreciably decreasing in numbers as long as the buffaloes come amongst them periodically, but gradually dwindling in numbers, and at last altogether disappearing within a few years of the final extinction of those animals, in spite of the continued presence of other kinds of game.

Although Mr. Reid saw no "flies" between

[1] An old Zambesi trader of great experience.

Leshuma and Kazungula either in 1885 or in 1888, there were still a few lingering there in the latter year. There were so few in the early part of 1888, however, that probably none were to be seen during June and July, when the nights were very cold, but later on in this same year they increased very rapidly in numbers, as I think, owing to the fact that my own and Mr. Reid's cattle deposited a great deal of dung all along the waggon track leading down to Kazungula. It was in June of that year (1888), after I myself had crossed the Zambesi on an expedition to the north, that Jan Weyers, an old Dutch hunter, took my waggon by night through the old "fly" belt between Leshuma and Kazungula in order to trade with the natives living on the Zambesi, sending the oxen back to Leshuma the following night. In the same month, or a little later, Mr. Percy Reid and his party brought their waggons to Leshuma, and their oxen pulled them backwards and forwards several times between that place and Kazungula. There was thus a great deal of cattle dung, which is, of course, precisely the same as buffalo dung, all along this short stretch of waggon road. For some reason this driving of cattle backwards and forwards between Leshuma and the Chobi caused an extraordinary increase in the number of tse-tse flies. All the natives who travelled the road remarked upon it, and both they and Jan Weyers assured me that they had thought the "fly" was almost absolutely extinct in this district, as in the previous year, even in the hot weather before the rains, very few had been seen.

However, when I went down to the river in August (1888) on my way to the Barotse country, I found a good many tse-tse flies along the track, and by November they had become very numerous. As Mr. Reid and his party did not return to Pandamatenka by way of Leshuma, but went along the southern bank of the Zambesi to the Falls, they were unaware of this sudden increase in the numbers of the tse-tse flies.

I am still quite unable to account for the sudden and rapid increase in the number of tse-tse flies along the waggon track between Leshuma and Kazungula between August and November 1888, as it is quite certain that up to the latter month they had taken no toll of blood from the cattle which had been driven backwards and forwards along the road either by night or during the cold weather in June or July.

I knew that my friend the late Dr. Bradshaw used to hold the view that the tse-tse fly deposited its eggs in buffalo dung, and I thought at the time that the cattle dung had been taken as a substitute. The very important researches, however, of Lieutenant-Colonel Bruce in Zululand have shown that "*the 'tse-tse' fly does not lay eggs as do the majority of the Diptera, but extrudes a yellow coloured larva, nearly as large as the abdomen of the mother.*" The perfect insect does not hatch out for six weeks, so that the increase by generation from a small number of individuals in the course of a few months would not be very great. I can only think, therefore, that all the tse-tse flies throughout the bush through which the ten miles of road led from Leshuma to the Chobi must have been attracted to its neighbourhood by the smell of the cattle dung, which no doubt they mistook for that of buffaloes, the animals with which they have always been so closely associated in the countries to the south of the Zambesi. I am, however, not at all satisfied with this explanation.

I was obliged to keep my waggon standing on the bank of the Zambesi (waiting for ivory to be brought down from the Barotse valley) until late in November 1888, so that when I was at last able to send my oxen down to the river to bring it through the "fly," which now infested the waggon track leading from Leshuma to Kazungula in considerable numbers, the nights had become very warm, and although we did not start till after eleven o'clock, and ran the oxen to the river and brought the waggon back as quickly as possible, every one of them, twenty-one in all, got "fly-stuck" and died within six months.

After 1888 the tse-tse flies again rapidly diminished in numbers between Leshuma and Kazungula, and have long since absolutely ceased to exist there; so that here again we have another instance of a country in which, at no very distant time, both buffaloes and tse-tse flies literally swarmed, but from which both have now long since completely disappeared, although other animals, such as antelopes of various kinds and baboons, cannot yet be altogether extinct.

The same diminution and eventual disappearance of the tse-tse fly has also followed the extinction of the buffalo on the Okavango to the north of Lake N'gami.

As has been recorded by C. J. Andersson and other travellers and hunters, both buffaloes and tse-tse flies existed in great numbers along the Teoge (Okavango) river between Lake N'gami and Libèbè's in the early 'fifties of the last century. At that time the Batauwana tribe were living at Lake N'gami. These people gradually acquired firearms and drove the buffaloes northwards up the Okavango, and the fly did not long remain in the countries which these animals ceased to visit. In 1884, after having been twice attacked by the Matabele, the Batauwana abandoned their settlements at Lake N'gami and retreated several days' journey to the north along the Okavango, where they built a new town, which they named Denukani (on the river). From this point they have now been hunting through all the country farther north for more than twenty years, and I have been lately informed that a waggon road has been cut from Denukani to Libèbè's, and from thence to the Quito, the whole length of which is entirely free from tse-tse fly, which insects there seems every reason to believe have died out owing to the disappearance of the buffaloes from their former haunts.

But the facts which I have already stated, and which seem to me to show that in Africa to the south of the Zambesi there has always been a close connection between the buffalo and the tse-tse fly, by no means exhaust the evidence on this point.

When Sebitwane, the great chief of the Makololo, and Umziligazi, the founder of the Matabele nation, led their clans, the one to Linyanti between the Chobi and Zambesi rivers, the other to the high plateau near the sources of the Gwai and Umzingwani rivers, they found the whole country south of the Zambesi, between the Daka and the Gwai, occupied by an unwarlike and agricultural people akin to the Makalaka, and if any value can be placed on native testimony, these people were rich in cattle.

Attacked first by the Makololo and later on by the Matabele, these unfortunate people were killed in great numbers and gradually dispossessed of their lands, all their cattle being taken from them. Those that escaped death fled across the Zambesi, where their descendants are living to this day.

Now I have no doubt that long ago, before the country between the Gwai and the Daka rivers was settled up by natives, it had been a "fly"-infested country full of buffaloes. At any rate, as soon as the natives had been killed or driven out of it, buffaloes and all other kinds of game took possession of it, moving in no doubt from the countries both to the east and the west, and with them came a few tse-tse flies, which must soon have increased and multiplied in so favourable an environment.

In 1873 I was hunting elephants at the junction of the Gwai and Shangani rivers, and through all the country westwards to beyond the site of the present coal-mine at Wankies. At that time all this country was full of buffaloes and tse-tse flies.

Fifteen years later, however, the Matabele, who had then for a long time been in the possession of firearms, had driven the buffaloes out of all the country on either side of the river Gwai, and as these animals went farther north and east, the tse-tse fly gradually disappeared.

The last time I saw Lo Bengula alive—early in 1890—I spent the greater part of two days talking to him on many subjects, especially game, for he loved to talk about wild animals, having been a great hunter in his youth. He told me that there were then no more buffaloes anywhere in the neighbourhood of the Gwai and Shangani rivers, and that with the buffaloes the "fly" had gone too, and that as the buffaloes and the "fly" had died out, he had gradually pushed his cattle posts down both the Gwai and Shangani rivers, and that at that time, 1890, he had actually got a cattle post at the junction of the two rivers, where seventeen years before I had found buffaloes and tse-tse flies both very numerous.

The history of the country lying between the lower course of the Chobi river and the Zambesi has been very similar to that of the territory to the south of the Zambesi between the Gwai and the Daka.

When Livingstone and Oswell visited the chief Sebitwane in 1853, they first took their waggon during the night through the narrow strip of "fly"-infested country which ran along the southern bank of the Chobi, and swam their bullocks to the other side of the river before sunrise the next morning. Just where they struck the southern branch of the Chobi there were no trees or bushes on its northern bank, only open grass lands and reed beds to which the tse-tse flies never crossed, although the river was only fifty yards broad, and they simply swarmed all along the wooded southern bank.

At this time, 1853, Sebitwane, who possessed great numbers of cattle, was living not in the open grass country, which has always been free from "fly," but at Linyanti, which was situated beyond the northern branch of the Chobi and was surrounded on all sides by sandy ridges on which grew forest trees and bushes. In 1861 Linyanti was again visited by Dr. Livingstone, in company with his brother Charles and Dr. (now Sir John) Kirk. Sekeletu, the son of Sebitwane, was then the chief of the Makololo, and these people were still rich in cattle. After Sekeletu's death a civil war broke out between two rival claimants to the chieftainship which so weakened the Makololo, that a coalition of the remnants of the various tribes they had conquered and reduced to servitude some forty years previously rose in rebellion against their rulers, and under the leadership of Sepopo, the uncle of Lewanika, the present chief of the Barotse, absolutely destroyed them as a people, killing every male down to the new-born infants, but sparing all the young females and girl children, who were subsequently taken as wives by their captors.

After the destruction of the Makololo tribe, the country between the Chobi and the Zambesi was once more given back to nature.

In 1879 I crossed both branches of the Chobi and visited the site of the once important native town of Linyanti. I there found several relics of the ill-fated Makololo mission party (sent to that tribe by Dr. Livingstone's advice), in the shape of the iron tyres and nave bands of waggon wheels. At that time the surrounding country had been uninhabited for some fifteen years, and I found great herds of buffaloes grazing undisturbed all round and over the site of Linyanti, where once had pastured the cattle of the Makololo. With the buffaloes too had come the tse-tse flies, which swarmed all over this district, though when the former left the forest and bush and went into the reed beds and open grass lands between the two main branches of the Chobi, the latter did not follow them. There can be no doubt, however, that when the Makololo first crossed from Sesheke on the Zambesi to the northern branch of the Chobi river, they must have found both buffaloes and tse-tse flies numerous in the district where later on their chief Sebitwane built his principal town. The buffaloes must have first been driven to the west, and the fly must subsequently have died out, before the natives were able to introduce cattle into this part of the country. After the destruction of the native population about 1864, the buffaloes moved back into the country from which they had whilom been driven, and the tse-tse flies came with them. The rinderpest which passed through the country in 1896, I believe, killed all the buffaloes left anywhere near Linyanti, and probably the tse-tse fly has also long since died out in that district,[1] into which cattle may have been once more introduced by the natives, though I do not know that this is the case.

But although it would seem, from the historical facts I have just related, that in Africa, to the south of the Zambesi river, *Glossina morsitans* has always been dependent upon the Cape buffalo for

[1] A reference to the letter I have already quoted from my friend Mr. Percy Reid shows that in 1899 he found neither buffaloes nor tse-tse flies in the neighbourhood of Linyanti, where both were very numerous on the occasion of my visit in 1879.

its continued existence, certain climatic and other conditions which have never yet been satisfactorily explained have always prevented tse-tse flies from spreading into all parts of the country in which buffaloes were once found. In Southern Africa the tse-tse fly has always been confined to a strip of country along the south-east coast, and the hot, well-wooded valleys of the Zambesi and Limpopo rivers and their tributaries. Apparently the tse-tse fly (*Glossina morsitans*) requires a certain degree of heat in the atmosphere, or can only stand a certain degree of cold; for along the east coast it seems never to have existed to the south of St. Lucia Bay, in the 28th parallel of south latitude, although buffaloes were once plentiful far beyond this limit, all through the coast lands of Natal and the Cape Colony, as far as Mossel Bay. Nor are these insects ever found at a high altitude above the sea. "Fly" country is usually less than 3000 feet above sea-level, though in places such as the district to the north of Hartley Hills, in Mashunaland, tse-tse flies ascend to a height of nearly 3500 feet. Nearer the equator, they are able to live at a higher level, and I have myself met with tse-tse flies near the upper Kafukwe river at an altitude of at least 4000 feet above the sea.

The tse-tse flies spread with the buffaloes from the sea-coast all along the Limpopo to beyond its junction with the Maghaliquain, but were not able to accompany them to higher ground. The buffaloes, however, spread right up to near the sources of the Limpopo and its tributaries, crossed the watershed to the reed beds of the Molopo, and from thence spread through Bechwanaland as far south as the Orange river, hundreds of miles away from the nearest "fly"-infested area. Even in the midst of low-lying districts full of buffaloes, and, speaking generally, full of tse-tse flies as well, all open pieces of grass country, where there are neither trees nor bushes, and all reed beds of any size, will be found to be free from these insects. When buffaloes feed out into such places from the surrounding forests, the "flies" soon leave them and return to the shelter of the trees. Similarly, if one side of a river be covered with bush and forest down to the water's edge, and if, along this forest-covered bank, tse-tse flies swarm, these insects will never cross even a narrow channel to open reed beds or grass land on the other side. Dr. Livingstone has mentioned how, though he found tse-tse flies swarming along the southern bank of the Chobi river in 1853, his oxen were perfectly safe from these insects in the open grass lands on the other side of the river; and in my own experience, although I have often crossed this same part of the Chobi by canoe, and seen numbers of "flies" on meat, or on the natives or myself, as we left the southern bank, I never knew one of them to cross the river with us. As soon as we got to a short distance from the southern bank, they all left us and flew back to the shelter of the trees and bushes. But the most extraordinary thing about the tse-tse fly is, that in certain low-lying countries away from the wooded banks of the larger rivers, these insects were not found everywhere, but only in certain forest areas, known to the early South African pioneers as "fly" belts. I am speaking now, of course, of the time when natural conditions and the balance of nature had not been upset by North Europeans; for no charge of this kind can be made against the Portuguese, who were always poor hunters.

No one, I think, has ever been able to explain why the tse-tse flies never spread from the "fly" belt which was crossed by the old waggon road to the Zambesi, a few miles to the south of Daka, to the "fly"-infested forest, which lay across the same road a little to the north of Pandamatenka. The country between these two "fly"-infested areas was exactly similar in its vegetation, its altitude above the sea, and in every other particular, as far as one could see, to the "fly" belts which bounded it to the north and south, and during the rainy season buffaloes must have wandered through the intermediate country, as well as through the two "fly" belts. That tse-tse flies used to be found in the greatest numbers along the wooded banks of rivers such as the Chobi, the Zambesi and many of its tributaries, was owing, I think, to the fact that buffaloes had become excessively plentiful in the same districts, not because the near neighbourhood of water was necessary to them; for many "fly" belts, *e.g.* those extending across the road to the Zambesi, were absolutely destitute of water during several months of every year.

The tenacity with which tse-tse flies cling to certain tracts of country, or even narrow belts of forest, is wonderful, but they sometimes move beyond their usual limits nevertheless. About forty years ago, a waggon track was made by elephant hunters from Matabeleland to Hartley Hills in Mashunaland. Not more than ten miles to the north of the points where this waggon road cut the Umzweswe and Umfuli rivers, the country was always frequented by buffaloes and infested with tse-tse flies. In my own experience, I have often known large herds of buffaloes to come south along the Umfuli river up to and beyond the waggon road. I hunted and shot them there on horseback for the last time in 1885, and used my waggon and oxen to bring the meat and skins to my camp; and as my cattle did not suffer in any way, there could not have been any "flies" about.

The tse-tse flies, however, used always to come with the buffaloes for several miles beyond their usual boundary, but gradually left them, and in my own experience I never knew them to quite reach the waggon road.

It will thus be seen that although "fly"-infested areas are, as a rule, well defined and well known to the natives, the movements of large herds of buffaloes may carry these insects—sometimes in great numbers—for a short period of time, for a few miles beyond their usual limits. Within a large area of country throughout which tse-tse flies exist, such as the level forest country in the valley of the Zambesi intersected by the lower courses of the Sanyati and Panyami rivers, or the country near the east coast, in the neighbourhood of the Pungwe river, tse-tse flies used to move about, so that in a place where they were found in great numbers on a certain date, hardly any would sometimes be met with in the same place a month later. In my experience, in such cases the tse-tse flies always moved about with the buffaloes, within these areas, where all other conditions were suitable to their existence.

In "fly"-infested areas where these insects are not very numerous, comparatively few or possibly none at all will be seen during the months of May, June, and July, when the days are short and not excessively hot and the nights are bitterly cold. In fact, it is quite possible to pass through a good deal of "fly" country during these months without ever becoming aware of the existence of these insects. But as the days get longer and hotter, and the nights less cold, if there are any tse-tse flies in a district at all they will be found to increase very rapidly in numbers. They become most numerous and most troublesome, I think, in October and November, just before the commencement of the rainy season. During the rainy season they are perhaps not quite so exasperating, but my experience has been that they were both numerous and troublesome at that season too. They are not so active in cloudy weather as in bright sunshine, and if a strong wind is blowing they hardly show themselves at all.

It is perhaps worth mentioning that the fact of the disappearance of the tse-tse fly from all countries to the south of the Zambesi, very soon after the complete extinction of buffaloes in the same regions, cannot be attributed to the settling up and cultivation of the land by Europeans; for the tse-tse fly has never existed in any part of Africa south of the Zambesi where malarial fever was not and is not still rife. Whatever may be the case to-day, up to 1896, long after the disappearance of both buffaloes and tse-tse flies, the Boers had never been able to establish themselves and live all the year round in the Northern Transvaal along the valley of the Limpopo, although they used to graze their cattle there during the winter; nor, as far as I am aware, although mining operations have been carried on for nearly twenty years within what was once "fly" country to the north of Hartley Hills in Mashunaland, has there been any settlement of families on the land in that district.

The word "tse-tse" (pronounced by the natives "tsay-tsay" and by colonists "tetsy") is simply the word used by natives of the Bechwana clans for the deadly fly known to scientists as *Glossina morsitans.* The Matabele—as well, I believe, as the Zulu—name for the same insect is "impugan." With the Matabele any kind of fly is an "impugan," but it is the only word they ever employ for the tse-tse.

As is well known, the tse-tse fly, when with its long proboscis it "sticks," as the Boers say, a domestic animal, introduces into the blood of the latter certain minute blood parasites (Trypanosoma), which, though constantly present in the blood of wild animals living in the "fly"-infested regions of Africa, does them no harm. These Trypanosomes, if introduced into the blood of domestic animals in any quantity, at once set up a disease, which almost always ends fatally. Cattle when "fly-stuck" soon begin to run at the eyes, and the glands behind the ears and in the throat swell. Although continuing to feed well, they become thinner and weaker day by day, and should they be exposed to cold or wet weather, their coats stare, as if they were suffering from lung sickness. According to the number of Trypanosomes in their blood, cattle will live a shorter or longer time. They will succumb within a month if kept constantly in country where tse-tse flies are numerous during that time. On the other hand, they will sometimes live for nearly a year if only "stuck" by one or a few flies whilst passing through a "fly"-infested belt of forest of small extent. I have known a young ox, though it showed every sign of having been impregnated with the "fly" disease—possibly it had only been "stuck" by one "fly"—to recover completely after remaining very thin for more than a year. Horses and donkeys, when "fly-stuck," run at the eyes and swell at the navel, and soon get thin and lose all their strength.

In 1877 I took three donkeys with me up the Chobi. They lived in a swarm of tse-tse flies day after day and all day long. The first of them to succumb only lived a fortnight; the second died in five weeks; but the third lived for nearly three months, and carried a buffalo head back to my waggons at Daka—some eighty miles from the Chobi.

For about ten days before the second donkey died I remained in the same camp. By this time it had grown very thin and was too weak to carry anything, but it did not seem to suffer in any way, and whenever I could observe it, was always feeding on the young green grass at the river's edge. I never tied it up at nights, but every evening it used to come and roll in a large heap of ashes behind my camp. One evening it came and rolled in the ashes as usual, but was too weak to get on its legs again, and on the following morning was dead. Apparently it enjoyed its life to the very last.

During 1887 some friends and I took four horses and five donkeys into the "fly" country on the Angwa river, in the northern part of Mashunaland. There were a good many buffaloes and a fair number of tse-tse flies in this district at that time, but not one for every hundred of either that I had met with along the Chobi river in the early 'seventies. My own horse cut its career short by galloping with me into an open game pitfall and breaking its back, and the other three, although they were well fed with maize morning and evening, were too weak to gallop after game in a fortnight. After a month they were too weak to carry a man at all, and they were then shot. The five donkeys all got thin, and swelled at the navel, and ran at the eyes, but none of them died, although they remained in the "fly" country for more than a month. By the end of the following rainy season they had quite recovered their condition and were well and strong again. These same five donkeys were taken down to Zumbo on the Zambesi the following year by the late Bishop Knight-Bruce. But they all died from the effects of this journey, during which they must have suffered great hardships and also been exposed to the attacks of thousands of tse-tse flies on the lower Panyami river.

When visiting the old Portuguese settlement of Zumbo on the Zambesi, in 1882, I found the few

Portuguese residents as well as the natives living there in the possession of great numbers of pigs. These animals were sent out every morning into the country round the settlement, and called back in the evening — those which belonged to the Portuguese—by a few notes on a horn. A little maize was then scattered on the ground for them to pick up, after which they were shut up for the night in a walled enclosure. As tse-tse flies were numerous along the bank of the Zambesi on both sides of Zumbo, and it was quite impossible to keep cattle there on account of them, or any other domestic animals besides the pigs, except the small native goats, the former must have been equally as resistant to "fly" poison as the latter. These domestic pigs certainly did not owe their immunity to the "fly" disease to the fact that they were fat, for they were miserably thin long-snouted looking brutes. Although the pigs I saw at Zumbo probably did not go very far away from the settlement during the daytime, I feel sure that they must have been constantly bitten by tse-tse flies, as these insects were numerous quite close up to the native village, which is built amongst the ruins of the old Portuguese town.

All the natives living in "fly"-infested districts of South Africa keep small, miserable-looking dogs, as well as goats of a small, indigenous breed, and the natives outside such infested districts also keep goats of the same kind. These goats take no harm from the tse-tse flies; but the large Cape goats, which are descended from European breeds, as well as Angora goats, are not resistant to the "fly" disease. Nor are any dogs of European breeds.

In 1891 my two horses were suddenly attacked by tse-tse flies as I was riding with a companion along the bank of the Revue river, where the local Kafirs had told me these insects did not exist. Luckily, being so well acquainted with the peculiar "buzz" made by a tse-tse fly, I believe I heard the first one that came to my horse, and immediately dismounted. In the next few minutes we caught sixteen flies on the two horses, most of them by pinning their feet with a knife blade, as they are very difficult to catch with the hand. I then made the Kafirs cut branches, with which they kept the flies off the horses until we had got them away from the river, and beyond the "fly" belt. Most of these flies were caught immediately they settled on the horses, but two or three managed to fill themselves with blood. My horses, however, which were in very good condition, were never affected in any way.

Tse-tse flies are most active and troublesome in hot weather. During the winter months in South Africa (May, June, and July) none will be seen until the sun is high above the horizon, but later in the season they begin to bite early in the morning. After sunset in the evening they seem to become lethargic, and will often crawl up between one's legs or under one's coat as if for shelter, and from such positions will often "stick" one long after dark. On cold nights they probably become quite benumbed, and do not move at all, but on warm nights they are sometimes very active and hungry. As before related, I lost twenty-one oxen by driving them backwards and forwards in one night through a "fly" belt ten miles in width. This was in the month of November, and the night was very warm.

On the 25th of August 1874, when returning from the pursuit of a wounded elephant, I struck the Chobi river late at night, and had to walk several miles along the bank before getting to my camp. It was a bright moonlight night, and fairly warm. My only clothing consisted of a shirt, a hat, and a pair of veld shoes, and as I walked along near the water's edge the tse-tse flies kept flying up from the ground and biting my bare legs, and from the loud slaps behind me I knew they were paying similar attentions to my Kafirs. Now, these "flies" were undoubtedly resting on the bare ground, for we were walking, not through bushes, but along the strip of open ground between the forest and the water's edge. The bite of the tse-tse is very sharp, like the prick of a needle, but in a healthy man it causes no swelling or after irritation, like the bite of a midge or a mosquitoe. Speaking generally, the bites of a moderate number of tse-tse flies may be said to have no appreciable effect on a human being. Still, I am of opinion that if one is exposed to the attentions of swarms of these insects for months at a time, the strongest of human beings will find himself growing gradually weaker. Explorers or traders may sometimes be exposed to the bites of great numbers of tse-tse flies for a few days together, but they will soon pass through such districts. Only an elephant hunter, I think, would ever be likely to remain for any considerable period of time in a country where tse-tse flies were very numerous. I cannot think that many Europeans have suffered from tse-tse fly bites as much as I have. In 1874, and again in 1877, I spent the whole of the dry season, from June till November, on the southern bank of the Chobi river, and lived during the greater part of those two seasons in a swarm of tse-tse flies. Up to that time I had had no fever, and my constitution was unimpaired in any way. Towards the end of both those seasons, however, not only I myself but all my Kafir attendants became excessively thin, and seemed to be getting rather weak. The natives, too, who lived in the reed beds where there were no tse-tse flies, but who used to come to the southern bank of the river to collect firewood and look at their game traps, all said that they could not live there because of the tse-tse, which made them thin and weak, or, as they expressed it, the tse-tse "killed them," just as they say in times of famine that hunger is killing them.

In 1882 I met with a curious experience, for which I cannot quite account. During that year I had made an expedition from the high plateau of Mashunaland to Zumbo, on the Zambesi, and had had a somewhat hard time and gone through a severe attack of fever. I had also been very much bitten by tse-tse flies on the lower Panyami and Umsengaisi rivers. Towards the end of the year I got back to the Mission Station of Umshlangeni in Matabeleland, and was given a warm welcome by my old friends the Rev. W. A. Elliott and his wife. I reached the Mission Station late in the evening, after a ride of fifty miles in the hot sun. I was fairly well, having recovered from the attack of fever, but perhaps a little run down.

Soon after I had turned in on the bed Mrs. Elliott had arranged for me, I felt my nose coming on to bleed. Not wanting to disturb any one, I pulled a newspaper I had been reading from the chair by my bedside, and spreading it on the floor, let my nose bleed on to it. It bled a good deal, and the next morning I was surprised to see that the blood which had come from me was not like blood at all, but slimy, yellow-looking stuff. When I showed it to Mr. Elliott, I said to him that it looked to me exactly like the blood of a "fly-stuck" donkey which I had shot some years before at Daka, and I laughingly suggested that I was "fly-stuck" too. That something had affected the red corpuscles of my blood seems certain, but whether innumerable tse-tse fly bites or fever, or both combined, had done it I cannot say. Ever since I received an injury in the head in 1880, I have been rather subject to bleeding from the right nostril, but I have never again lost any blood which bore the slightest resemblance to that which came from me in Mr. Elliott's house after my trip to Zumbo in 1882.

CHAPTER X

NOTES ON THE BLACK OR PREHENSILE-LIPPED RHINOCEROS

Character of the black rhinoceros—Its practical extermination in South Africa at a very trifling cost to human life—No case known to author of a Boer hunter having been killed by a black rhinoceros—Accidents to English hunters—Harris's opinion of and experiences with the black rhinoceros—Seemingly unnecessary slaughter of these animals—Large numbers shot by Oswell and Vardon—Divergence of opinion concerning disposition of the two so-called different species of black rhinoceroses—Experiences of Gordon Cumming, Andersson, and Baldwin with these animals—Victims of the ferocity of the black rhinoceros extraordinarily few in South Africa—The author's experiences with these animals—Sudden rise in the value of short rhinoceros horns—Its fatal effect—Dull sight of the black rhinoceros—Keen scent—Inquisitiveness—Blind rush of the black rhinoceros when wounded—An advancing rhinoceros shot in the head—Author chased by black rhinoceroses when on horseback—Curious experience near Thamma-Setjie—Black rhinoceroses charging through caravans—Coming to camp fires at night—Author's doubts as to the extreme ferocity of black rhinoceroses in general—Testimony of experienced hunters as to the character of the black rhinoceros in the countries north of the Zambesi—Captain Stigand severely injured by one of these animals—Experiences of Mr. Vaughan Kirby—Extraordinary number of black rhinoceroses in East Africa — Experiences of A. H. Neumann and F. J. Jackson with these animals—Views of Sir James Hayes-Sadler—Great numbers of rhinoceroses lately shot in East Africa without loss of life to hunters—Superiority of modern weapons—President Roosevelt's letter—Mr. Fleischmann's remarkable account of a combat between a rhinoceros and a crocodile—Possible explanation of seeming helplessness of the rhinoceros.

In a previous chapter I have spoken of the difficulty of understanding the true character of the African black or prehensile-lipped rhinoceros; but perhaps I ought to have said "my own" difficulty, for never having had my life seriously endangered by any one of the many animals of this species which I met with at a time when they were still fairly numerous in the interior of South Africa, I have always found it very difficult to credit the vast majority of these stupidly inquisitive but dull-sighted brutes with the vindictiveness and ferocity of disposition that has often been attributed to the whole race. I am, it must be understood, now speaking only of the black rhinoceros in Africa to the south of the Zambesi. In other parts of the continent I have had no experience of these animals.

In Southern Africa the black as well as the white rhinoceros has been almost absolutely exterminated during the last sixty years. During that period, thousands upon thousands of these animals have been killed, at a cost to human life so trifling, that I submit it is impossible to contend that, speaking generally, the hunting and shooting of black rhinoceroses was an exceptionally dangerous undertaking.

When a young man I was personally acquainted with several of the most noted of the old Boer hunters — Petrus Jacobs, Jan Viljoen, Martinus Swart, Michael Engelbreght, and others — who were amongst the first white men to penetrate to the wondrous hunting-grounds beyond the Limpopo; but I never heard of any Boer hunter having been killed by a black rhinoceros.

Amongst the early English hunters, who were probably more reckless and less experienced than the Boers, a few accidents certainly happened, but, considering the number of rhinoceroses they killed, they must have been favoured with extraordinarily good luck to have got off as cheaply as they did, if anything like a large proportion of these animals had habitually attacked them without provocation, as soon as they saw or scented them, or even made a point of charging immediately they were interfered with.

During his wonderful hunting expedition to the interior of South Africa in 1836-37, Captain (afterwards Sir Cornwallis) Harris met with an extraordinary number of rhinoceroses of both the black and the white species. He shot great numbers of both, but never seems himself to have been in any serious danger from a black rhinoceros, though one of his Hottentot servants was knocked over by one of these animals, and his companion, Mr. Richardson, seems to have had a very narrow escape from another.

Speaking of this incident, Harris says: "My companion the next morning achieved a 'gentle passage of arms' with the very duplicate of this gentleman;[1] but *his* antagonist could not be prevailed upon to surrender to superior weapons, until it had considerably disfigured with the point of its horn the stock of the rifle employed in its reduction. Aroused from a siesta in a thick bush by the smarting of a gunshot wound, the exasperated beast pursued its human assailant so closely, that Richardson was fain in self-defence to discharge the second barrel down its open throat!"

In a further paragraph Harris wrote: "As we advanced, the species (the black rhinoceros) became daily more and more abundant, and I shall hardly gain credence when I assert that in the valley of the Limpopo specimens were so numerous that on arriving in the afternoon at our new ground it was no uncommon thing to perceive a dozen horned snouts protruded at once from bushes in the

[1] Another rhinoceros shot by Captain Harris.

immediate vicinity. No sooner were the teams unyoked than the whole party, in the regular routine of business, having assumed their weapons, proceeded to dislodge the enemy, and right stoutly often was the field contested. But where is the quadruped that can stand before the grooved rifle? it will take the conceit out of the most contumacious, and like a sedative, will calm his ruffled temper in a minute. Every individual came in for a share of cold lead and quicksilver; and the stubborn brute that would not quietly withdraw, satisfied with the mercurial dose he had received, was ultimately badgered to death as a matter of course. Daily almost two or three were thus annihilated within view of the camp."

Personally, I find it impossible to believe, nor does it seem to be implied, that any great danger attended this oft-repeated and senseless slaughter of animals, which were undoubtedly attracted to the waggons by nothing more reprehensible than inquisitiveness; just as, when crossing the high downs between the Zambesi and Kafukwe rivers with a train of pack-donkeys in 1888, I was upon several occasions accompanied by herds of wildebeests, which ran alongside of my caravan for considerable distances, their sense of danger entirely overcome by the stronger passion of curiosity.

It is very evident from Harris's description of the white rhinoceros that he considered this species to be almost equally as dangerous as the black. He states that he found it "subject to the same paroxysms of reckless and unprovoked fury," and "often fully as troublesome as its sable relative."

The black rhinoceros is often spoken of as a beast of so savage and morose a temper that it will not only attack any animal which may approach it, but in default of anything better, will vent its senseless rage on bushes or other inanimate objects.

But is there any authority for such a charge? Harris says: "Nineteen times out of twenty shall you see the crusty old fellow standing listlessly in the society of gnoos, quaggas, and hartebeests"; and I myself have often seen black rhinoceroses drinking peaceably in close proximity to buffaloes and other animals.

Mr. William Cotton Oswell, who between the years 1844 and 1853 made five hunting expeditions into the interior of South Africa, met with and shot great numbers of rhinoceroses of both the black and the white species. In one season alone, he and his companion Mr. Vardon shot no less than eighty-nine of these animals. Oswell, who was a man of a very bold and fearless disposition, was badly injured by a black rhinoceros on one occasion, and on another had his horse gored to death by a wounded animal of the white species.

It is worthy of remark, I think, that Harris took the correct view that all the prehensile-lipped rhinoceroses he encountered belonged to one and the same species, although showing individually very great divergencies in the relative length of the two horns. In a footnote to his description of the black rhinoceros he says: "In no two specimens of this animal which came under my observation were the horns built exactly upon the same model. Disease or accident had not unfrequently rendered the anterior horn the *shorter* of the two."

Oswell, however, as well as many other travellers and hunters, adopted the native view that those prehensile-lipped rhinoceroses in which the posterior horn was equal or nearly equal in length to the anterior belonged to a distinct species, and in view of the fact that all naturalists and sportsmen are now agreed that all prehensile-lipped rhinoceroses throughout Africa belong to one and the same species, the differences in their horns being merely individual variations of no specific value, it is interesting to note the divergence of opinion between well-known writers as to the comparative aggressiveness of the two supposed species.

Oswell speaks of the borili—the prehensile-lipped rhinoceros in which the second horn was short—as being "as a rule the only really troublesome member of his family," whilst Andersson and Chapman considered the keitloa—the variety in which both horns were of equal or nearly equal length—as the more dangerous variety.

Gordon Cumming speaks of both varieties of the black rhinoceros as "extremely fierce and dangerous," and says "they rush headlong and unprovoked at any object which attracts their attention." Although, however, this great hunter must have seen and shot large numbers of these animals, I cannot gather from his writings that he ever treated them with the respect which the character he gives them ought to have inspired, or ever seemed to think there was much danger to be apprehended in attacking them. Having approached the first black rhinoceros he ever saw very closely, it heard him and advanced towards where he was hiding. Gordon Cumming then, "knowing well that a frontal shot would not prove deadly," sprang to his feet and ran for cover, upon which the rhinoceros charged and chased him round a bush. The animal then stood eyeing the hunter, but "*getting a whiff of his wind, at once became alarmed and ran off*." This last remark is interesting to me because it has so often been stated that black rhinoceroses charge as a rule immediately they scent a human being, whereas my own experience agrees in this particular with that of Gordon Cumming. With the exception of this adventure, a careful perusal of Gordon Cumming's writings does not reveal the fact that he was ever again in any great danger from a black rhinoceros. He was once chased when on horseback by one which he had wounded, but from the account he gives of this incident he could hardly have expected anything else. He writes: "Becoming at last annoyed at the length of the chase . . . I determined to bring matters to a crisis; so, spurring my horse, I dashed ahead and rode right in his path. Upon this the hideous monster instantly charged me in the most resolute manner, blowing loudly through his nostrils."

C. J. Andersson, who travelled in Western South Africa in the early 'fifties of the last century, was also a mighty hunter. He states that he killed "many scores" of rhinoceroses—as many as sixty in one season alone. He gives the black rhinoceros a very bad character, saying that animals of this species are not only of "a very sullen and morose disposition," but that they are also "subject to sudden paroxysms of unprovoked fury, rushing and charging with inconceivable fierceness animals, stones, bushes—in short, any object that comes in their way."

Except, however, upon one occasion, when Andersson was badly injured one night and nearly lost his life as the result of closely approaching and throwing a stone at a black rhinoceros which he had previously wounded, he does not seem to have met with any further adventures or suffered any inconvenience from the unprovoked fury of any other individual of the species.

About the same time that Andersson was travelling and hunting in Damaraland and Ovampoland, Baldwin was leading an almost precisely similar life first in Zululand and Amatongaland, and later on in the countries lying to the north and north-west of the Transvaal as far as the Zambesi river and Lake N'gami. Baldwin must have encountered a considerable number of rhinoceroses of both the black and the white species, and records the shooting of a good many of these animals in the most matter-of-fact way. From cover to cover of the very interesting book he wrote describing his hunting adventures, *African Hunting from Natal to the Zambesi*, he never speaks of the black rhinoceros as being a savage and ferocious animal, given to sudden paroxysms of fury, nor does he ever appear to have thought it a more dangerous animal to attack than one of the white species. Indeed, on several occasions he simply records the fact that he shot a rhinoceros, without saying to which species it belonged. One rhinoceros came at him after having been wounded, but was stopped by a shot in the forehead. As this animal—a cow with a very small calf—is spoken of as having a very long horn, it was probably a white rhinoceros, which would have charged with its nose close to the ground, and would therefore have been much easier to kill with a shot in the forehead than one of the black species, whose head would necessarily have been held somewhat higher owing to the shortness of its neck.

My own personal experience of the black rhinoceros in Southern Africa compels me to believe that, although a small proportion of animals of this species may have been excessively ill-tempered, and were always ready to charge anything and everything they saw moving, and even to hunt a human being by scent, that was never the character of the great majority of these animals. At any rate, the rage of the black rhinoceros in the countries to the south of the Zambesi has been singularly impotent and ineffective. In the thirty-five years which elapsed between the date of Harris's travels through Bechwanaland and the north-western portions of what is now the Transvaal Colony and my own first visit to South Africa in 1871, thousands of black rhinoceroses must have been killed; a very large proportion of them by white—principally Boer—hunters, for up to the latter date the natives only possessed a very few firearms. Yet how many hunters were killed or injured during the killing-off of this enormous number of creatures, which have been so often described as not only excessively savage and dangerous when interfered with, but also subject to sudden paroxysms of unprovoked fury? I think I have read all recent books on South African hunting, but I cannot recall any mention of a white man or a black man having been killed by a black rhinoceros in any one of them, though both Oswell and Andersson were badly injured and came very near losing their lives in encounters with individuals of this species. I do not say that between 1836 and 1871 no human being was killed by a black rhinoceros in South Africa. All I wish to convey is that such incidents must have been exceedingly rare, for I cannot remember either to have read any account of such a catastrophe or to have heard any of the old Boer hunters mention such a case.

Between 1872 and 1890, the period during which both black and white rhinoceroses were practically exterminated in all the countries between the Limpopo and the Zambesi rivers, I can, however, positively assert that no white hunter was killed or even injured by a black rhinoceros in any part of the immense territories comprised in the present Southern Rhodesia and the Bechwanaland Protectorate, for no such accident could have happened without my having heard of it; nor did I ever hear of a native hunter having been killed by one of these animals during that time, although one of the old traders—George Kirton[1]—told me that in 1868 a black rhinoceros had charged through his string of porters, and driven its horn through both

[1] An elder brother of Argent Kirton, who was killed with Allan Wilson in the Matabele War of 1893.

thighs of one of them, throwing him up in the air. Fortunately no bones were broken and the injured man quickly recovered from his wounds. Another instance of the same kind happened in the experience of my old hunting companion, George Wood. One day, as he and two companions—David Napier and, I think, James Gifford—were riding along on elephant spoor in Mashunaland, a black rhinoceros suddenly charged through them, overturning Napier's horse and throwing it and its rider to the ground. Napier was not hurt, but I forget whether or no the horse was killed. These two incidents serve to show that in the parts of Africa in which my own experience was gained, certain black rhinoceroses were undoubtedly dangerous and aggressive; but such animals were, I am convinced, exceptional. I do not think that rhinoceroses were ever so plentiful on the northern watershed between the Limpopo and Zambesi rivers as Harris found them in the valley of the former river in 1837, but nevertheless in the early 'seventies, throughout all the uninhabited portions of the territory now known as Southern Rhodesia, rhinoceroses of both the black and the white species were very plentiful. The countries through which I hunted in 1872 and 1873 were practically virgin ground, as the Matabele were then only just beginning to acquire firearms in any quantity. As I have recorded in my book *A Hunter's Wanderings*,[1] when hunting elephants during those two years I encountered almost daily one or more prehensile-lipped rhinoceroses, often seeing five, six, or even eight in one day, and in addition to these, I met with many of the square-mouthed or white species as well. As I was hunting elephants for a living and could not therefore afford to run the risk of disturbing these valuable animals by firing indiscriminately

[1] First published in 1881.

at any other kind of game, unless I really wanted meat, I seldom killed rhinoceroses. But had these animals been valuable, and had I been hunting them for a living instead of elephants, I think that by watching at their drinking-places, and following up fresh tracks, as well as shooting all those I came across casually, I might easily have killed a hundred of each species during those two years. During each of the years 1874, 1877, 1878, 1879, 1880, 1882, 1883, 1885, and 1887, I came across black rhinoceroses, but never in any one of those years in anything like the numbers I had met with these animals in 1872 and 1873.

In the country to the north-east of Matabeleland, between the Sebakwe and the Hanyani rivers, both black and white rhinoceroses were still fairly numerous in 1878, during which year I one day saw five of the latter all together, and it was only after 1880 that the numbers of both species commenced to be seriously reduced in this part of South Africa. About that time rhinoceros horns—of all sorts and sizes—attained a considerable commercial value, probably through some freak of fashion in knife-handles or combs or what not in Europe. But whatever was the cause of it, this sudden rise in the value of small rhinoceros horns sounded the death-knell of these creatures in the interior of South Africa. By the year 1880, ivory had become very scarce in that portion of the continent, and the traders in Matabeleland then for the first time began to employ native hunters to shoot rhinoceroses for the sake of their horns—no matter of what length—and their hides, which latter were made into waggon whips and sjamboks. One trader alone told me that he had supplied four hundred Matabele hunters with guns and ammunition, and between 1880 and 1884 his large store always contained great piles of rhinoceros horns—of all sorts and sizes, often the spoils of over a hundred of these animals at one time, although they were constantly being sold to other traders and carried south to Kimberley on their way to Europe. I do not know for a fact that all these rhinoceros horns were sent to Europe. They may have been shipped to China or India.

Although many hundreds of native hunters—poorly armed with smooth-bore muskets for the most part—must have taken part in the practical extermination of both the black and the white rhinoceros, throughout all the uninhabited tracts of country lying between the high plateau of Matabeleland and the Zambesi river, as far as I know no single man was either killed or injured in the process, although they must have killed between them at least a thousand black rhinoceroses alone during the five years before 1886. After that there were very few rhinoceroses left to shoot to the west of the Umfuli river, beyond which the Matabele hunters seldom ventured.

Black rhinoceroses always appeared to me to be very dull of sight, but quick of hearing and excessively keen scented, and I have never known an instance of one not immediately running off on getting my wind. I have often seen them, too, take alarm and run off when warned by the tick-birds that so often accompanied them, although they had neither seen nor smelt me. These tick-birds, which may often be seen accompanying buffaloes and other animals as well as rhinoceroses, always flutter about and give well-understood warning cries on the approach of a human being. On the other hand, I have seen many black rhinoceroses, when suddenly disturbed by the noise made by my Kafirs and myself, as we walked past them, come trotting up towards us snorting loudly. Such animals had not got our wind or they would have run off—at least I think so. Whenever rhinoceroses came trotting towards us snorting, my Kafirs used to run to the nearest trees and call to me to do the same; but I never did so, and I was never charged by one. These animals, after first trotting quickly towards me, would stand looking intently at what must have been to them the unaccustomed sight of a figure with a shirt and a hat on it, then snort again and trot up nearer; but with one exception they always turned round and trotted off sooner or later, carrying their heads and tails high in the air. Sometimes I had to shout and throw sticks and stones at them before they wheeled round and made off.

It sometimes happened that a rhinoceros which I had disturbed came trotting towards me, at a time when I wanted meat, and I then took advantage of the opportunity, and kneeling down, fired a four-ounce ball into its chest from my muzzle-loading elephant gun. In such cases they would usually come rushing straight forwards at a gallop, puffing and snorting furiously, and on several occasions have passed within a few yards of where I was standing. However, I never thought that these wounded animals were charging, but believed them to be rushing blindly forwards after having received a mortal wound. I have, however, often heard such blind rushes described as terrific charges.

The one occasion on which I had to fire at an advancing black rhinoceros because I could not make it turn was on April 25, 1878. At that time I was making my way from the Zambesi river to Matabeland, through an uninhabited piece of country which had never previously been traversed by a white man. I was very weak and ill from fever and privation, and on meeting with a black rhinoceros early in the morning, was anxious to kill it for the sake of the meat. When the animal, however, an old bull, first came trotting towards me, I did not fire at it, as I thought I could make more certain of killing it with a shot through the lungs as it turned to run off. But it would not turn, but kept advancing steadily towards me without taking any notice of my shouts, until it was so near that I determined to try and kill it with a shot in the front of the head. I was at that time armed with a single-barrelled ten-bore rifle, which was carefully sighted and shot very accurately, and when the rhinoceros was within fifteen yards of where I stood, and still slowly but steadily advancing, I put a bullet past its horns and into its forehead. It fell to the shot and rolled on its side, but almost immediately raised its head and brought it down again on the ground with a thump. I saw that it was only stunned, just as the one had been which I had lost some five years previously, after having hit it in almost exactly the same place with a four-ounce bullet; so I ran close up to it and killed it with a bullet behind the shoulder, just as it swung itself up into a sitting position. What this rhinoceros would have done if I had not fired I do not know. I think it very likely, however, that had I turned and run for a tree, it might have rushed after me and struck at me with its horn. Some of the others, too, which had trotted up towards me in previous years might have done the same thing, if they had suddenly seen me running close in front of them. I have twice had the same experience as that described by Gordon Cumming when he galloped in front of a black rhinoceros which he had wounded, that is to say, I have been smartly chased by two of these animals. The first was a cow with a nearly full-grown calf. These two animals went off at a swift trot as soon as they scented me, breaking into a gallop when I pressed them. I then tried to pass them, so as to get a broadside shot; but directly my horse drew level with her, the cow charged in the most determined manner, snorting furiously and chasing me for a considerable distance. This incident occurred in 1880. In 1883, when hunting on horseback just outside the "fly" country on the upper Sabi river, I one day came across an old bull black rhinoceros which, though it ran off in the first instance as soon as it saw or scented me, turned and chased me smartly, with the usual accompaniment of snorts and puffs, as soon as my horse drew level with it. It chased me certainly for over a hundred yards, and pressed my horse pretty hard. As it swerved off and stopped snorting, I brought my horse round, and dismounting, gave it a shot in the ribs; but on galloping up near it again, it gave me another smart chase. Two more bullets, however, finished this plucky old animal.

Besides these two, I can only call to mind eight other black rhinoceroses which I chased on horseback, and none of these showed any fight at all, but kept continually sheering off as the horse drew level with them, making it almost impossible to get anything but a stern shot. In November 1874 I chased a black rhinoceros bull out into an open expanse of ground near Thamma-Setjie, on the old waggon road to the Zambesi, and in trying to get a broadside shot, rode it round and round in a large circle, until it presently stood still with its mouth open, evidently completely done. Even when I dismounted and shot it at close range—I only had an old smooth-bore gun—it never attempted to charge.

Several times, when hunting elephants in the early 'seventies of the last century, black rhinoceroses rushed snorting either close in front of or close behind myself and my small party of Kafirs. They had undoubtedly been alarmed by hearing or smelling us, and were, I think, trying to get out of danger; but I believe that, should a rhinoceros get the wind of the foremost man amongst a long string of porters, and on starting off to run away from the disagreeable smell, suddenly find itself confronted by another portion of the caravan, it will not turn back, but rush snorting through the line, sometimes perhaps injuring a man in its passage. It is, I think, owing to the fact that travellers, traders, and hunters in East Africa have always employed very large numbers of porters, who marched in single file in a line often extending to several hundred yards in length, that incidents of this kind have been so frequent in that country. But when a black rhinoceros just rushes through a long line of porters without singling out and following any particular man, I think such a proceeding is more the result of panic than anything else. My view is that the wind blowing obliquely across the line being taken by a caravan may reach a rhinoceros lying or standing some distance away. This animal at once takes alarm and runs off, at first perhaps at right angles to the direction from which the wind is blowing; but on again turning up wind, as rhinoceroses almost invariably do, it comes right on to another portion of the straggling line of porters. Confronted by this line of men, whom it had at first tried to avoid, it will probably not turn back, but rather charge through them and continue its flight. The sight of the black rhinoceros is certainly very bad, and in cases where these animals have charged against waggons in South Africa, and trains on the Uganda Railway, it is difficult to say whether they were animated by pure bad temper or ran against these obstacles because they suddenly saw them moving right across their path, when they were endeavouring to escape from some other danger.

Upon three occasions during 1873 black rhinoceroses came close up to my camp at night, snorting loudly, and upon one occasion, as I shall relate in a subsequent chapter, a white one did the same thing. On all these occasions, I think the curiosity of these rhinoceroses must have been aroused by the sight of the camp fires, or else the smell of blood and meat must have excited them. I fired into one of the black rhinoceroses as he was coming very close, and drove off the other two by shouting at them.

That a certain proportion of the vanished race of South African rhinoceroses of the prehensile-lipped species were of a morose and savage temper, and therefore dangerous animals to encounter, I will not for one moment attempt to deny, for there is a great deal of evidence that this was the case. But what I do think is that many writers have taken the character of the exceptionally vicious animals they met with as typical of that of the whole species. But, unless at least a very considerable proportion of black rhinoceroses were neither savage nor dangerous, I fail to understand why it was that none of those that I myself encountered behaved in a manner befitting their reputation ; how it has come about that the whole race has been practically exterminated in South Africa at so infinitesimal a cost to human life ; why Gordon Cumming, who shot so many of these "hideous monsters," only appears to have met with two adventures—both of a very mild character—with these animals ; and why Baldwin never seemed to have the least idea that they were either dangerous to attack or subject to sudden paroxysms of unprovoked fury.

Hitherto I have only spoken of the black rhinoceros in South Africa ; but the testimony of the most experienced hunters, in other parts of the continent, seems to show that the character of this animal has always been essentially the same throughout its entire range. Everywhere it seems to have been and to be a stupid, blundering, bad-sighted, but keen-scented beast; in the great majority of cases doing its best to avoid human beings, but always liable to become savage when wounded, like elephants, lions, and buffaloes, and sometimes being really bad-tempered and savage by nature, and ready to charge unprovoked at the sight or scent of any one approaching it. My own experience proves at least that it is quite possible to come across a great number of black rhinoceroses without ever encountering a really vicious one.

In those countries which now form part of North-Western Rhodesia, through which I travelled many years ago, black rhinoceroses were by no means plentiful. In fact, though I from time to time came across their tracks, I never actually saw a rhinoceros in the flesh to the north of the Zambesi. Throughout British Central Africa, too, I believe I am correct in stating that these animals have never been found in any great number. It was somewhere in this territory that my friend Captain C. H. Stigand was severely injured by a black rhinoceros. I have heard the story of this misadventure from his own lips, and I think there can be no doubt that the animal which suddenly charged and tossed him without provocation was one of those vicious, dangerous brutes whose exceptionally savage tempers have given a bad name to the whole species.

In a footnote to the article on the black rhinoceros contributed to the *Great and Small Game of Africa* by Mr. F. Vaughan Kirby, that writer says, in speaking of the character of this animal: "I know an instance of a native being charged and killed, and another whom I met personally who was chased and regularly hunted by a wounded one, which caught and fearfully mutilated him."

Judging by his own personal experience, Mr.

Kirby came to the conclusion that, "although naturally timid, and certainly not dangerously aggressive, the black rhinoceros is of most uncertain temper, and when wounded and encountered at close quarters, can and will charge most fiercely, and occasionally is as vindictive as any buffalo." The adjective "vindictive" here used by Mr. Kirby does not appear to me to be quite the right or fair one. If an elephant, buffalo, lion, or rhinoceros should be attacked and grievously injured by a human being, and is brave and stubborn enough to resent such treatment and make a fight for its life, it seems like adding insult to injury to speak of it as vindictive.

In many parts of both British and German East Africa black rhinoceroses were quite recently, and in some cases probably still are, extraordinarily numerous. Here, as in other parts of Africa, a certain number of accidents have occurred in hunting these animals, and there have been a good many instances of their charging through a line of native porters. However, although it is unquestionable that in East Africa, as elsewhere, black rhinoceroses have sometimes shown themselves to be really vicious, and therefore very dangerous animals, there seems to be a consensus of opinion amongst those men who have had the greatest experience with them, that these were the exceptions to the general rule.

Few men, if any, could have had a wider experience with the black rhinoceros in East Africa than my friend the late A. H. Neumann, whose recent death I shall never cease to deplore, and I therefore make no apology for quoting a few sentences from the very interesting and informing article contributed by him to the *Great and Small Game of Africa* on the subject of this animal. Neumann says:

As has often been pointed out, the rhino is the most intensely stupid of animals, and marvellously blind. So much so, that it may often be approached even on a bare plain with little trouble *up wind.* It is their very stupidity and blindness which makes these beasts a source of danger to passing caravans; for should the wind be blowing *from* them, and unless they be accompanied by tick-birds, as they often are, which alarm them and cause them to make off, they frequently remain unconscious of the approach of a caravan until it is close to them, when, being suddenly confronted with a long line of porters, they will sometimes charge straight through it, apparently under the impression that there is no other way of escape open. On the other hand, they are keen-scented; and if the wind be blowing in their direction they start away at a quick trot as soon as the taint reaches them, and while yet a long way off.

As regards the much-disputed question, to what degree the rhinoceros is a dangerous beast, the result of my experience and observations is very decidedly to convince me that, under ordinary circumstances and with proper caution, there is not very much risk in shooting him, and that the danger is not to be compared in any way with that attending the pursuit of the elephant. At the same time, there is always a possibility that one may charge, and there is therefore a certain amount of excitement in the sport; and instances are not rare of men having been badly injured by these beasts. . . .

The Ndorobos kill these animals with their elephant harpoons, or trap them in the same manner as elephants. Those I have been among have far less fear of rhinoceroses than of elephants, and as a consequence it is a rare thing to see a rhino in country much frequented by such of these people as have much skill and courage in elephant-hunting. The same applies to Swahilis, many of whom think nothing of shooting a "faro," though they would not dream of attacking elephants.

The only other man whose experience with rhinoceroses in East Africa has been equal to that of Arthur Neumann is Mr. F. J. Jackson, C.B., who for some years past has been a most able administrator of the territories in which he first made a name as a hunter and a naturalist. Mr. Jackson's testimony concerning the character of the black rhinoceros as he has known that animal appears to me to coincide very closely with that arrived at by Neumann, his great friend and only rival as a hunter in East Africa. Like Neumann, Jackson fully realises that black rhinoceroses are sometimes vicious and dangerous, but his experience has been that, as a rule, these animals avoid and run away from human beings if they can, and that even when they rush snorting through a long line of native porters, they are usually trying to escape from rather than viciously attacking these men. In the course of the very interesting article on the black rhinoceros contributed by Mr. F. J. Jackson to vol. i. on *Big Game Shooting* of the Badminton Library, he states: "When alarmed, the rhinoceros becomes easily flurried, appears to do things on impulse which other animals endowed with more sagacity would not do, and is by no means the vicious and vindictive brute which some writers have found him to be in South Africa and the Soudan. In the majority of cases, where a rhinoceros is said, by men who perhaps have not been very well acquainted with his peculiarities, to have charged in a most determined and vicious manner, I believe this so-called charge to have been nothing more than the first headlong and impetuous rush of the beast in a semidazed state, endeavouring to avoid an encounter rather than court one."

In the course of the Report made to the Earl of Elgin on the game of the East Africa Proctectorate by the Chief Commissioner, Captain (now Sir

James) Hayes-Sadler, dated "Commissioner's Office, Nairobi, September 28, 1906," the following passage occurs: "This interesting Pachyderm (the black rhinoceros), though sometimes a dangerous, is always a stupid animal, and, from his bulk and the nature of the country he inhabits, with but few exceptions falls an easy prey. My experience of him, too, is that in fairly open country he is easily driven away, and that therefore the necessity of shooting to protect life is not nearly so frequent as has sometimes been alleged."

The opinion expressed in the above paragraph concerning the black rhinoceros and the danger of its pursuit has, I think, been proved to be fairly accurate by the experience of the many sportsmen (most of them utterly inexperienced in hunting large and dangerous animals) who have visited British East Africa in recent years; for since Mr. B. Eastwood was very badly injured, and indeed had a most miraculous escape, near Lake Baringo, in October 1902, from a rhinoceros which he thought he had killed, but which got on to its feet again and charged him after he had walked close up to where it was lying, I have not heard of any other accident having occurred in the hunting of these animals, although during the three years ending on March 31, 1906, no less than 308 black rhinoceroses were killed under sportsmen's and settlers' licences in British East Africa, besides twenty-three others which were shot on the border of the same territory by the members of the Anglo-German Boundary Commission.

The big-game hunter of to-day is armed with weapons which are vastly superior to those which the old pioneer hunters of South Africa had to rely upon in bygone times, and the dangers of big-game hunting are, in consequence, now very much less than they were then; but still, judging from my own experience (and in 1872, 1873, and 1874 the clumsy old four-bore guns I used were very inferior even to the two-grooved rifles possessed by Harris, Oswell, or Gordon Cumming) and all I heard from many old Boer and native hunters, I feel convinced that the character of the black rhinoceros was originally painted by picturesque writers in colours which, although they may have been appropriate to a certain small proportion of these animals, were quite undeserved by the great majority of the species. I will conclude these notes on the black rhinoceros with a letter which I have lately received from President Roosevelt, covering a most remarkable and excessively interesting description of a struggle between a crocodile and a rhinoceros in the Tana river, in British East Africa. Before making any comments on this extraordinary incident, I will first give both President Roosevelt's letter to myself and his correspondent's communication, as I have full permission to do.

THE WHITE HOUSE, WASHINGTON,
September 27, 1907.

MY DEAR MR. SELOUS—I don't know whether the enclosed letter and photographs will be of any value to you in your book or not. Both relate to an occurrence so remarkable that I thought I would send them to you. Fleischmann is a man of good standing, entirely truthful, and he had no conception of the importance of what he was telling me. I told him that the "authorities in Africa" who informed him that the crocodile might have gotten a purchase by wrapping its tail around something sunken were doubtless in error, and advised him to leave it out of the letter which he wrote me, which I told him I was going to send to you. But he put it in, and I am sending it along. It is the only part of his letter which is mere hearsay or guesswork. I had no conception that crocodiles would tackle a rhinoceros. But you may remember in Samuel Baker's *Wild Beasts and Their Ways* that he speaks of seeing crocodiles in Africa with the girth of a hippopotamus. In any event I send you the letter.

The other day, in reading *Big Game*, in the Badminton Library, I noticed that Oswell, the South African hunter, speaks of trying to cut off a cheetah, and that the latter distanced his horse with the utmost ease. This tends to confirm me in the opinion that the cheetah for a half mile or so can readily distance a horse, and that when pursued by you the two animals you overtook at first simply tried to keep ahead of you, not trying to exert themselves, and that after a half mile was passed their wind was gone and then they gave out.

When do you think you will publish your book?

Sincerely yours,

THEODORE ROOSEVELT.

MR. FREDERICK C. SELOUS,
Heatherside, Worplesdon,
Surrey, England.

CINCINNATI, *September* 23, 1907.

MY DEAR MR. PRESIDENT—I take pleasure in sending you under separate cover to-day, as per your request, the enlarged photographs of the encounter between a rhinoceros and crocodiles in the Tana river, British East Africa; also another photograph showing a large herd of hippopotami in the Tana river, which I believe may prove of interest to you.

I shall also undertake to give you a brief description of the attack of the crocodile upon the rhino, which resulted in the latter's death. While encamped on the Thika river, about one hundred yards above its junction with the Tana, the attention of the members of our hunting party was called to the loud cries of the porters. A moment later "Ali," the Somali headman, came running in to tell us that a mamba (crocodile) had seized a faro (rhinoceros), as the latter stepped into the river to drink. "Ali" was concealed in the bushes on the side of the river opposite the scene at the time the rhino came down to drink. When our party arrived, about fifty of our porters were on a sandbank leading out into the Tana river. The rhino was held by its left hind-leg, which had been seized by the crocodile just as the big beast was leaving the river after drinking. At least half a dozen of the porters, who had been lying in the bushes near the scene, in reply to my questions, agreed as to the manner the rhino was attacked.

When we neared the point of attack, the rhino appeared panic-stricken, making very little noise—simply straining and heaving in its efforts to release its leg from the jaws of the crocodile. While making but little headway, the rhino did for a time succeed in holding its own, keeping in shallow water, as the photos 1 and 2 show. A moment or two later, however, blood appeared on the surface of the water, leading us to believe that the crocodile had been reinforced by other mambas which had been attracted to the scene by the blood and lashing of the water. The struggle continued on down the stream, the combatants having moved quite a distance from the original point of attack. The rhino still managed to keep on its feet, facing either down stream or toward the opposite bank, and for a distance of at least one hundred yards down stream had made no perceptible loss of ground. Shortly afterward, however, apparently maddened by the pain it was undoubtedly suffering (for now much more blood and pieces of flesh appeared on the surface of the water), the rhino evidently lost its head and attempted to cross through the deep water to the opposite shore, as shown in photo 3. This move was the beginning of the rhino's end, for as soon as it turned and met with deeper water, it lost the advantage of a firm foothold in the shallow water, and the animal was quickly drawn beneath the surface.

PHOTOGRAPHS OF A STRUGGLE BETWEEN A RHINOCEROS AND A CROCODILE.

No. 1.

Shows the Rhinoceros holding its own, but unable to reach the bank.

No. 2.

Shows the Rhinoceros still struggling, but in deeper water.

No. 3.

Shows the Rhinoceros after it had turned round, and just before it got into deep water and was pulled under.

The rhino was a full-grown female with a horn which we estimated to be about twenty inches in length. It was the opinion of authorities in Africa to whom I told the story of the struggle, that a very large crocodile had taken hold of the rhino's leg and wrapped its tail around some sunken obstacle, thus giving it a purchase, as it were, which enabled it to successfully hold on until reinforced by other crocodiles.

These enlarged photographs were made from $3\frac{1}{4} \times 4\frac{1}{2}$ negatives, the "snaps" being taken by my valet, who was acting in charge of the commissary department of the caravan.

I trust that these photos will reach you in good condition.

With my sincere regards, I have the honour to be,

Yours respectfully,

MAX C. FLEISCHMANN.

TO HONORABLE THEODORE ROOSEVELT,
Washington, D.C.

Remarkable and unusual as was the occurrence witnessed by Mr. Fleischmann, there can be no doubt as to the truth of his most interesting story. The three photographs—all of which are reproduced in this book—showing the rhinoceros straining against something which was gradually pulling its hind-quarters deeper and deeper into the water, must convince the most sceptical. I fully agree with President Roosevelt that the theory, that the crocodile held the rhinoceros by getting a purchase with its tail round some sunken log, is not tenable, especially as Mr. Fleischmann states that "the struggle continued on down the stream, the combatants having moved quite a distance from the original point of attack."

Personally, I find no difficulty in believing that if

a very large crocodile were to seize a rhinoceros by the one hind-leg, and was sufficiently powerful to hold that limb off the ground, the largest of these animals would become almost helpless; for if either hind-leg of a rhinoceros be broken by a bullet, the animal is rendered immediately almost incapable of movement, and very soon assumes a sitting position. I imagine that a rhinoceros would easily be able to pull the largest of crocodiles out of water, if it was harnessed to one of these reptiles, and so could get a fair pull at it from the chest and shoulders; but I think that the paralysing effect of the crocodile's hold on one of its hind-legs would be sufficient to account for the helplessness of the animal whose struggles and ultimate death Mr. Fleischmann witnessed in the Tana river.

CHAPTER XI

NOTES ON THE GIRAFFE

Appearance of the giraffe—Not a vanishing species—Immense range—Habitat—Native mounted hunters—Destruction of giraffes and other game by Europeans—Necessity of restraining native hunters—Discussion as to the possibility of the giraffe existing for long periods without drinking—Water-conserving tubers—Wild water-melons—Habits of elephants after much persecution—Possible explanation of the belief that giraffes can dispense with water—Giraffes seen in the act of drinking—Giraffes absolutely voiceless—Partial to open, park-like country—Difficult to approach on foot—Giraffes very keen-scented—Hunting giraffes with Bushmen trackers—Exhilarating sport—Pace of the giraffe—The easiest way to kill giraffes—Driving wounded giraffes to camp—Two curious experiences with giraffes—"Stink bulls"—Excellence of the meat of a fat giraffe cow—Height of giraffes—Giraffes only occasionally killed by lions—Young giraffe attacked by leopards.

"UNGAINLY" is an epithet which has often been applied to the giraffe; but "stately," I think, would be a far more truly descriptive word, and there is certainly no animal in Africa which adds so much to the interest of the parched and waterless wastes in which it is usually found as this tallest of mammals. The sight of a herd of giraffes walking leisurely across an open piece of ground, or feeding through a park-like country of scattered trees and bush, is one which, once seen, must ever linger in the memory; for there is a something about the appearance of some few of the largest mammals still extant upon the earth which stirs the imagination as the sight of smaller but more beautiful animals can never do. When watching a moose bull standing knee-deep on the edge of some swampy lake, amidst the silence and the gloom of sub-Arctic pine forests, I always seem to be carried back to some far distant period of the world's history; and I remember that when hunting with Bushmen amidst the dull monotony of the sun-scorched, silent wastes of Western South Africa, the sight of giraffes always stirred the same thought. My rude companions were palæolithic men, and we were hunting strange beasts in the hot dry atmosphere of a long past geological era.

Giraffes are often spoken of as a scarce and fast vanishing species, but this I cannot believe to be really the case. There are vast areas of country, extending right across the whole width of the broadest part of Africa from Senegambia to Somaliland, and from thence southwards to the northern border of British Central Africa, throughout the whole of which one or other of the different races into which giraffes have lately been divided is to be found, often in great abundance. Throughout the greater part of this immense range, these magnificent, strangely beautiful creatures will, in my opinion, continue to live and thrive for centuries yet to come; for the giraffe is, as a rule, an inhabitant only of countries which, owing to the extreme scarcity of water, can never be settled up by Europeans, nor support anything but a sparse and scattered population of native herdsmen. Here they will never be hunted to any great extent by Europeans on horseback, nor shot down in large numbers for the sake of their hides, whilst their keenness of sight and great range of vision will protect them very effectually from all danger of extermination at the hands of native hunters as long as these latter are only armed with primitive weapons.

Even in the countries to the south and west of the Zambesi river, though there the range of the giraffe has been sadly curtailed since the time when the emigrant Boers first crossed the Orange river in 1836, these animals are far from being a vanished species, or one which is on the verge of extermination. True, there are now no giraffes left in large areas of country where thirty years ago they were plentiful, but these animals are still to be found in Western Matabeleland, throughout the greater part of Khama's country, as well as in the Northern Kalahari, and thence northwards to far within the boundaries of the Portuguese province of Angola. The whole of this vast extent of country is, like so much of Northern Africa to the south of the Sahara and Abyssinia, a semidesert, impossible of settlement by Europeans; for although it is covered for the most part with trees of various kinds, or thorn scrub varying in height from two or three to twelve or fifteen feet, the soil is almost everywhere deep soft sand, and for several months in the year there is little or no surface water, except in the large rivers, which are few in number and far apart. Throughout the greater part of these arid, sun-scorched wastes, giraffes are, I think, likely to hold their own for a long time to come, if only some check can be put upon the operations of the native mounted hunters, belonging to the Bakwena, Bamangwato, and Batauwana tribes, who are now practically their only enemies.

For the extermination of the giraffe in the Transvaal, Bechwanaland, and the country immediately to the north of the Limpopo, Europeans are entirely responsible. The Boers killed most of them, of course, because up to 1890 Boer hunters were always in the proportion of at least ten to one to white hunters of any other nationality. But, man for man, English hunters were quite as destructive as Boers. The fact is, the pioneers of all the white races of North-Western Europe in new countries are tarred with the same brush, as far as the extermination of wild animals is concerned. In North America the western frontiers-men, who were largely of British descent, exterminated in a few short years the countless herds of bison ; in South Africa the Boers have exterminated or brought to the verge of extinction many species of animals which but a few decades ago were spread over the face of the land in seemingly inexhaustible numbers; and to-day the inhabitants of Newfoundland are hard at work destroying as fast as they can the great herds of seals which annually assemble in the early spring to bring forth their young on the ice floes off the coast of Labrador.

When human greed of gain is added to the old love of hunting, and both are unrestrained by legislation, the speedy extermination of any beast or bird which has any market value must necessarily follow. The errors of the past can never be retrieved, but it is to be hoped that now that every part of the world has been taken under the protection of some civilised state, no species of animal or bird which still survives in any considerable numbers will be allowed to become extinct. The white man, whether Boer or Briton, is now effectually restrained from taking any further part in lessening the numbers of the giraffes in the countries to the west of Southern Rhodesia and to the north of the Limpopo, which are under British protection, and if only the native Bechwana hunters from Molipololi, Palapye, and Denukana—who are well-mounted and armed with breech-loading rifles—were forbidden by their chiefs to kill more than a certain fixed number of giraffes annually, and severely punished for exceeding the limit allowed, I see no reason why these most interesting animals should not survive for all time, throughout all those great areas of South-Western Africa where, owing to the scarcity of water, no human beings other than a few scattered families of wandering Bushmen can ever make their home.

The belief is very general, both amongst white and native hunters in South Africa, that giraffes are capable of going for months at a time without drinking, and the fact that they are to be found during the driest season of the year in the most arid districts, far away from any place where surface water exists, lends colour to this belief. But yet it seems to me impossible that an animal of the size of the giraffe, which during the dry season is exposed day after day to a sun-heat of 165° (Fahrenheit), and which browses on leaves and twigs which at that time of year contain but little moisture, can really live for long periods without drinking. When hunting with Bushmen in the country to the south of the Mababi river, which towards the end of the dry season is quite waterless, my savage companions would often halt suddenly on perceiving a certain thin, grass-like leaf protruding from the ground, and squatting down, commence digging vigorously with their spears in the soft sandy soil. They would presently unearth great white tubers—often as big as a man's head—white in colour and looking something like very large turnips. These tubers contained as much water as a juicy orange, and were, as the Bushmen said, "metsi hela" (that is, "nothing but water"). They told me, and I think with truth, that they were able to live and hunt in the country where these tubers grew without requiring water to drink. They also informed me that elands, gemsbucks, and other antelopes which live in the desert were in the habit of pawing away the sand from and then eating these tubers, which rendered them independent of actual drinking water. There are probably other water-conserving tubers, known to animals which live in the waterless parts of Western South Africa; and at certain times of year a kind of small water-melon grows in the Kalahari in great profusion, which, as long as it lasts, renders all wild animals entirely independent of drinking water. Oxen and horses soon get accustomed to these wild melons and thrive on them, and human beings can make tea or coffee from their juice.

Now, the occurrence of wild melons and tubers which contain a great deal of water, probably explains the otherwise unaccountable fact that large antelopes and other animals are able to exist in the most arid portions of South-West Africa at a time of year when there is absolutely no surface water; but in the country to the south of the Mababi the Bushmen stated emphatically that giraffes never dug up the water-containing tubers of which I have spoken. My own belief is that, although they must be able to go without water for a much longer time than most animals, they must nevertheless drink periodically throughout the year. It is possible that in the recesses of the Kalahari the giraffes may obtain the fluid they require from the wild water-melons like other animals, or in periods of prolonged drought they may migrate to the neighbourhood of the Botletlie and other rivers. To the east and north of the Botletlie, a glance at a good map will show that giraffes could never be more than fifty or sixty miles from permanent water. When I was hunting elephants on the Chobi river, in the 'seventies of last century, elephants were in the habit of drinking early one night in that river, and then travelling straight away into the waterless country to the west, and I am sure they got their next drink, either twenty-four or possibly forty-eight hours later, in the overflow of the Okavango, known by the natives living on the Mababi as the Machabi. These elephants, which had become excessively wary, through much hunting, I believe never quenched their thirst twice running in the same river ; and as giraffes would not require to drink nearly as frequently as elephants, they would be able to range over far more extensive areas of country than those animals, drinking at intervals at points far distant one from another, and between which there was absolutely no surface water. I cannot help thinking that the idea that giraffes can go for months together without drinking, in countries where there is but a small percentage of fluid in the food they eat, and in which the heat and dryness of the atmosphere are so intense that one's nails become as brittle as glass and the hairs of one's beard are constantly splitting, must be a mistaken one. It is, however, only right to say that many very experienced African hunters hold the view that giraffes are quite independent of water, and that they can and do exist for months at a time without drinking.

Giraffes certainly show no aversion to water, as I have frequently seen them drinking, and watched them as they gradually straddled their forelegs wide apart, by a series of little jerks, until they at length got their mouths down to the surface of the pool.

Many herbivorous animals are, as a rule, very silent, but all antelopes are capable of making, and do occasionally make, certain vocal sounds. But the giraffe appears to be absolutely voiceless. At any rate, I have never heard one make any kind of noise, and that was the experience of my friend the late Mr. A. H. Neumann; whilst Mr. H. A. Bryden, as well as other men who have hunted these animals, have put the same fact on record.

Although giraffes often feed through dense thickets of wait-a-bit thorns on their way from one part of a country to another, they are more partial, I think, to open park-like surroundings than to thick forest. In portions of Khama's country—both near

Lopepe and Metsi-butluku—I have upon more than one occasion seen giraffes and springbucks at the same time. In such districts, before the days of the modern long-range, small-bore rifles, it was very difficult to get within shot of the former animals on foot, as, owing to the great height of their heads above the ground and their quickness of sight, they were always able to see anything approaching them, when still a long way off. Giraffes are also very keen-scented, as any one will agree who has often followed on their spoor with Bushmen trackers. Pointing to the ground, on which they have read as in a book that just here the giraffes have commenced to run, these quick-sighted savages will suddenly dash off along the spoor with right arms extended, crying, "Sabili; ootlili pevu"[1] ("They've run away; they've got our wind"). Running on the tracks of the disturbed animals at a pace which it requires a sharp canter to keep up with, it is seldom that these wiry sons of the desert will not bring the mounted hunter in sight of the giant quarry. "Tutla, tutla ki-o" ("The giraffes; there are the giraffes"), they cry, pointing eagerly forwards with glistening eyes. And then it is for the white man to do his part and secure a plentiful supply of meat for his savage friends.

The chase of the giraffe on horseback lacks, of course, the fierce joy and the soul-stirring excitement which accompanied elephant- and lion-hunting, with the rude muzzle-loading guns used by professional African hunters some forty years ago; for the giraffe is a most harmless and inoffensive animal, in no way dangerous to human life. The same thing may, however, be said of the fox and the wild red deer of Exmoor, the pursuit of which animals, it is generally conceded, affords some of the most exhilarating sport procurable in this country.

[1] Literally, "They've *heard* the wind."

Personally, in the old days when giraffes were very plentiful, and when, with the thoughtless optimism of youth, one failed to realise that they would ever become scarce, and when, moreover, a large supply of meat was constantly required to feed one's native followers, I always looked upon a good, reckless, breakneck gallop after a herd of giraffes as a most exhilarating experience. The giant quadrupeds looked so splendid as they dashed along at tremendous speed, with their long black tails screwed up over their backs. Nothing checked their pace, as they tore their way through dense thorn jungles, or crashed through the branches of forest trees, ever and anon dipping their lofty heads with the most unerring judgment so as just to pass beneath some horizontal limb, which almost seemed to graze their shoulders. One took lots of chances in giraffe-hunting, and got many a heavy fall when galloping *ventre à terre* across open ground full of ant-bear holes, or deep sun-cracks hidden from view by thick tussocky grass, and when one saw the branches of two neighbouring wait-a-bit thorn bushes, each covered with hundreds of little hard black hooks, suddenly close together with a swish behind the disappearing stern of a giraffe, it needed considerable resolution to follow in its wake.

I have often had the greater part of my shirt—for I never wore a coat—torn off and my bare arms very severely scratched whilst chasing giraffes through thick wait-a-bit thorn scrub. I have had some heavy falls too, and once knocked one of my front teeth clean out of the socket, through galloping into an ant-eater's hole and falling on my heavy ten-bore rifle. On another occasion my horse rolled over on me, and cracked the tibia of my right leg, so that some of the serum ran out and formed a lump on the bone. However, I never hurt myself seriously, and the risk of such little misadventures when galloping after giraffes through thick forests and over ground where the holes were hidden by long grass always added zest to the pursuit of these animals.

The pace of the giraffe, when pressed, is very great, and in my own experience, which has been considerable, I have found that it is only an exceptionally fast South African shooting horse which can actually gallop past an unwounded giraffe in open ground. The young Boer hunters used always to think a lot of a horse which was fast enough to enable them to "brant," *i.e.* "burn," a giraffe. This meant firing into one of these animals when galloping level with it and at a distance of only a few paces. Such a practice is, however, not to be recommended, as it takes too much out of a horse, upon which one has to depend to keep one's camp in meat throughout a long hunting season, and the easiest way of killing giraffes is not to press them too hard, but to jump off behind them whenever a suitable opportunity occurs and aim for the root of the tail. A bullet so placed, even from one of the old low velocity rifles of forty years ago, would penetrate to the heart and lungs, and soon prove fatal.

A wounded giraffe will usually, if not invariably, run against the wind, and if one's waggon or camp is anywhere in the direction for which it is heading, it is possible, by galloping alongside and shouting, to alter its course to a certain extent, and so drive the unsuspecting animal close up to the place where it can be most conveniently killed and cut up. I have driven many giraffes quite close up to my waggons before killing them ; but I have also found that if a wounded giraffe takes a course exactly opposite to that in which you want it to go, no power on earth will make it turn right round and run in the other direction. In the nature of things one cannot have an adventure with a giraffe, but I have had two somewhat curious experiences with these animals.

During 1876, when my friend George Dorehill and I were hunting in Western Matabeleland, some Bushmen one day came to our camp and asked us to shoot them a giraffe for the sake of the meat; so, on the following morning, we went out with them, and before long crossing the fresh tracks of a big old bull, followed them, and presently came up with the animal itself. After a short gallop, I wounded it, and it then very soon came to a halt and stood quite still. Wishing to drive it to our camp, I rode slowly towards it, waving my hat and shouting, but it never moved. I was sitting on my horse quite close to where the giant beast stood towering above me, when I heard the crack of my friend's rifle close behind me. At the same instant, the whole seventeen feet of giraffe lurched over and came tumbling towards me, perfectly rigid and without a bend in legs or neck. I don't think I had hold of my horse's reins when my friend fired and shot the giraffe through the head from behind, and the sudden fall of the huge beast was so unexpected that my horse never moved till the great head crashed to the ground close to its forefeet. I am sure that I am not exaggerating when I say that the short thick horns of this dead giraffe only missed my horse's neck by less than six inches. Had the giraffe only been a little taller, or had my horse and I been a little nearer to it, there would have been more than one dead animal on the ground soon after my friend's very accurate shot.

On another occasion, during the same year, Dorehill wounded a giraffe—a good-sized but not full-grown bull—which, after running a little distance, stopped and then knelt down, in the position of an ox or a camel at rest, and never moved when we rode up and dismounted close to it. "I'll bet you, you won't get on to its back," said my friend. We were both of us very young men then, which perhaps does not excuse the thoughtless cruelty of the act; but in answer to my friend's challenge I at once vaulted on to the giraffe's back, and sat astride it just behind the withers. Immediately I touched it the startled animal struggled to its feet and started off at a gallop. Clasping it round the neck, I had no difficulty in retaining my seat, and my remembrance is that the motion of my tall steed was easy. I was not carried very far, however, and there were fortunately no trees, but only a low growth of scrubby bush for a good distance in front of us. After carrying me at a swinging canter for a short distance, the giraffe once more knelt gently down, and I hastily dismounted. This giraffe was not mortally wounded, but a bullet had injured its hip or pelvis, though, as far as I can remember, no bone was actually broken.

The body of an old bull giraffe gives out an excessively strong, pungent odour, which can be smelt by a human being at a considerable distance. These old bulls, which are always so dark in colour that they look almost black, used to be called by the old Boer hunters "stink bulls." The meat of such animals was never eaten by white hunters, but every scrap of it was either consumed when fresh, or dried for future consumption, by one's Kafir or Bushman followers. The tongue of an old bull giraffe, which is the only part of such an animal that I have ever eaten, I have, however, always found to be excellent.

During the rainy season, when giraffes are able to obtain without much exertion a plentiful supply of sweet and nourishing food, the full-grown cows get into very good condition, and are sometimes so fat in the early part of the dry season—May and June—that they probably never get into bad order for the remainder of the year. I have shot giraffe cows whose sides when the hide was peeled off them were covered with a thick layer of white fat, from half an inch to over two inches in thickness from shoulder to rump. There is no finer meat to be got in the whole world than that of a fat giraffe cow, and the soft white fat when rendered out is equal to the best lard. The tongue and marrow-bones are also great delicacies, and the hide is valuable for waggon whips, sjamboks, and the soles of boots. No wonder the South African frontiersmen, whether Boers or Britons, were always keen giraffe hunters.

It has often been stated that giraffe bulls in South Africa grow to a height of 19 feet, whilst the cows attain to a stature of from 16 to 17 feet. I unfortunately only measured the standing height of two bull giraffes; both of which, however, were old animals, and seemed to me to be fine specimens of their kind. One of these, the head of which I still have in my collection, measured, when his legs and neck had been pulled out into as straight a line as possible, just 17 feet, the measurement having been taken between two stakes, the one driven into the ground at the base of the forefoot, the other at the top of the short horns. This giraffe was undoubtedly a very large animal, and I remember very well Mr. Rowland Ward remarking on the size of its skull, compared to one which had lately been brought from Somaliland by the late Mr. F. L. James, as they both lay side by side in Piccadilly. The other giraffe I measured—also a big bull, or, at any rate, an old one—could only have stood 16 feet 6 inches in height, in a straight line from the heel of the forefoot to the top of the horns. The original old South

African bull giraffe, too, which once used to stand in the Mammalian Gallery of the Natural History Museum at South Kensington, and which always appeared to me to be a magnificent specimen in point of size, only measured as set up 17 feet 5 inches from the ground to the top of the horns. I took this measurement myself with the aid of a ladder. I know that in the Tring Museum the Hon. Walter Rothschild has a specimen of a giraffe from Southern Angola, which measures 18 feet 4 inches as it stands. But I am not convinced that the animal actually stood that height when alive. In modern taxidermy a framework model of an animal is first built, and the skin then stretched over it. The man who shot and preserved the skin of the giraffe now in the Tring Museum said that it stood 18 feet 4 inches, and it has been set up to that height; but if the measurement was taken carelessly, or over the curves of the animal's body, there would be no difficulty in stretching the skin so as to obtain the height required. My esteemed friend the late Mr. A. H. Neumann, than whom there never lived a better authority upon African game, when speaking of the northern giraffe in *The Great and Small Game of Africa,* says: "It may possibly be somewhat smaller (than the southern species), for the height of the full-grown males I have shot averaged about 16 feet, that of the cows 14 feet." And he further says: "And though I have not found these dimensions exceeded respectively in any of the southern specimens of either sex I have myself killed anywhere, I have read in the accounts of other hunters of considerably taller animals being obtained in parts of South Africa."

Personally, grounding my belief on the size of the magnificent old bull giraffe which once stood in the Mammalian Gallery of the Natural History Museum at South Kensington, and the measurement I myself took, immediately it was dead, of a very fine old bull which I shot in Western Matabeleland in 1880, I should say that the average height, at any rate of giraffe bulls in South Africa, cannot be more than 17 feet, and that of the cows about 2 feet less. I have never measured a cow giraffe, but in a herd of these animals an old black bull always towers above the tallest cows. Exceptional specimens in both sexes may, of course, grow much taller than the average height of the species.

Giraffes are, I think, less troubled by lions or other carnivorous animals than any other African mammal, with the exception of the elephant, rhinoceros, and hippopotamus. That giraffes are occasionally killed by lions is, of course, a well-known fact, but my own experience leads me to believe that such cases are quite exceptional. There are two reasons, I think, for this, the first being that giraffes spend most of their time in very dry, semidesert countries, far away from water, into which lions do not often penetrate; and the second, that, owing to their great size and strength and the thickness of their hides, giraffes cannot be easy animals for even lions to pull down, and, as a matter of fact, I think they are seldom molested in parts of the country where game of other kinds, such as zebras, buffaloes, or large antelopes, are plentiful.

An instance of a young giraffe being attacked by two leopards once came within my own experience. I was riding with some Bushmen—more than thirty years ago now—near the course of the Upper Tati river in Western Matabeleland, when a single giraffe cow ran out into the open from a cluster of mimosa trees through which we were passing. Immediately I saw the giraffe, I put spurs to my horse and galloped after it, but had only just reached the edge of the mimosa grove when my horse put his foot in a hole, and not only fell, but rolled over on me, breaking the thin thong attached to my belt from a ring on the bridle. I was not hurt, but I was unable to extricate myself and regain my feet as quickly as my horse, and he, not being a very well-trained animal, trotted away in the direction taken by the giraffe before I could get hold of the bridle. I now for the first time saw a very young giraffe calf, which I do not think could have been more than a day or two old, running between my horse and its mother, but much nearer to the former than the latter. I suppose this little calf, being so very young, had been purposely left by its mother lying hidden amongst the bushes to await her return, but that we had frightened it and caused it to jump up and run off. As we watched it we saw it run close up to my horse, and as long as it was in view it appeared to be running close behind it.

I now told two of my Bushmen to run after my horse, and try and get in front of it and then catch it and bring it back to me. This they succeeded in doing before very long, as, after having trotted away for a mile or so, my recreant steed had commenced to feed. When we met, the Bushmen told me that the giraffe cow had come round and taken off the calf before they came up with my horse.

Since this giraffe calf was evidently very young and weak, I thought it would be an easy matter to catch it alive, so I told my Bushmen to take up its spoor at once. We had been following the tracks of both the cow and the calf for perhaps a mile, when I saw the head and neck of the latter rising out of some tussocky grass in an opening in the forest. Galloping up to it, I found that the poor little creature's hind-legs were stretched out straight behind it, as if its back were broken. It was also bleeding from a few scratches. My Bushmen were now examining the ground round the injured calf; and I heard one of them say, "Ingwi, ingwi mabele"

("Leopards, two leopards"). They soon explained to me exactly what had happened. As the giraffe calf was following its mother, two leopards had attacked it. They must, however, have been driven from their prey very quickly, as I could only find a few claw-marks upon the body of the calf. Its mother had evidently struck at the leopards with her forefeet, as we found several freshly-made marks where her sharp hoofs had struck the hard ground. Unfortunately, one of these terrific blows, very probably the first aimed at the leopard which had attacked the calf, had struck the little creature on the loins and broken its back, or at any rate paralysed its hind-quarters. I searched all round for the leopards, but could not find them, and was obliged to kill the calf, for it could only have died a lingering death if I had not done so, or been torn to pieces sooner or later by leopards or hyænas.

I don't think giraffes ever give birth to more than one calf at a time. The calves are born, in South-Western Africa, towards the end of the dry season or early in the rainy season, that is, during the months of September, October, November, or December.

CHAPTER XII

A JOURNEY TO AMATONGALAND IN SEARCH OF INYALA

The inyala, a rare and beautiful animal—Seldom shot by Englishmen—Account of, by Mr. Baldwin—Further observations of, by the Hon. W. H. Drummond—Inyala-shooting and fever almost synonymous—Distribution of the inyala—Curious antelope shot by Captain Faulkner—Start on journey in search of inyalas—Reach Delagoa Bay—Meet Mr. Wissels—Voyage to the Maputa river—Depredations of locusts—Elephants still found in the Matuta district—A quick run up the river—Reach Bella Vista—Talk with Portuguese officer—Hippopotamuses seen—Change of weather—Longman engages four lady porters—Start for Mr. Wissels's station—Sleep at Amatonga kraal—Description of people—Cross the Maputa river—Reedbuck shot—Rainy weather—Reach Mr. Wissels's station.

Of all the various species of antelopes still to be found in the southern portion of the great African continent, the inyala is perhaps at once the most beautiful and the least known to naturalists and sportsmen. This handsome animal, although it had been previously shot by some few Boer hunters, was first described and brought to the notice of European naturalists by Mr. Douglas Angas, by whom it was named *Tragelaphus angasi*, or Angas's bushbuck, though it is more generally known at the present day by its native Zulu name of inyala.

Inyala horns are often met with in collections, but such trophies, it will be found, have almost invariably been obtained from the natives, few living Englishmen having actually shot this very local and retiring animal; whilst, as far as I am aware, but two of these have, since Angas's first description, given us any information concerning its haunts and habits.

That tough old sportsman the late Mr. William Charles Baldwin met with the inyala on his first visit to Amatongaland in 1854. He writes:

> Hearing from the Kaffirs that there were inyalas in the bush, I sallied out, but without success, until nearly sunset, when, as I was returning home, the Amatongas showed me two inyalas feeding, the first I had ever seen. I succeeded in bagging the stag, a most beautiful dark silver-grey buck, with long mane and very long hair like a goat. He is of the bushbuck species, but on a much larger scale than the inkonka of the colony, with long spiral horns, tanned legs, very long hair on his breast and quarters—a beautiful animal, weighing from 250 lbs. to 300 lbs., and very fierce when wounded. They inhabit the coast from this to Delagoa Bay, and are numerous. The does are often to be seen in large herds, and are likewise very beautiful, resembling a fallow deer, but are of a much darker red, striped and spotted with white. They have no horns, and are half the size of the stag; and nowhere else in Africa have I met with them.

Baldwin was evidently very much struck with the beauty of these antelopes, for, referring to the first of the species which he shot, he says: "When I at last secured him I thought I should never sufficiently admire him." On another occasion he says: "I wounded an inyala doe, and had a long chase after her, but eventually lost her. They are wild and wary, and it requires the greatest caution to get a shot at them."

The only other author, besides Angas and

Baldwin, who, as far as I know, has written anything concerning the inyala from personal experience is the Hon. W. H. Drummond, who was travelling and hunting in Zululand and Amatongaland from 1867 to 1872, and who subsequently recorded his observations on the wild animals he met with in those countries in a book entitled *The Large Game and Natural History of South and South-East Africa.* As his remarks concerning the inyala are very much to the point, I think they are well worth quoting. He writes concerning this antelope as follows :—

Perhaps the most beautiful of all the antelopes that I have seen is the inyala, the white lines with which it is striped being more numerous, more regular, and much better defined than those of either the koodoo or the striped eland, which, as far as I know, are the only two animals which possess them at all. Unfortunately, it does not exist except in the low, fever-stricken districts of the Bombo range, about the 28th degree of south latitude. It frequents the densest thickets it can find, and is wary and difficult to stalk ; indeed, I should fancy that more people have caught fever by hunting this antelope than in the pursuit of any other animal in Africa, except perhaps the elephant. Of course, as with most game, early morning and evening are the best times during which to look for it, and early dawn implies being wet through to above the waist by the heavy dew and the subsequent drying of one's things by the heat of the sun—a pretty certain method of getting fever ; evening, on the other hand, means not getting home till hours after dark, and breathing during that period the fatal miasma, which, as soon as the sun sets, begins to rise from all over the great lagoons and dotted plains where this antelope is chiefly found. Inyala-shooting and fever are all but synonymous ; but to those who have already had the latter, and with whom the mischief as regards constitution is already done, ample amends are made by the graceful beauty of the antelope and the magificence of its skin. Its horns almost exactly resemble those of a koodoo of eighteen months or two years old, though, if anything, they have a broader spread.

The range of this beautiful animal is very limited, and even yet has not been quite accurately ascertained. Angas first met with it on the northern shores of St. Lucia Bay, in latitude 28 degrees south, which seems to be its extreme southern range. North of St. Lucia Bay it is, or was, plentiful in the neighbourhood of all the rivers which flow through the wooded plains that lie between the Lebombo Hills and the sea as far north as Delagoa Bay, being particularly numerous in the thickets which border the Pongolo, Usutu, and Tembe rivers. North of Delagoa Bay its distribution is very imperfectly known; but, as it has been shot on the lower course of the Oliphants river, it doubtless exists along the Limpopo between the point where the former river joins it and the sea. To the north of the Limpopo it is probably found along the coast-line wherever conditions suitable to its habits exist, namely, dense jungle in the immediate neighbourhood of swamps and rivers, as far north as the great Sabi river. At any rate, several Kafirs whom I have questioned in the De Beers compound at Kimberley, and who were natives of the coast country near Inyambani, were evidently well acquainted with it, describing it accurately and giving it the Zulu name of inyala.

North of the Sabi, and between that river and the Zambesi, the inyala has, I believe, never been met with. Personally, I have never come across any trace of it, nor obtained any information concerning it during my travels on the lower course of either the Zambesi, Pungwe, or Buzi rivers, the latter being the first important stream met with flowing into the Indian Ocean north of the great Sabi river.

Thus, until quite lately the range of Angas's bushbuck was supposed to be confined to the coast-line between St. Lucia Bay and a point somewhere to the south of the great Sabi river; but amongst a parcel of skins sent from Nyasaland in 1891 by Mr. (now Sir Alfred) Sharpe to Dr. P. L. Sclater, the well-known zoologist, was the unmistakable hide of a male inyala, and subsequent research has brought to light the fact that this beautiful antelope, whose habitat had hitherto been supposed to be confined entirely to the country immediately north and south of Delagoa Bay, is also an inhabitant of the jungles on the central course of the Shiré river. In a consular report concerning the state of Nyasaland, published some years ago, Sir H. H. Johnston, amongst his most interesting notes on the fauna of the country which he had so ably administered, wrote: "In the west Shiré and lower Shiré districts only is found the very handsome inyala antelope."

Concerning the skin previously mentioned, which was obtained by Mr. (now Sir Alfred) Sharpe, Dr. P. L. Sclater wrote as follows:—

> Mr. Sharpe brings a flat skin of what is apparently a male of this antelope (the inyala), hitherto not known to occur so far north. He gives the following notes on it: "This antelope is found in a piece of thick, scrubby country bordering the Moanza, which enters the Shiré on the right bank near the Murchison cataracts. I have never seen it alive myself, but have heard of it frequently from the natives, by whom it is called bo, the 'o' being pronounced very long. It frequents the thick scrub, and only occasionally comes out to the edges of the grass flats. I have never heard of it in any other part of Nyasaland."

However, although the fact of the existence of the inyala in Nyasaland was only established as lately as 1891, I think that a specimen of this antelope was undoubtedly shot near Cape Maclear, on the shores of Lake Nyasa itself (where apparently it is not now known to exist), by the late Captain Faulkner in 1866. In his narrative of a journey to Lake Nyasa, in connection with the Livingstone search expedition sent out from England under the command of Lieutenant Young in that year, Captain Faulkner has written, in a little-known work entitled *Elephants' Haunts*: "I had walked a long way without seeing anything, and as it was getting late, was about returning, when I saw a beautiful antelope feeding near a narrow strip of swamp." This antelope he killed, and then described it in the following words: "He was in splendid condition, and a distinctly different animal from any I had hitherto seen; height at shoulder, 3 ft. 4 in.; spiral horns, 21 in. long, slightly curved forward, skin of a greyish colour, and covered with white spots, belly white."

Now, either this antelope shot by Captain Faulkner on the shores of Lake Nyasa was an inyala, or it belonged to a species still unknown to science. Seeing that it has now been ascertained that the inyala is an inhabitant of certain thickets on the banks of the Shiré river, at no great distance from the place where Captain Faulkner shot his unidentified specimen, I am inclined to think that the former supposition is the most probable, and that a mistake was made in describing the animal as covered with spots; for if this sentence had read: "Of a greyish colour, and covered with white stripes, or white spots and stripes," the whole description, meagre though it is, would have been applicable to a male inyala, which the length and shape of the horns, and the standing height at the shoulder, seem to show that it was. It certainly was not a bushbuck, with which animal Captain Faulkner was well acquainted; and as the Kafirs chopped off its horns, and the skin went rotten and was not preserved, and the description of the animal in question may have been written from memory by a man who was not a trained observer, some want of accuracy was to be expected. The fact that the shaggy hair which hangs from the neck and chest, and fringes the flanks of the male inyala, and is such a very noticeable characteristic of this species of antelope, was not mentioned by Captain Faulkner, is certainly very curious; still, I am inclined to the belief that the animal which he shot on the shore of Lake Nyasa was an inyala. If not, there exists in that district a nearly allied species still unknown to science, which I do not think is likely, though it would be worth while to make careful inquiries amongst the natives living near Cape Maclear as to all the antelopes of the bushbuck tribe with spiral horns with which they are acquainted, in order to clear up the mystery.

The foregoing notes represent all the information I have been able to gather from the works of travellers and sportsmen concerning the habits and distribution of the inyala, and I will now give a short account of a journey undertaken by myself to the Usutu river, in Amatongaland, in search of these antelopes, during which I was able to obtain some knowledge of them at first hand.

It had long been my ambition to add the head of an inyala, shot by myself, to my collection of hunting trophies, but year after year had rolled by, without my having been able to spare the time to undertake a special journey to the country near Delagoa Bay in search of it, until I recognised that, unless I made a determined effort, my large collection of South African antelope heads would for ever remain incomplete and unsatisfactory, ungraced as it would have been by the spoils of one of the handsomest species.

Thus I left Matabeleland in September 1896, at the conclusion of the native rebellion in that country, with the fixed resolve to do my best to kill a male inyala before quitting South Africa.

Leaving my wife in the care of kind friends at Kimberley, I proceeded by the shortest route, viz. by rail *viâ* Pretoria to Delagoa Bay, and found myself in the now important town of Lourenço Marques on the evening of Monday, September 21.

There I was fortunate enough to make the acquaintance of Messrs. Gould and Edixhoven, two gentlemen who were most kind and obliging to me in every way, and who spared no pains to render me all the assistance in their power to enable me to carry out the object I had in view. They introduced me at once to a trader from Amatongaland, who had lately come down to Delagoa Bay, and who was just about to return to his station near the junction of the Pongolo and Usutu rivers. Mr. Wissels (the gentleman in question), a Cape colonist of German extraction, I found was about to return to his station by boat on the following day; and when he heard that I wished to shoot an inyala, he told me that these animals were plentiful in the neighbourhood of his station. Then he most kindly offered to take me there with him, and to find Kafirs who knew the haunts and habits of the antelopes in question to go hunting with me.

I had but very little preparation to make for the journey before me, but before I could leave Delagoa Bay it was necessary for me to get a passport from the authorities to travel in Portuguese territory, and also to obtain a licence to carry arms. Thanks to the ready kindness of Mr. B. Cohen,[1] and the courtesy of the Portuguese governor of Lourenço Marques, I obtained all the necessary licences in an unusually short space of time, and was ready to embark on

[1] At that time the British Consul at Delagoa Bay.

Mr. Wissels's large, open sailing-boat by four o'clock on the afternoon of Tuesday, September 22. The same evening, after a good dinner at a small hotel on the opposite side of the bay, we ran out to sea with the tide, by the light of a most glorious full moon, and after passing a reef of rocks which projects into the sea from the southern shore of the bay immediately opposite Reuben Point, on which there is a lighthouse, we anchored about midnight in quite shallow water to wait for the morning breeze, by the help of which Mr. Wissels expected we would be able to run right into the mouth of the Maputa river, in time to catch the inflowing tide.

After a not too comfortable night, passed on mealie bags which had not been arranged to serve as a bed, we awoke just as the day was breaking, but before the moon had quite set, and found that a strong breeze had sprung up, before which we ran right into the mouth of the Maputa river in a very short space of time. The Maputa is the name given to the united streams of the Pongolo and Usutu, below their confluence, and carries to the sea the muddy water of the former commingled with the clear stream of the latter, which takes its rise amongst the far-off hills of Swaziland. As the height of the country above sea-level at the junction of these rivers is, I believe, under 400 feet, it follows that the Maputa runs through a very level tract of country. Like all rivers flowing into the Indian Ocean, on the east coast of Africa, it is a tidal stream fringed on both banks along its lower course by monotonous, dismal-looking mangrove swamps.

The country between the Maputa and the Tembe —which latter is the river flowing into the southern portion of Delagoa Bay—is reputed to be very fruitful, and to carry a large native population, who, however, have suffered terribly of late years owing to the depredations of locusts. The district is called Matuta. To the south the land does not appear to be so rich, and must be more sparsely populated, as elephants are said to still maintain a precarious footing there. After entering the mouth of the Maputa, both wind and tide being favourable, we ran up its course at racing speed, and by ten o'clock had passed the limit of the mangrove swamps. So far the only sign of life we had seen was numerous large flocks of curlews feeding on the mud-banks on both sides of the river. These birds appeared very similar to the species so familiar to British shore-shooters, and were equally wary and shy of close acquaintanceship.

About eleven o'clock we reached the Portuguese military station of Bella Vista, in charge of an officer, who, after he had inspected my papers and found them all in order, was very civil, and invited us to join him at the late breakfast which is one of the two substantial meals partaken of by the Portuguese in Africa.

Our host seemed to be something more of a sportsman than most of his countrymen, and only the day previous to our arrival had shot a fine reedbuck ram, and a short time before a bushbuck ram, having killed both with buck shot. He also possessed a good pair of inyala horns, which, he told me, had been obtained from the natives on the Pongolo river. We remained at Bella Vista for a couple of hours, conversing in French on various topics, especially the late Matabele rebellion, in which our host seemed to take a great interest. He was very emphatic in his condemnation of the policy of raising a police force from amongst the natives of a conquered country. "However," said he, "it is the English way; they have done it in Natal and Zululand too, and may yet live to regret it; qui vivra verra." "But," said I, "you Portuguese surely do the same thing, for wherever I have travelled in your possessions, I have always met with your black soldiers." "That is true," said he, "but still our policy is very different from yours; for we never employ natives as police or soldiers in their own country; all the black troops you see in our East African possessions being recruited in Angola, and *vice versa*, and thus all native levies in the Portuguese service are looked upon as foreigners by, and are themselves out of sympathy with, the tribes amongst whom they find themselves."

After bidding adieu to our host and resuming our journey, we continued to make very good progress, with the help of wind and tide, and although we now and then lost a little time by sticking on a sandbank, we had done so well by sundown that Mr. Wissels expected to make a record run up to his station. During the afternoon we passed a few hippopotamuses and an odd crocodile; but they were few and far between, and appeared to be very wild and wary. Our luck, however, was not to last, for during the hour which intervened between the setting of the sun and the rising of the moon (which was now but one day beyond the full) the wind veered right round, and commenced to blow fresh and cool from the south. We soon found it impossible to make any further progress, even with the oars, after the sail, which had done us such good service throughout the day, had been lowered; for the strength of the wind blew us in under the bank. So, yielding to necessity, we made our heavy craft fast to a tree for the night, and then, after having made a hasty meal, washed down by a cup of tea, we turned in under our blankets, which were once more spread on the top of the mealie bags.

On the following morning, just at daybreak, two

hippos passed down the river close to our boat. They were very wary, however, and gave but little chance of a shot, even had we wished to kill them, which I, at any rate, did not. The weather had now completely changed, the sky being overcast with an unbroken sheet of cloud, whilst the temperature had become quite cool and pleasant, with a strong breeze blowing from the south. It looked to me as if we were going to have a day or two of cloudy weather, which would end in rain when the wind dropped; but as it was very early in the season for rain, Mr. Wissels thought it was only a cool spell which would blow off again in a day or two. However, all progress by boat being impossible as long as the southerly wind lasted, my companion, knowing that my time was limited, advised me to get some carriers and push on at once on foot to his station, which was about thirty miles distant, and in the vicinity of which inyala were to be found. This proposition entirely coinciding with my own wishes, one of our two Zulu boatmen, an excellent fellow named Longman, was sent off to engage four carriers, and soon after midday returned with four Amatonga women; for, in in this part of the country, the women act almost exclusively as porters.

Of the ladies who, after a considerable amount of haggling, at length agreed to carry my baggage to the junction of the Usutu and Pongolo rivers, three were already in the afternoon of life—gaunt, bony, wrinkled, hideous hags. The fourth was a younger and pleasanter-looking woman, who, in addition to her load, which weighed about forty pounds, carried a two-year-old child, slung in a goatskin, at her back. It took some time to arrange the price which was to be paid for their services, but at last, after testing the weight of the loads, they agreed to carry them to Mr. Wissels's store for a certain price. This, however, had to be paid in advance, in accordance with a custom which is general throughout every portion of the Portuguese dominions in South-East Africa—a custom which is most humiliating to the pride of an Englishman, as it seems to say, "By bitter experience we black people have learnt that white men will cheat us if they can, and therefore we do not trust them."

At last everything was ready, and I was able to start on my journey at about two o'clock, accompanied by my four lady carriers and Longman, the Zulu, whom Mr. Wissels had most kindly given me to act as guide and headman. That afternoon we walked for about three hours, and slept at a small Amatonga kraal on a rise above the Maputa river. The country through which we travelled was neither flat nor hilly, but consisted of a succession of undulating rises separated by boggy streams. The soil on the surface was of pure white sand, which rendered the walking very heavy. These sandy rises were for the most part free of trees or bush, though patches of thorny scrub were to be seen here and there, as well as some large thorn trees in the hollows.

The Amatonga about here seem to live in families rather than in large communities, as we passed several kraals, none of which contained more than half-a-dozen huts. Each little community seemed to possess a few head of cattle of a small breed, which is probably identical with that found throughout Eastern and South Central Africa, though in certain localities it has become very dwarfed. At the time of my visit to Amatongaland the people were very badly off for food, as for several successive years their crops had more or less been destroyed by a wing of that mighty army of locusts by which the whole of South-Eastern and South Central Africa has been devastated continually ever since 1890.

Arrived at our destination for the night, a hut was placed at my disposal by the headman of the village, which I found perfectly clean, and free from anything which might have made it interesting to an entomologist. Indeed, I will here say that I found all the Amatonga huts in which I slept during this trip perfectly clean and comfortable. The people themselves are too well known to need any detailed description. They are nearly allied to the Zulus in race, language, and general appearance, and most of them understand and speak pure Zulu. In their own dialect, which I was not able to follow, the letter "h" is very noticeable; for instance, the Zulu word "inkuku," a fowl, becomes "huku" in Satonga. I found no difficulty in understanding them when they spoke Zulu, or in making them understand "Sintabele," the native language with which I am best acquainted, and which is itself a dialect of Zulu.

On waking the following morning, I found that the weather looked very threatening, as the clouds had become quite thick, and rain was evidently near at hand. However, after a good deal of opposition on the part of my lady porters had been overcome, we made a fairly early start, and soon reached the Maputa river at the place where we had to cross it in a native ferry boat, which proved to be merely a very disreputable-looking old dug-out canoe.

On our way here we passed along the edge of a marsh, and as we were doing so I heard a reedbuck whistle, but as the morning was very dull and misty, neither Longman nor I could at first see any sign of the animal that had thus needlessly betrayed its existence. However, after walking a short distance in the direction from which the sound had proceeded, we made out three reedbucks, which, as they ran from behind some reeds into the open ground, I saw were a ram and two ewes. They almost immediately stood, the ram with his hind-quarters towards us; so, judging the distance between us to be about three hundred yards, I put up the third sight, and sitting down took a careful shot at him. I thought I heard the bullet strike, but as he ran lightly behind the two ewes without showing any sign of being hit, I began to think I must have been mistaken. Before going far, however, he stopped suddenly for a few moments, and then rolled over on his side, apparently dead. On walking up to him, however, we found him still alive, although on examination the bullet proved to have passed through the lower part of his heart, having first hit him in the belly between the hind-legs and gone forwards through the whole length of his body.

Whilst Longman and I were cutting up the reedbuck, the lady porters took their loads to the ferry, which was close at hand, and then returned for the meat; and when we had got everything down to the river, we shouted for the ferryman to take us to the other side.

It was some time before the native Charon made his appearance, and, whilst we were waiting for him, my lady porters ate up about half the reedbuck, and I also made a good breakfast, and skinned the head, which was a pretty good one. Just where we crossed the river we saw some elephant spoor which looked fairly recent, and the natives told us that a herd of these animals roamed over the country between the Tembe and Maputa rivers, and sometimes passed close to their kraal on their way to drink in the latter stream. The banks of the river presented a very pretty appearance at the time of our crossing, as all the bushes were covered with convolvulus creepers in full bloom.

It was past midday when we again resumed our journey, and light showers had already begun to fall, and continued to do so during the remainder of the day, becoming heavier towards evening, so that by the time we reached the little kraal where we intended to pass the night, I was pretty damp, though not exactly wet through. With the aid of a big fire, however, I got my things dry again before nightfall, and spent a comfortable night in a clean native hut.

During the night it rained a good deal, but when day broke no rain was actually falling, although heavy watery-looking clouds were coming up fast from the south. Taking advantage of the temporary respite, I managed to get my traps packed up, and my unwilling porters under way, as I knew that I should not be able to persuade them to start if rain were actually falling. We had not proceeded far, however, before being caught in a soaking shower, which soon wetted me to the skin, as, not expecting rain, I had not brought a waterproof coat with me, and was only lightly clad. There was nothing for it but to push on to Mr. Wissels's store. It proved to be farther off than I had anticipated, as it was one o'clock before Longman and I arrived there, whilst my lady porters did not turn up until three hours later, in a very bedraggled condition.

During the morning's walk we had passed a large fresh-water lake or lagoon, on which there were numbers of spur-winged geese, one of which I should have tried to shoot for food, had I not been so cold and wet that my one idea was to reach Mr. Wissels's store as soon as possible. After passing the lagoon we crossed a broad marshy plain, where I saw three reedbucks, and also the spoor of two waterbucks, which I am afraid are almost the last of their species in this part of the country, where not many years ago these animals must have been very numerous. On at length reaching the store, I found that the white man—

a German sailor, whom Mr. Wissels had left in charge, and whom I had expected to find there—had gone down to the Maputa river with carriers to bring up some bags of maize, and was not expected back till the following day. Thus, I only found some Amatonga natives looking after the store, who, although they were civil and obliging enough after Longman had told them all about me, were yet unable to give me the same kind of welcome that one white man always extends to another in the wilds of Africa. For instance, had Mr. Wissels's friend been at home I should have borrowed a shirt and trousers from him whilst I dried my own; but, in the nature of things, the naked Amatonga were unable to oblige me in this way; however, they did the next best thing, and built a big fire beneath a large thick-foliaged tree; and by the help of this I managed to get myself tolerably dry in the course of the afternoon.

CHAPTER XIII

A JOURNEY TO AMATONGALAND (*concluded*)

Receive information concerning the haunts of the inyala—Heavy thunderstorm—Start for Gugawi's kraal—Cross the Usutu river—Reach Gugawi's—Go out hunting—Crested guinea-fowl seen—Two inyalas shot—Angas's description of the inyala antelope—Inyala skins prepared for mounting—Now safe in Natural History Museum—A third inyala shot—One missed—Move farther up the Usutu river—Country denuded of game—Bushbucks scarce—Hippopotamuses in river—Heavy thunderstorm—Two more male inyalas shot—Start on return journey to Delagoa Bay—Tedious journey—Intense heat—End of trip—Slight attacks of fever.

THERE were now abundant signs that I was approaching the haunts of the beautiful antelope I had come so far to seek, as inyala skins and horns were very much in evidence round Mr. Wissels's store, and several of the latter had manifestly been but recently killed. All these animals, Longman assured me, had been shot by the Amatonga within a short distance of the store, in the dense jungles lying in the angle between the Usutu and Pongolo rivers, which I could now see covering some low ridges at a distance of not more than six or seven miles from where we stood. Had it not been for the rain, I should have gone on the same afternoon; however, I gathered a good deal of information and arranged for a start with fresh carriers as early as possible the following day—my objective point being the kraal of an Amatonga headman named Gugawi, who, I was told, lived a few miles up the Usutu river, on the very edge of the jungle where inyalas were said to be plentiful. I noticed, however, that my informants were not over confident about my being likely to shoot any of these animals. When I asked if I should be sure to see some, they replied, "The imbala-intendi (the local name in this part of Amatongaland for the inyala) is very cunning; he lives in the very densest jungle, and never comes into the open except at nights; he is very cunning; he is a witch is the imbala-intendi." They all agreed, however, in declaring that there were plenty of them, although they were difficult to get a sight of. Well, there was nothing for it but to do my best, and deserve success even if I could not attain it.

That night we had a most tremendous thunderstorm, the rain falling in torrents; and as the place in which I was sleeping was not water-tight, I had rather a bad time of it, and was very glad when day broke.

The thunderstorm had cleared the air, and Sunday, September 27, dawned bright and clear, with every prospect of its being a fine day. I had all my things packed up pretty early, and with four new women carriers, and accompanied by two men who knew the way to Gugawi's kraal, managed to get off about an hour after sunrise, and reached my destination before ten o'clock. On our way we crossed the Usutu river—here a clear, swift-flowing stream, about two hundred yards in breadth, running over a bed of sand. We waded across it, and found the water quite shallow for the most part, and never more than three feet deep.

On reaching the kraal we were making for, I told Longman to cook me some breakfast; and whilst he was frying me some reedbuck steaks, I had a talk with the headman Gugawi and told him the reason of my visit. He replied that the "imbala-intendi" were numerous in the jungle just behind his kraal, and promised to do his best to help me to secure the specimens I wanted, though, like every one else, he said the animals were very cunning and difficult to get a sight of. As soon as I had had my breakfast, I asked Gugawi to give me a man who was well acquainted with the habits of the inyala, as I wished to go into the bush after them without any loss of time. He gave me one of his sons, and, accompanied by Longman and one of the Kafirs who had come from Mr. Wissels's store, we forthwith entered the jungle, which extended to within a few yards of the kraal. From this we were not distant more than two hundred yards before we saw fresh inyala spoor plainly imprinted in the wet ground. The rain at least had done us this service, that it had washed out all old spoor and rendered any fresh tracks quite conspicuous.

We now commenced to creep very cautiously through the thick thorny bush, making our way for the most part through tunnels made by hippopotamuses during their night excursions in search of food. We had usually to walk bent nearly double, often having to creep on our hands and knees; and, as the air was very hot and steamy, we were soon bathed in perspiration. Now and again we came to little open spaces in the bush, and in one of these, which we passed through soon after leaving the kraal, I saw a very handsome crested guinea-fowl, the same species, no doubt (*Guttera edouardi*), as that met with on the central Zambesi, to the east of the Victoria Falls.

We had been creeping about the bush in the uncomfortable manner I have described for about an hour, when we came suddenly upon a little circular opening some fifty or sixty yards in diameter. As we approached the edge of this open space, advancing very cautiously in a stooping attitude down a hippopotamus path, my guide suddenly dropped to the ground. As he did so, I got a clear view past him, and saw, standing amongst the grass and bush, just on the further side of the opening, what I knew was an inyala doe, as I could distinctly see it was reddish in colour. I could see no other animal near her, and as I required two specimens of inyala does, the one for the British and the other for the South African Museum, I lost no time about firing at the animal in question, which I saw drop instantly to the shot. But even as she did so, there appeared in her place, or very close to where she had stood, a great black shaggy form, which, indistinctly as I could see it in the deep shadow of the bush, I knew was a male inyala—the first that my eyes had ever looked upon in the flesh. My rifle was a single-barrelled one; and before I could fire the shot that might make that rare and beautiful beast mine, I had to open the breech of my rifle, take another cartridge from my belt, slip it into the chamber, close the breech again, and then raise the rifle to my shoulder and take aim. All this meant time and noise. Would the inyala, which stood like a statue by the dead body of his mate, give me the few seconds I required to take his own life too? I little thought he would, but he did; and as I raised my rifle once more, and took a quick but careful sight on his dark shoulder, I felt, as I pulled the trigger, that he was mine.

As the report of the rifle sounded, he plunged madly forward, and was instantly lost to sight in the thick scrub. But I felt sure he carried death with him; and so it proved, for we found him lying dead not twenty yards from where he had stood when the bullet struck him. The fatal missile had

"I KNEW IT WAS A MALE INYALA—THE FIRST THAT MY EYES HAD EVER LOOKED UPON."

passed right through his shoulders, and having expanded on impact, had torn his heart to pieces. I had the dead female brought to where the male had fallen, and laid them side by side; then stood admiring them for a long time before I could bring myself to skin them. To thus secure a very handsome pair of inyala antelopes — whose excellently mounted skins are now safe in the Mammalian Gallery of the Natural History Museum at South Kensington—on the very first day I had ever hunted for them, and after little more than an hour's search—was indeed a most glorious and exceptional piece of good fortune, which, however, has been balanced by many and many a day that I can remember of unrequited labour in search of game.

I think I had here better give Mr. Angas's very careful descriptions of the inyala antelope, male and female, as they are so detailed and precise that they cannot be improved upon—except that, for a reason which I shall refer to presently, I imagine that the male whose skin he described could not have been fully adult.

Mr. Angas tells us that his notes "were drawn up from recently killed specimens which he in vain attempted to purchase from the Boers who possessed them," and are as follows: "The adult male is about 7 feet 6 inches in total length, and 3 feet 4 inches high at the shoulder. Though elegant in form, and with much of the grace of the solitary koodoo, the robust and shaggy aspect of the male bears considerable resemblance to that of the goat. Legs clean, hoofs pointed and black, with two oval cream-coloured spots in front of each fetlock, immediately above the hoof. Horns of the specimen in question, 1 foot 10 inches long,[1] twisted and

[1] It may be remembered that the unidentified antelope shot by Captain Faulkner on the shore of Lake Nyasa, near Cape Maclear, stood 3 feet 4 inches at the shoulder, whilst the length of its horns was 1 foot 9 inches.

sublyrate, very similar to those of the bushbuck, but rather more spiral; very sharp polished extremities of a pale straw colour, rest of horns brownish black, deeply ridged from the forehead to about half the length of the horn. Prevailing colour, greyish black, tinged with purplish brown and ochre; on the neck, flanks, and cheeks marked with several white stripes like the koodoo. Forehead brilliant sienna brown, almost approaching to orange; mane black down the neck, and white from the withers to the insertion of the tail; ears, 8 inches long, oval, rufous, tipped with black, and fringed inside with white hairs. A pale ochreous circle round the eyes, which are connected by two white spots, forming an arrow-shaped mark on a black ground; nose black; a white spot on each side of the upper lip; chin and gullet white; and three white marks under each eye; neck covered with long shaggy hair, extending also under the belly and fringing the haunches to the knees; two white spots on the flanks, and a patch of long white hair on the interior portion of the thigh; a white tuft under the belly, and another on the dewlap. On the outer side of the forelegs is a black patch above the knee surrounded by three white spots; legs below the knee bright rufous colour; tail, 1 foot 8 inches long, black above, with tip and inside white." This most detailed description is, I think, that of an animal not fully adult, as in the three full-grown male inyalas which I saw in the flesh all the buff, ochreous, and orange tints described by Mr. Angas had turned to greyish black, except to a slight extent below the knees, whilst none of them had any white stripes on the cheeks or neck; and, as the general ground colour of the young male is reddish brown, and that of a full-grown male greyish black, it goes without saying that, as the young animal grows from kidhood to maturity, the former colour gradually gives place to the latter—till, in a very old male, there is no buff or ochre left except on the legs below the knees. Of the female, Mr. Angas's description is as follows: "Smaller than the male, and without horns; total length, 6 feet; nose, to insertion of ear, 10 inches; length of ear, 6½ inches; height from forefoot to shoulder, 2 feet 9 inches; tail, 1 foot 3 inches in length; becoming very pale on the belly and lower parts and white inside the thighs; a black dorsal ridge of bristly hair extends from the back of the crown to the tail; nose black; the white spots on various parts of the body nearly resembling those of the male, only the white stripes on both sides are more numerous and clearly defined, amounting to twelve or thirteen in number; tail, rufous above and white below, tipped with black."

As soon as I had stripped the skins, with the leg-bones still attached, from my two beautiful specimens, I had them carried, together with the skulls, to Gugawi's kraal, on the edge of the bush, and there spent the remainder of the day in preparing them for mounting. Of the meat, which was all brought in, I sent a couple of haunches over to Mr. Wissels, and then, after keeping a small piece for myself, gave the remainder to Gugawi, to divide amongst his people as he thought fit.

Next morning I was up and out in the bush just as day was breaking, accompanied only by my guide of yesterday and Longman, who, however, kept some distance behind, in order to allow my guide and myself to approach our game as noiselessly as possible. We had been creeping about in the dense jungle for some three hours without having seen anything, although there was a good deal of fresh spoor about, and twice we had heard inyalas dash away through the bush without getting a sight of them, when suddenly my guide crouched to the ground, at the same time pointing towards a large ant-heap growing out of the dense scrub, and itself covered with undergrowth. Following the direction of his arm, I made out a reddish patch not fifteen yards away in the gloom of the bush; and, taking it for an inyala doe, I fired into it point-blank, as I required another specimen for mounting. At the shot, the animal fell, and on creeping up to it, I found that it was a young male. It was something less in size than a full-grown female, from which it did not differ in any way in coloration and the number and distribution of white stripes and spots. It was thus interesting, as showing that the male inyala changes in general colour from bright red to dark grey, only losing the rufous and orange tints on the ears and forehead—which were still conspicuous in the type specimen described by Mr. Angas—when fully adult.

As it was now getting on for midday, I had the young inyala carried forthwith to the kraal, where I remained until about four o'clock, then again sallied forth, and did another two hours' jungle-creeping before dark. I saw an inyala doe, and could have fired at her, but, thinking there might have been a male accompanying her, did not care to do so too hurriedly, and whilst I was straining my eyes peering into the bush all around her, she either saw or winded me, and bounded off, quite alone as far as I could make out.

Early the following morning I was again in the bush, and just after sunrise came on a male inyala close to the river. He was standing behind a mass of tree stems, with just his tail showing on one side and part of his head on the other. He was evidently looking at us, and as I knew he would be off in a moment, giving but little chance of a shot, I thought I had better try and put a bullet into him through an interstice amongst the tree stems, where I could see what I took to be part of his neck. I made a bad shot, however, as my bullet, instead of passing through the opening, imbedded itself in the wood of one of the tree stems, and the inyala went off uninjured.

On returning to the kraal, Gugawi proposed to take me to a spot some few miles higher up the Usutu, where he said there were plenty of inyalas, whilst at the same time the bush was not so dense as near his kraal. Being by this time thoroughly sick of crawling about bent nearly double, I hailed with delight the idea of finding the game I was seeking in a country where I could walk upright, and visions of inyalas feeding through open glades passed through my mind—visions, alas, which were never realised, for in my small experience I never found these antelopes anywhere except in dense bush. However, I was glad of the change, and soon had everything ready for a move.

In the afternoon we travelled some five or six miles up the river, and pitched camp in a bit of jungle near the water's edge. The Usutu river is here very broad, and reminded me strongly of parts of the Chobi; but whereas the banks of the latter river, as I knew it in the early 'seventies, abounded in game of many descriptions, from the elephant downwards, there was not a track to be seen along the Usutu of any kind of animal with the exception of the inyala. All the wealth of wild life which Baldwin saw in this same district in 1854 had melted away before the guns of the native Amatonga hunters; for, be it noted, this is a country in which but very little game has been killed by white men. Rhinoceroses, buffaloes, koodoos, waterbucks, impalas, lions,—all are gone, the only game left being the inyalas, which owe their preservation to the dense jungles in which they live; and even they are being rapidly killed off, as the natives are always after them, lying in wait for them in the paths made by the hippopotamuses or creeping stealthily through the bush in their pursuit.

Curiously enough, in these thickets, where inyalas are so numerous, there are very few bushbucks, although the surroundings are in every respect suited to their requirements. I can only account for the scarcity of the bushbucks, where inyalas are plentiful, by supposing that the latter animals will not tolerate the former—considering them too nearly akin to themselves to make good neighbours; for a male bushbuck might be excused, I think, for making love to an inyala doe, which scarcely differs from one of his own females in any way except size, and that probably not to a sufficient degree to stop his advances during the rutting season; which, of course, would be resented by the male inyala, and the latter being the more powerful animal, has been able to drive his rival out of his preserves. If jealousy is not answerable for the scarcity of bushbucks in these jungles where inyalas are so plentiful, I fail to understand why the former animals should be so numerous lower down the river under exactly similar conditions, except that there there are no inyalas.

In the open expanse of water, some half a mile in breadth, just opposite our camp, several hippopotamuses were grunting and playing about on our arrival, and as long as we remained here there were always some of these animals in sight. In the evening I went out after inyala, but though I saw plenty of spoor, I did not catch sight of one of the animals themselves. Soon after dark a heavy thunderstorm came up from the south, and continued with much lightning and torrents of rain till long after midnight. Having neither a tent nor a waterproof sheet, I, like my native companions, of course got soaking wet; and we had to sit shivering in our drenched blankets until daylight, as the heavy rains had put our fires out and we could not get another alight, everything being wet.

Soon after dawn, however, we managed to get a fire under way, and I then had a cup of warm coffee. Just as the sun was rising I went out into the dripping bush, and returned to camp dry and warm before midday. In spite of what Gugawi had said as to the bush being more open round this camp than near his own kraal, I found but little difference, and should describe all the bush in which I hunted on the Usutu river as dense jungle. In the course of the morning I just caught a glimpse of an inyala—a male evidently by his colour—but failed to get a shot at him. I also saw a large number of the beautiful crested guinea-fowls, which in this district seem to be more numerous than the common South African species. During the heat of the day I remained at our bivouac, and, as the sun was intensely hot, managed to thoroughly dry all my belongings, which had got so wet during the previous night's rain. In the evening I again went out into the bush, and just at dusk caught sight of the hind-quarters of an antelope amongst the thick scrub ahead of me. The light was fast failing, and although I felt sure it was an inyala, as there were apparently no other kinds of antelopes in the district, yet I could not in the least tell whether it was a male or female, but, hoping for the best, fired, and saw nothing more.

On forcing my way through the scrub to where the animal had been when I fired, I found a fine inyala doe lying on the ground, just on the point of death, the bullet having struck her in the left thigh and passed through the whole length of her body into the cavity of the chest. Although disappointed that it was not a male, I skinned her carefully for mounting; and she now forms part of the fine collection of South African mammalia which is in the Museum at Cape Town.

It would be but tedious reading were I to continue to describe in detail my further bush-crawling experiences in search of inyalas. Suffice it to say that, on October 1 and 2, I secured two more fine males, whose heads I preserved for my own collection. Although I should have liked to have got a fourth male for the South African Museum, I did not think it prudent to remain any longer in my camp on the edge of a swamp, where I knew the air must be reeking with malarial poison, as, besides the exhalations from the marsh, the ground (from which I was only separated at nights by a little dry grass and a blanket) had been soaked to the depth of two feet by the recent rain, thus rendering the conditions more than usually unhealthy. The weather, too, was now again looking very threatening, and I did not relish the idea of any further lying out in the rain; as I knew, from former experience, that I should probably have to pay for the wettings I had already suffered, by some attacks of fever—a disease from which I had been entirely exempt for seven years, but the poison of which I knew was still in my blood, and would be likely to be again stirred into activity by my recent exposure to unhealthy conditions.

Hence, on Saturday, October 3, I packed up my things and returned to Gugawi's kraal, walking on in the afternoon to Mr. Wissels's store. At Gugawi's I met an Englishman, who informed me that he had come down from Barberton, and was travelling about amongst the Amatonga, buying skins of wild cats, jackals, etc., which he hoped to sell again at a profit to the Kafirs working in the mines in the Transvaal. He seemed much surprised when I told him that I had only come to Amatongaland in order to shoot an inyala, and frequently remarked in the course of our conversation, "Well, I'm ——; so you've come all this —— way to shoot a —— buck." He also informed me that he was not very well, as he had been "on the burst" for the last three days; but this confidence was superfluous, as no one could have approached within ten yards of him without realising his condition.

On my arrival at the store I was disappointed to find that Mr. Wissels was absent, having again returned to Delagoa Bay for another cargo of maize. Had he been at home, I should have endeavoured to obtain a specimen of Livingstone's antelope—a species which I have never shot, and which Mr. Wissels had informed me was numerous in most of the jungles near his store. These little animals are very similar in habits to the diminutive blue buck of Natal, and as they inhabit dense bush, are not often shot, except by driving, and Mr. Wissels had promised that when I returned to his station he would collect a lot of Kafirs and get up a drive for me. However, as I did not know when he would return, and was anxious to get back to Kimberley as soon as possible now that I had accomplished the main object of my journey, I did not care about waiting for him, but determined to get on as quickly as possible. Had Mr. Wissels been at home I should probably have returned to Delagoa Bay by boat, but now I had the prospect of an eighty-mile walk. I had no difficulty in getting carriers, as Gugawi's men, who had brought my things to the store, and with whom I had been associated for the last week, volunteered to go on with me to Delagoa Bay; and it pleased me very much to find that they did not insist on being paid beforehand, but trusted to my honour to deal fairly with them.

On the evening of the day on which I returned

to Mr. Wissels's store, the weather looked very unsettled; but on the following morning all signs of rain had cleared off, and the sun rose red and fiery in a cloudless sky. I got away early, and on the evening of the third day slept within sight of the lights amongst the shipping in Delagoa Bay. During those three days the heat had been intense, and in those eighty miles I never put my foot on a piece of firm ground, but plodded painfully through deep white sand, like the soft sand of the sea-shore. Indeed, all this flat country to the south of Delagoa Bay must once have been at the bottom of the sea—from which it has been upheaved probably at no very distant time, geologically speaking, as I noticed that the patches of sandy soil which were under cultivation were full of oyster and other sea-shells. Water seemed to be everywhere close below the surface, but was not good—having an unhealthy, slimy taste, and making bad tea. Indeed, except in the actual stream of the Usutu river, I never tasted anything but swamp water during this trip. As I tramped along mile after mile in the deep sand and beneath the blazing sun, I could not but think regretfully of my elephant-hunting days of over twenty years before, when I used to do the same sort of work day after day and month after month without feeling it, and got up every morning without an ache or pain, fresh and ready for the next day's work. But one cannot last for ever; and on this long weary tramp there were moments when I would have given a good deal for a horse, or even a donkey, and on the first day's walk the sun gave me a bad headache.

On the evening of the first and the morning of the second day we passed through some quite uninhabited country, and here I shot two duiker antelopes and a steinbuck. I also saw some quite fresh elephant spoor, and just caught a glimpse of a little

Livingstone's antelope, whose local name is "schlengarn," in a patch of thich bush. The country was looking fresh and green, with the sprouting grass after the recent heavy rains; and hundreds of beetles were now running over the sand, which was a good deal more than warm. Indeed, it was so hot that I think a baboon would have hesitated to sit down on it.

But my weary tramp came to an end at last, and early on the morning of October 7 I crossed the Bay of Delagoa to the town of Lourenço Marques, and, thanks to the kind assistance of Mr. Edixhoven, got all my specimens packed and conveyed on board the *Pembroke Castle* the same day, for transport to England, where they duly arrived in very good order.

The same evening I left Delagoa Bay by train for the Transvaal, and finally reached Kimberley on October 10. Here I had a slight attack of malarial fever—a matter of a few hours only—succeeded by two more in Cape Town, and a final attack on board ship on my way to England. But these attacks were very slight and only lasted for a few hours at a time, and I can only say, with Drummond, that ample amends have been made for any little inconveniences I may have suffered, by the pleasure of the thought that I have not only added a pair of inyala heads to my own private collection, but have also enriched our National Museum of Natural History with two beautiful specimens of this rare and handsome antelope.

CHAPTER XIV

NOTES ON THE GEMSBUCK

Number of African antelopes—The eland—Roan and sable antelopes —The greater koodoo—Other antelopes—The gemsbuck—Limited range—Habitat—Keen sight—Speed and endurance —Chase after four gemsbucks—Two shot—Sight of vultures—Oxen frightened—Horse wounded by lioness—Gemsbuck bull shot—Visit from natives—Gemsbucks and zebras—Gemsbucks ridden to a standstill—Fine specimens shot—Length of horns —Character of the gemsbuck—Probably unaffected by the rinderpest—Likely to survive for long time.

THERE is such a wealth of splendid-looking antelopes to be found on the great African continent that it is hard, nay, impossible to say which amongst them is the grandest prize of all that can fall to a hunter's rifle. In bulk nothing approaches the eland, and an old bull of this species, with his massive form, low-hanging dewlap, and great neck surmounted by a striking and beautifully proportioned head, is in truth a noble animal, but at the same time one that looks fitter in every way to adorn a park than to be hunted to the death. The eland is, in fact, one of those beasts that ought to have been trained to the service of man, and would have been in all probability had it existed in Asia instead of in Africa. Such an animal few can slay without a certain feeling of regret, for even when desperately wounded, nothing but reproach can be read in its mild dark eyes.

How different is the quiet resignation shown by

the dying eland to the fierce defiance of every look and gesture of a roan or sable antelope brought to bay and fighting desperately to the very last. These two latter animals are amongst the finest of all the African antelopes, and by many sportsmen the last named is considered the noblest of them all. The magnificent greater koodoo, too, has many warm admirers, whilst the inyala, lesser koodoo, and Grant's gazelle, if not amongst the grandest of the several genera to which they belong, are certainly some of the most beautiful.

But there is yet another species, whose praises have of late years been sung by few, the successful pursuit of which has always given me more satisfaction than that of any other of the larger antelopes of Southern Africa. This is the gemsbuck, the grandest of all the handsome oryx family. Cornwallis Harris, Gordon Cumming, Oswell, Baldwin, and others of those fortunate Englishmen who travelled and hunted in South Africa when the last century was only middle-aged have all written enthusiastically of the chase of the gemsbuck and the joy of securing a good head of this species.

But with the spread of European settlements and the steady advance of civilisation, these beautiful animals have been driven from many of their former haunts, and are now only to be found in the most arid districts of Western South Africa; and though their range extends from the north-western portion of the Cape Colony in the south to the southern part of the Portuguese province of Angola in the north, there can, I think, be but few districts left where they are to be met with at the present day in anything but small and widely scattered herds. At least, a herd of about fifteen is the greatest number that I have ever seen together, though it must be remembered that I have only met with the gemsbuck in the more easterly portions of its range, and it is quite possible that in the recesses of the Kalahari it may at certain seasons of the year collect into larger droves than anything that I have ever seen.

Compared with other South African game, I have shot but few gemsbuck—only twenty-five, I find by reference to my note-books—partly because I have done the greater part of my hunting in the more easterly parts of the country where these animals are unknown, but also for the reason that even when in countries where they existed I never found them anything but scarce.

The gemsbuck, as I have said before, is an inhabitant of Western South Africa, and lives and thrives in parts of the country where not only are there no running streams, but where for months together every year there is absolutely no surface water at all. In such districts there are almost limitless expanses of level plains covered with low scrub and thorny bush studded with small glittering white salt-pans, and intersected by forest-covered country, with sometimes a thick undergrowth amongst the trees, and it is in such surroundings that the gemsbuck is at home.

As a rule, they confine themselves to the arid, scrub-covered plains, but sometimes wander into the forests. If the sun is not shining full upon them—when they look almost white—the pale grey colour of their coats harmonises wonderfully well with all their surroundings, for the soil on which they stand is generally much the colour of their hides, whilst the parched and thorny scrub around them is always of a pale neutral tint, for it is usually leafless, and even when in leaf the leaves are rather grey than green.

Like the striping of the zebra, the brilliant black and white markings of the gemsbuck's face can be plainly seen when near at hand, but are inconspicuous at any distance over four hundred yards, and the presence of these animals is often first betrayed by the sun glinting on their long black horns. The sight of the gemsbuck is very keen, and the Bushmen say that, like the ostrich, he trusts more to this sense for his safety than to scent, which is no doubt the case as long as he is in country of an open character. There is no more splendid sight than that of a herd of gemsbucks galloping over the arid wastes of their desert home; for, owing to the fact that the cows have longer horns than the bulls, every individual member of the herd looks as if it carried a head worth winning. They run at a steadier pace than any other animal with which I am acquainted, holding their heads rather low, so that their long black horns stand well up, only slanting slightly backwards. As they gallop, their long bushy black tails almost sweep the ground, as they swing from side to side.

In comparing the speed and endurance of various species of South African antelopes, it is first of all necessary to eliminate all cows heavy with calf, as these are so heavily handicapped that they do not afford any criterion of the real powers, under ordinary circumstances, of the species to which they belong. Every one who has ridden after sable and roan antelopes in August or September knows how easy it is at that time of year to bring the heavier cows to a standstill, but I have never yet been able to gallop down a bull of either species, though I have had many a good try.

The gemsbuck is often spoken of as the fleetest and most enduring of all the South African antelopes. My own experience is not sufficient to justify me in dogmatising on this subject, but all those I have shot I have galloped after, and I have also had a considerable experience in riding after most other South African antelopes; and my verdict is, that although gemsbuck run with great speed and endurance, they are inferior in these respects to the tsessebe, Cape hartebeest, Lichtenstein's hartebeest, blue and black wildebeest, and to the blesbok. I should put their running powers much on a par with those of the sable and roan antelope.

Gemsbucks being usually found in open country, as a rule get a good start, and I can well believe that a man mounted on a horse in low condition or only grass-fed would never get up to them at all; but a good South African shooting pony, in hard condition and fed regularly morning and evening on maize, ought to carry a twelve-stone man up to a herd of gemsbucks every time.

I have twice found gemsbucks in company with a herd of Burchell's zebras, and on both occasions in very open ground. On sighting me the former animals at once took the lead and galloped off, closely followed by the latter. On the first occasion they had a long start, and husbanding my horse, I only drew up to them gradually. There were only four gemsbucks—three cows and a bull—and about a dozen zebras; and these latter, when I at length drew up within a hundred yards, entirely prevented my getting a shot at the more coveted game. The horse I was riding had a very good turn of speed, so I then let him out as hard as he could go, and galloped right through the zebras, which scattered to either side of me, and then reforming in one herd, went off by themselves. The gemsbucks were now going at their utmost speed, and when I had passed the zebras were still sixty or seventy yards in front of me. The bull was only to be distinguished from the cows by his somewhat heavier build and shorter though stouter horns. Pulling my horse in as quickly as possible, I jumped to the ground, and aiming for the centre of the black patch which bedecks the hind-quarters of

"THE GEMSBUCKS WERE NOW GOING AT THEIR UTMOST SPEED, AND WHEN I HAD PASSED THE ZEBRAS WERE STILL SIXTY OR SEVENTY YARDS IN FRONT OF ME."

these antelopes, fired. My shot, as it turned out, struck him exactly right, an inch or so above the root of the tail, and must have broken or injured the vertebral column, as his hind-quarters gave way at once, bringing the doomed animal into a sitting position, from which he was unable to recover himself. My after-rider, a light-weight Griqua lad, was now close up behind me, so shouting to him to despatch the bull (whose head I wanted for my own collection), I galloped on after the cows, the best of which I wished to secure for our National Museum of Natural History, for which I had already got a good bull.

They had now, however, got a long start, and as the chase soon led me across a succession of broad sandy ridges entirely free from all vegetation but a little coarse grass, the going became terribly heavy, and I began to think I should never get within shooting distance again. At last, however, the gemsbucks got out of the heavy sand and raced into a broad open plain, where the ground was fairly firm. They were still going strong, and were some three hundred yards ahead of me. I now made what I knew would have to be my last effort, and gradually drew nearer and nearer to the hindmost antelope, until at length I was not more than 120 yards behind it. Just then the leading gemsbuck swerved somewhat to the left, and the other two following in its tracks, gave me—for I had pulled in and jumped to the ground directly I saw the leader turn—a somewhat better chance for a shot than had been offered as long as the chase had remained exactly tail-on-end. Had I missed I should have pulled in and given up the hunt, as I did not want to overtire my horse; but I distinctly heard the bullet tell, and so remounted and galloped on again. For the next half-mile the wounded animal showed no signs of being hit, but held on close behind her companions. Presently, however, she began to fall behind, and suddenly coming to a halt, turned broadside and stood looking at her pursuer. She let me ride up to within fifty yards of her without moving, and it was only when, after having pulled in and dismounted, I had given her a shot through the heart, that she made a short rush forward and then rolled over dead.

I was now at least two miles from where I had disabled the bull, and as I knew that it would be a long time before my after-rider could come up with the Bushmen, I set to work to skin the animal just killed. She was a beautiful beast, but it was a terribly hot job skinning so large an animal without any assistance in the open shadeless plain, for it was already past midday and the heat of the sun was simply intense, and I was somewhat hungry and very thirsty as well, since I had left my waggon (which was standing at a pool of water on the road between Bamangwato and the Mababi) just at daybreak. At last my task was ended, and I then disembowelled the carcase of the dead antelope, and covered it as well as I could with dry grass, an operation that took some time, as grass only grew in scanty tussocks anywhere near at hand. I was also careful to throw sand over all the blood-stains on the ground, these precautions being necessary to keep off vultures, for although none of these birds were at the moment in sight, I was afraid that they might collect and destroy the meat after I had left, and before the Bushmen came for it.

I have satisfied myself over and over again that, in South Africa at least, vultures are guided to their food entirely by sight, and not at all by scent; for should an animal be killed in the midst of dense bush, it will often lie there for days, untouched by vultures, no matter how many of these birds may be circling about overhead; but unless the carcase of an animal killed on an open plain should be quickly hidden from view with branches of trees or grass, it will not remain long unvisited, for one or other of the vultures constantly flying round, perhaps at such a height as to be invisible to the human eye, is sure to spy it ere long, and then—something in its mode of flight no doubt suggesting that it is bent on serious business—is itself seen and followed by others, which in their turn are observed, till all the vultures in the neighbourhood are presently assembled at the feast. The Bushmen say that it is useless covering up a carcase and leaving blood-stains on the ground round about, as vultures can see these signs of slaughter at an incredible distance, and will always come down to investigate such tell-tale marks, whether the meat of the slain animal has been removed or not.

Having secured the skin of the gemsbuck (with the skull and leg-bones still attached) to my saddle, I commenced to lead my horse along his back tracks, but had not proceeded far when I met my after-rider, who, after having despatched the gemsbuck bull, had followed me up with half a dozen of the Bushmen. These latter I sent on to bring in the meat of the cow, and they overtook us again just as we had finished cutting up the bull. It was late in the afternoon when we got back to the waggon, but after a good meal, washed down with the best part of a kettleful of tea, I set to work, and before turning in got the headskin of the bull, as well as the complete skin of the cow, cleaned and prepared for mounting, with arsenical soap. The latter now stands in the Mammalian Gallery of the Natural History Museum at South Kensington, and the former is in my own collection.

As there was but little game in the desert country surrounding the pool where I was encamped—nothing, in fact, but a few giraffes, ostriches, gemsbucks, springbucks, and hartebeests—and the Bushmen had told me that there were absolutely no lions in the district, I had allowed my cattle, donkeys, and horses to feed and lie loose at nights. On this evening I was lying reading in the waggon after having prepared the gemsbuck skins, when I suddenly heard my troop of cattle (some thirty in number, including cows) galloping. They must have been feeding or lying down a few hundred yards behind the waggon, when something startled them and they came rushing towards the waggon in a solid phalanx; but on the driver and some of the boys running towards them and shouting, they halted close down to the edge of the pool. That something had frightened them, there could be no doubt, and as I have never known oxen show any fear of hyænas, I couldn't help thinking that, in spite of what the Bushmen had said, there was a lion about. I therefore had my oxen at once tied up, and taking the lantern, called up some of the Bushmen and went out to look for the rest of my live stock. We soon found the two horses that had been ridden that day and the donkeys, but of my third horse, a very powerful stallion, we could find no trace, though he had had his feed of maize at sundown with the others. I went back to the waggon therefore, feeling very anxious about him.

At daylight the next morning I saddled up my best horse, and accompanied by some of the Bushmen, rode round to the spot from which the oxen had stampeded. The ground was very hard, as the pool of water by which we were encamped was situated in a limestone formation, and for some time we could discover nothing; but on riding back along the waggon track for about a mile to sandy ground, we there at once found the spoor of a lion, or more probably a lioness, as the tracks looked small. These tracks even the Bushmen were unable to follow over the limestone; but about a mile away on the other side of the pool we found the stallion lying down, and soon discovered that he had been both bitten and clawed during the night. I believe that his assailant must have been a very old and weakly lioness, which had found him lying down and attacked him whilst he was in that position. He had been somewhat severely bitten in the back of the neck, and clawed on the left shoulder and in both flanks, but being a very powerful animal, he had managed to throw his assailant off. I at once syringed out the stallion's wounds with a very strong cauterising solution of carbolic acid, and they never sloughed at all, but healed up very rapidly, though if the bite of a lion is not cauterised it takes a long time to heal.

The strangest part of this experience is that I never saw or heard anything more of this lion or lioness. With a dozen of the finest trackers in the world to help me, nothing could be done on the hard limestone ground, which in one direction extended for miles; nor, though I remained in the same camp for a week, did the baffled beast ever make any further attempt to interfere with my cattle. Possibly the stallion, after shaking his assailant off, had given him or her a kick. The Bushmen told me that this was the first lion that had visited the neighbourhood of their camp for years, though a lion and lioness had together killed a cow giraffe near another permanent water, some thirty miles to the west, about a month before. No doubt the brute that had attacked my stallion—probably an old and half-famished lioness—had come a long way on the spoor of my cattle.

I secured my most beautiful gemsbuck head in April 1888, in the desert country between the lower course of the Nata river and the northern extremity of the great Makari-kari Salt-pan.

On the previous day I had come across a solitary bull in an open rolling sandy plain, destitute of any kind of vegetation but coarse tussocky grass. Owing to the very open nature of the ground in which I found him, this gemsbuck spied me from afar and went off with a very long start. I was, however, very well mounted, and after a long and exciting chase, at length got within shot of and killed him. Whilst racing along in full pursuit of this bull, I had seen in the distance quite a large herd of gemsbucks, and as I knew that there must be some fine heads among them, I had half a mind to take up their tracks later in the day, but gave up the idea, as I only had a sufficient number of Bushmen with me to carry the meat of the animal already shot.

On arriving at my waggon, I found a party of Matabele Kafirs there who had come to the Makarikari to collect rock salt, which they find there deposited in layers a couple of inches in thickness. This rock salt is reddish brown in colour, and very impure, containing apparently a great deal of lime. Although most of these Matabele carried guns, they told me they had scarcely seen a head of game since leaving home, and having shot nothing, had consequently had nothing to eat, after they had exhausted the small stock of grain with which they had started on their journey, but berries and tortoises, eked out with whatever they had been able to steal from the Bushmen. They certainly looked half starved, and on my presenting them with a hind-leg of the gemsbuck I had just shot, they very speedily devoured it, and then begged me to try and shoot them something on the following day, that they might lay in a stock of meat for their journey back to Matabeleland.

I promised to do my best for them, and at daylight the next morning, accompanied by a dozen

Matabele and several Bushmen, rode out in search of the herd of gemsbucks I had seen the previous day whilst chasing the bull. We took up their yesterday's tracks, and after following them for several hours, found that they had joined company with a herd of Burchell's zebras, with which animals they were still feeding when we at last overtook them. There were about fifteen gemsbucks (the largest number of these animals I have ever seen together) and as many zebras. The country where we found them being perfectly open, they, of course, saw us when we were still a long way off, and at once went off, with a long start, the gemsbucks leading and the zebras running close behind them.

The horse I was riding—the same with which I had chased the gemsbuck bull on the previous day—was one of the finest shooting horses I ever owned, and though no longer young, was both fast and possessed of great staying power. He was, too, a wonderfully sure-footed animal, and just now in splendid hard condition. Had the zebras been alone, they would have gone off at a leisurely pace, but being led by the gemsbucks, they kept close on their heels. These latter animals, according to my experience, when disturbed never run off in a leisurely way, nor even, if not pressed, do they keep stopping and looking back at their pursuer like almost all other antelopes, but go off at once at such a tearing pace, that although it is not the utmost speed they are capable of when hard pressed, is yet sufficiently fast to make it impossible to get near them at all without hard galloping. Owing to the long start they had got, I daresay I had galloped two, perhaps three, miles before my horse had carried me close up behind the zebras. These latter, running well together some fifty yards behind the gemsbucks, raised a tremendous dust, and, as in the former instance I have described, effectually hid the long-horned antelopes from my view. In fact, it was quite impossible to shoot a gemsbuck without passing the zebras. This I set myself to do, and before long I was galloping alongside of the hindmost animals, keeping above the wind so as to escape the dust they raised as much as possible.

In another few moments I think I should have fairly galloped past all the zebras, but they did not wait for me to do so, for suddenly the whole troop of them swerved off down wind and left me alone with the gemsbucks. These latter were all cows, and most of them carried good heads, but the horns of one seemed specially long and thin, and these I determined to secure. For some time, however, she kept well in front, and I could not get a chance of a shot at her, as she was always covered by one or other of her companions. When I passed the zebras, the gemsbucks were, I believe, going at their utmost speed, and I had kept them at it for another half-mile or so, when suddenly one of them swerved out from the rest, and facing round, came to a halt. I passed within ten yards of her, and she stood looking at me as I passed, and as she remained in the same place for some time, I think I may fairly say that she was ridden to a standstill. She appeared to be a fine full-grown cow, and was probably in calf; but as it would have been at least six months before she would have dropped her calf, this could hardly have affected her running powers. This is the second gemsbuck I have overtaken on horseback, the first having been a bull (with only one horn) which I fairly rode to a standstill in 1879.

At last I got a good chance at the long-horned cow as she swerved off to one side in the van of the herd, and my bullet, hitting her at the back of the ribs, and ranging forwards to the neighbourhood of the heart, brought her to the ground dead before she had run another hundred yards. She was indeed a beautiful animal, and her horns the handsomest, though by no means the longest, that I have ever seen. They were most perfectly symmetrical, and measured 43 inches in length; but being very thin and absolutely straight—gemsbuck horns usually have a slight turn backwards—looked longer than they actually were.

In 1879 I shot another gemsbuck cow near the Botletlie river with horns of exactly the same length; but these latter, being much thicker and having a strong bend backwards, do not look their full length. I think that I am correct in saying that gemsbuck horns measuring over 42 inches in length are quite exceptional. At any rate, I only remember to have seen three pairs exceeding 43 inches. The one measuring 44½ inches was shot by a Boer on the Botletlie river, and I purchased it from him for our Natural History Museum, where it now is; whilst I have seen another pair slightly longer which was shot in the Kalahari many years ago by the late Mr. W. Cotton Oswell. But the longest pair I have ever seen I found in the possession of a trader at Barclay West in December 1880. He told me that he had got them from a native hunter at Moroquain in the Southern Kalahari, and gave them to me, and I gave them to the late Mr. J. S. Jameson. I believe that this is the longest pair of gemsbuck horns known, their length being recorded in Mr. Rowland Ward's last book of horn measurements as 47½ inches. Besides these heads I have mentioned, a few more pairs are known in various collections which measure between 44 and 46 inches, but these are a few exceptionally long pairs that have been picked out in the course of many years from amongst the large number of gemsbuck horns which are annually shot by natives in different parts of the vast Kalahari desert, and brought either to Kimberley or to Cape Town *viâ* Walfisch Bay; and these few exceptions to the general rule only serve to show how very rarely gemsbuck horns attain to a length of 44 inches and upwards. The horns of the bulls sometimes attain a length of 42 inches, but are, as a rule, several inches shorter and a good deal stouter than those of the cows.

Although gemsbucks, when brought to bay, are doubtless dangerous antagonists to dogs, and very possibly sometimes kill lions which have attacked them incautiously, I should doubt their being as fierce an animal by nature as either the sable or roan antelope. At least, I have never seen any of those I have wounded make the same threatening demonstrations as the last-named animals always do when closely approached. I once fired at a bull gemsbuck which was galloping obliquely past me, and dropped him instantly, and as he was still lying motionless when I cantered up to him, I thought he was dead. I noted the position of the bullet-mark, rather high up just behind the shoulder, and thought it must have smashed the vertebral column and so caused instant death. I then dismounted beneath a neighbouring tree, and, placing my rifle against the stem, walked towards the dead animal—as I thought. I was within a few yards of its head, when suddenly, with scarcely a preliminary kick, it rose to its feet and stood facing me. I was so near it that I thought it would be sure to charge, as almost any roan or sable antelope bull would have done so in similar circumstances. But, much to my relief, after eyeing me steadily for a few seconds, it turned and galloped off, and might easily have got away altogether, had my horse not been a good one. When I eventually killed it, I found that my first bullet had only grazed the vertebral column, and momentarily paralysed the poor animal. But it had a splendid chance for vengeance, of which it altogether failed to take advantage, and I certainly would not care to afford another of its kind a similar opportunity.

I have not heard whether or not the plague of rinderpest which swept through South Africa in 1896, and worked such terrible havoc amongst both the cattle and game of that vast territory, affected the gemsbucks. But, isolated as they are in the arid wastes of the Kalahari, I should imagine not; and since they are protected from constant persecution by the inhospitable nature of their surroundings, I fancy that they will long outlive many other species of South African game, which but a few years ago were far more numerous. May this be so; for, though the gemsbuck will always be hard to find, and by no means easy to bring to bag when found, these difficulties enhance his value, whilst his head will ever be one of the most beautiful and coveted trophies to be won in the hunting-fields of Africa.

CHAPTER XV

SOME CURIOUS HUNTING EXPERIENCES

Contrast between Rhodesia to-day and long ago—The old days the best—White rhinoceroses and elephants drinking—A night on the Sikumi river—Abundance of big game—A white rhinoceros visits my camp—My queerest experience—Meet with two black rhinoceroses—A near approach—Rhinoceros knocked down—Apparently dead—Commence to cut it up—Rhinoceros regains consciousness — Gets on its legs — And runs off — Another curious experience—Buffaloes and tse-tse flies—Meeting with lioness—Hammer of rifle lost—Bushmen sent in search of it—Lions met with—Lion and lioness stand close to me—The chance of a lifetime—Rifle misses fire—Lions run off—Lion again seen—Rifle useless—Throw it at the lion—The irony of fate.

As I read almost weekly, in one or other of the papers devoted to South Africa, some account of all the marvellous changes which have recently been brought about, through the energy and intelligence of Britons, in the spacious country now known as Rhodesia, my thoughts often go back to the days when I first wandered and hunted through that land of stirring memories.

That was nearly forty years ago now, and Matabeleland was less known and more inaccessible then than is any part of Central Africa to-day, for at that time not a yard of railway had been laid from any coast town of the Cape Colony or Natal towards the interior of the country. Lo Bengula, a powerful chief of Zulu race, had but recently been elected king of the Matabele, and savagery seemed so firmly established throughout all the territory between the Limpopo and the Zambesi that I never dreamt I should live to see the destruction of that great chief's far-reaching power, and the defeat and dispersal of his brave but barbarous tribesmen, to be quickly followed by the founding of a European town near the site of the old native "great place," and the building of a railway through the wilderness to the north.

Ah! but the old days were the best, after all—or at any rate I think so. The traveller by rail to the Victoria Falls will journey at his ease, it is true, in a saloon carriage, with plenty to eat and drink, through seemingly endless wastes of low forest and scrubby bush, and will probably think it a terribly monotonous and uninteresting country; but no man will ever again sit by a camp fire near one of the little rivers the railway will cross, eating prime pieces of fat elephant's heart, roasted on a forked stick, nor watch the great white rhinoceroses coming to drink just before dark, nor lie and listen to herd after herd of elephants drinking and bathing in the river near their camp. On one particular night in 1873 which I shall never forget, the splashing and trumpeting of troop after troop of hot and thirsty elephants was kept up from soon after dark till long past midnight. This was at the little river Sikumi, which the traveller of to-day will cross by an iron bridge. There was no monotony about the country between Bulawayo and the Victoria Falls in those days. The abundance of big game—elephants, black and white rhinoceroses, giraffes, buffaloes, zebras, and many varieties of antelopes—made it always interesting alike to the hunter and the lover of nature. As I think of my early wanderings through those once well-stocked hunting-grounds in the days when I made my living by shooting elephants, I can recall many interesting experiences, some of a decidedly exciting nature, others only curious. I never had any narrow escapes from rhinoceroses, although I encountered numbers of these prehistoric-looking animals, but I do not think that the black rhinoceros of the interior of South Africa was ever of so aggressive a nature as he appears to be in many districts of East Africa to-day, though a wounded one was always likely to become savage.

One night in 1873, when camped on the borders of the hills which skirt the southern bank of the Zambesi to the east of the Victoria Falls, a white rhinoceros came to inspect my camp about an hour after dark. I had had my evening meal, and was sitting talking by a cheery log fire to one of my native attendants—for I had no white companion—when we heard a rhinoceros snort not far away, and soon afterwards, by the light of a young moon, we perceived one of these animals slowly approaching our camp. I told my boys to keep quite quiet, and we then sat watching our visitor. It advanced very slowly, holding its great square nose close to the ground, and every now and then stopped and snorted loudly. At last it was within twenty yards of our fires, and seemed determined to come closer still. Several of my Kafirs had by this time crept round to the back of the bushes which sheltered our camp and made for the nearest tree, whilst my favourite gun-carrier put my big four-bore elephant gun into my hands, and begged me to shoot the inquisitive beast before it charged in amongst us.

But in those days I was hunting elephants for a living, and as we were camped near a favourite drinking-place of these animals, and a shot in the night might have disturbed a herd approaching the water, I was determined not to fire at the rhinoceros if I could possibly avoid doing so.

However, something had to be done to stop it, as I was afraid that if it came any nearer e smell

"MY GUN-CARRIER HURLED ANOTHER LUMP OF BURNING WOOD AT OUR VISITOR."

of meat might excite it, and cause it to run amuck through the camp; so, plucking a good-sized piece of wood from the fire, I threw it with all my strength, and, just missing the rhinoceros's great ugly head, hit it on the neck or shoulder, and covered it with a shower of sparks. As the blazing brand fell to the ground, the rhinoceros backed a step or two and then seemed to be sniffing at it. At this moment my gun-carrier hurled another lump of burning wood at our visitor, with a somewhat better aim than mine, for he struck it full in the face—apparently right on the front horn—and lit up its head with a cataract of sparks. This was more than the rhinoceros could stand, and its curiosity being evidently fully satisfied, it spun round with a snort, and trotted off into the night, nor did it ever visit our camp again.

But the queerest experience I think I ever had with a rhinoceros was one which happened not far from the scene of the last adventure, and during the same year 1873.

Not having come across elephants for some time, my Kafirs and I were just out of meat—for in those days I seldom shot other animals as long as I had elephant meat to eat, for fear of disturbing the more valuable game—when we came one day on the fresh tracks of two black rhinoceroses, and after following the spoor for a short distance, suddenly sighted the animals themselves lying down in a rather open grassy piece of country. We all crouched down instantly, and as the rhinoceroses never moved, and the wind was favourable, it was soon evident that they had neither seen nor heard us, and were still quite unconscious of danger. Taking one of my heavy, clumsy, old four-bore muzzle-loading elephant guns—the only weapons I then possessed—I at once commenced to creep slowly towards them through the grass, which was not very long.

I had approached to within twenty yards or so of the sleeping animals, and had just raised myself to a sitting position for a shot from behind a small bush, when one of them, which I saw from the thickness of its horns was the bull, stood up, and commenced to walk slowly towards my very inadequate shelter. I do not think that it had any suspicion of my presence, but it was soon within ten yards of the little bush behind which I sat, and as it was still walking slowly towards me it was necessary to do something.

As its head was held in such a position that it covered its whole chest, I resolved to try and fire so as just to miss its horns, and strike it in the front of the head above the eyes. Even if I did not succeed in doing this, but hit one of its horns instead, which was very likely, considering the clumsy weapon I was using, I thought that the shock caused by the heavy bullet would be sure to discompose my opponent sufficiently to give me time to run back to the Kafirs and get my second gun before it thought of charging.

When I fired, the rhinoceros's legs seemed to give way under it, and it just sank to the ground, and then, rolling on to its side, lay quite still, and, as I thought, dead. "Tutu," shouted the Kafirs from behind me, meaning "It's done for," and all of them came running up, the cow having jumped up and made off immediately I fired at her companion.

We now all walked together to where the fallen animal lay apparently quite dead. My four-ounce round bullet had made a large hole in the front of its head, into which I and several of the Kafirs pushed our fingers as far as they would go. We then went to the nearest tree, some sixty or seventy yards away, and after resting my two elephant guns —the one still unloaded—against its stem, and placing all our scanty baggage on the ground in its shade, returned to cut up what we believed to be the carcase of a dead animal.

One of my Kafirs, by name Soga, a big strong Makalaka, at once plunged his assegai into the body of the prostrate rhinoceros and commenced to cut through the thick skin, pulling the blade of the assegai towards him with a sawing motion. This incision should have extended from near the top of the back behind the shoulder-blade to the bottom of the chest, and would have been the first step in peeling the whole hide from the upper surface of the body, preparatory to disembowelling the carcase and cutting up the meat; but when Soga had made a cut about two and a half feet long in its side, the limbs of the rhinoceros began to move spasmodically, and it suddenly raised its head and brought it down again with a thump on the ground.

From that moment it commenced to struggle frantically, and was evidently fast regaining consciousness. I shouted to Soga to try and stab it in the heart before it got on its legs; but as he only made a very feeble attempt to do so, I ran up, and snatching the assegai from him, endeavoured to stab the struggling animal to death myself. But it was now fast regaining strength, and with every effort to rise it threw up its head and brought it down on the ground again with a thump.

I managed to plunge the heavy assegai through the cut in its skin and deep into its side, but with a sudden spasmodic movement it broke the shaft in two, leaving a short piece attached to the blade sticking in its body. In another moment it was standing on its legs, but kept reeling about like a drunken man. I now ran to the tree where the guns had been left, and taking the loaded one, aimed a shot at the still staggering rhinoceros, but, as not infrequently happened in the old muzzle-loading days, it missed fire. I quickly put on a fresh cap, but as that missed fire too, I concluded that the nipple had got stopped up in some way, and so took up the gun with which I had originally wounded the rhinoceros, and commenced to reload it in frantic haste.

Just as I got the bullet rammed down, however, and before I could put the cap on the nipple, the rhinoceros, which all this time had been making a series of short runs, first in one direction and then in another, but had always been quite close to us, started off in a straight line, putting on more pace at every step; and although we ran as hard as we could, we never overtook it, and I did not fire at it again. My bullet no doubt passed above the animal's brain-pan, and must have lodged in the muscles of its neck, only stunning it temporarily; but it really seemed to be absolutely dead for so long a time after falling to the ground, that its recovery and eventual escape, after receiving a four-ounce bullet through the upper part of the head, and having a gash cut in its side at least two feet long, not to mention a deep stab in the region of the heart, is, I think, one of the most remarkable incidents I have ever witnessed during a long experience of African hunting.

Another equally curious, but far more exasperating experience occurred to me early in May 1877, when I was hunting with two friends, Dorehill and Kingsley, on one of the tributaries of the river Daka, about sixty miles to the south of the Victoria Falls of the Zambesi. At the time of which I am writing buffaloes literally swarmed all over this part of the country, and it was in order to shoot a few of these animals and lay in a supply of good fat meat, that we had left our waggons standing at a place known as the Baobab vley, and made an excursion to the east, necessarily on foot because of the tse-tse fly. Both buffaloes and tse-tse flies, I may say, ceased to exist in this district long long ago.

One evening I was coming home, and within a mile of camp—all my Kafirs and Bushmen carrying heavy loads of meat cut from two fat buffalo cows which I had shot during the day—when, whilst we were passing through a thick patch of scrubby thorn bush, a shot was fired a short distance to our right, immediately followed by a loud purring growl; then all was quiet again.

Calling to my Bushman gun-carrier to keep close, I ran in the direction of the sound, and soon came upon Kingsley quite alone and looking rather scared. Having a sore heel, he had remained in camp; but it appeared that having seen a buffalo bull crossing the open valley on the other side of which our camp was situated, he had gone after it all by himself. Being quite strange to the country and knowing nothing about hunting, Kingsley had lost sight of the buffalo amongst the thorn scrub, and not being able to follow its tracks, was making his way back to camp, when he suddenly saw an animal moving through the bush about twenty yards ahead of him, which he took to be an impala antelope, as he could only see it very indistinctly. He immediately fired at it through the scrub, when, to his horror, a lioness thrust her head into the open, and staring fixedly at him, gave a low growl. Kingsley said he stood quite still, but was afraid to reload his rifle or make any movement for fear of further exciting the savage-looking animal. The latter, however, after having gazed steadily at him for a few moments, turned and trotted off.

We now examined the place where the lioness had been standing when Kingsley fired at her, but could find no blood, and I have no doubt that he missed her. We then tried to track her; but her soft feet had left so little trace on the hard ground that even my Bushmen could not follow it, so we gave it up and all returned to camp together.

As I took my rifle from the Bushman who had been carrying it, I saw that the hammer was gone. This rifle was a single-barrelled ten-bore, with under lever action and a hammer. On examining it, I found that the screw that had held the hammer in place on the tumbler had evidently worked loose and fallen out, with the result that the hammer had dropped off. Now I felt sure that just before I had heard Kingsley's shot I had seen the hammer on the rifle, and believed that it must have fallen off whilst we were running a distance of not more than four hundred yards. I was very much annoyed at the prospect of having my favourite rifle put out of action indefinitely, although the Bushmen were confident that they would be able to find the lost hammer the next day. They said they would follow the tracks of my gun-carrier and myself, where we had been running, inch by inch on their hands and knees, burning the scanty grass as they went along. In spite of their confidence, I must say I had very little hope that they would be successful, and lay down to sleep that night with a heavy heart, for I thought that my well-tried and favourite rifle would have to be laid on the shelf for the remainder of the year.

On the following day, after having sent my gun-carrier and two other Bushmen to look for the hammer of my rifle, Dorehill and I went out hunting, leaving Kingsley in charge of the camp. On this occasion I took with me, in place of my ten-bore, a single-barrelled eight-bore weapon, which I had often used before, as I had only lately sold it to Dorehill. This rifle was fitted with a hair trigger, which one set by pushing the trigger forwards. I knew that my friend had taken the lock of this rifle to pieces, and cleaned and oiled it just before we left the waggons, but I did not know that he had done anything more than this. It afterwards turned out, however, that he had, as he said, "just touched the detenter" with a fine file, but unfortunately had taken enough off it to throw the mechanism connected with the hair trigger out of order. This, however, I only found out to my sorrow later on.

About two hours after we had left camp, we emerged from the open forest, with which most of the country was covered, upon a broad open valley, devoid of bush, but covered with a thick growth of yellow grass some four feet high. This open valley was bounded on its further side by a rocky ridge some twenty feet in height, which formed the edge of a level expanse of country covered with small scattered trees, and a very scanty growth of fine grass, of quite a different character to that growing in the valley below. Down the centre of the open ground ran a small stream of water, a tributary of the Daka river. We had just crossed this stream, and were within fifty yards of the steep ridge that bounded the further side of the valley, when two of our Kafirs, who had been after a honey-bird, and who were coming diagonally towards us through the long grass, and had just reached the stream about one hundred yards below us, suddenly shouted out "Isilouan, isilouan!" ("Lions, lions!"), and came running towards us. Seizing the eight-bore rifle from the shoulder of the Kafir who was carrying it just behind me, I ran towards them, calling out, "Where are they? Which way have they gone?" "They jumped out of the bed of the stream," they replied, "and went forward through the grass towards the ridge."

I did not wait to hear anything more, but ran to the ridge as hard as I could, closely followed by the Kafir who had been carrying my rifle. Climbing quickly to the top, I turned and looked eagerly for the lions, which I had hoped to be able to see from my vantage-ground in the grass below me. But I saw nothing, and so began to walk quickly along the edge of the low bluff, keeping my eyes as wide open as possible. Suddenly I heard a slight noise a little ahead of me, as of a small stone being moved; and turning my eyes in the direction of the sound, saw a lioness just emerging from the grass at the foot of the ridge. She was on a little game-path, and evidently intending to come up to the higher ground where I was standing; so, whispering the one word "aima" ("stand") to the Kafir behind me—a good staunch boy—I remained perfectly still, scarcely daring to breathe. The lioness walked slowly upwards and was immediately followed by a fine lion. One behind the other, these two magnificent brutes strolled leisurely up the steep path until they stood on the level ground above.

Just as they came to the top, the lion walked partially behind the lioness, whose hind-quarters then covered most of his head and shoulders. I don't think I was more than from twenty to thirty yards away from them, and there was not a bush or anything else between us but a scanty crop of short grass less than a foot in height, yet neither of them seemed at first to notice anything. I, on my part, remained absolutely motionless, not wishing to fire until I could get a clear view of the lion. After they had walked broadside on to me, for perhaps fifteen yards from the edge of the bluff, the lioness stopped, and turning her head, looked towards where I and the Kafir stood. The lion took another step or two forwards, and then also stopped and looked at us. They were standing exactly broadside on to me, close alongside of one another, the lion perhaps a foot in advance, so that he looked at us from just beyond his companion's head.

Now was my opportunity, and did ever hunter have such a chance before, I wonder? The eight-bore elephant rifle I carried could certainly have driven a bullet through two lions, and had I hit the lioness in the middle of the shoulder—and at thirty yards I could hardly have helped doing so—the bullet would have passed clean through her, and caught the lion just behind the shoulders, an equally fatal shot, as it would have passed through the big blood-vessels of both lungs. My rifle was already on full cock and the hair trigger set, and, raising it to my shoulder, I took a cool and careful aim and pulled the trigger. Click went the hammer, and just came down to the half-cock. This performance I repeated at least half-a-dozen times, but always with the same result.

All this time the lions stood perfectly still, watching me quietly and in rather a sleepy kind of way. Then the lioness walked forwards again, closely followed by her companion, but after taking a few steps they broke into a trot, which soon changed to a heavy lumbering canter. I ran after them as hard as I could, but soon lost sight of them amongst some small bushy shrubs.

Running into and through these bushes, I found myself close to the edge of the bluff again which skirted the open grass valley, for the lions had run round in a half-circle. Feeling sure they had descended to the lower ground, I ran on to the edge of the ridge, and at once saw the lion standing just below me at the foot of the bluff, and close to the edge of the long grass. The lioness I could not see. I don't think the lion was ten yards away from me. He had evidently heard me coming, and stood quite still looking at me whilst I tried three times to fire at him, but the hammer would not go beyond the half-cock.

Then realising my helplessness, and mad with rage and mortification, I caught my useless rifle by the barrel with both hands and threw it at the lion below me. It clattered down amongst the stones close to him, causing him to throw up his tail with a loud purr and disappear into the long grass. The rifle, though somewhat bruised and dinted, was not much the worse for its fall. I think this episode is about the worst piece of bad luck I have ever met with. No such chance of shooting two lions at one shot had ever been offered to me before or has ever occurred since, and it was surely the very irony of fate that this unique opportunity should have fallen to my lot on the one and only day when my favourite old ten-bore was useless to me, for the Bushmen not only found the hammer which I had lost the day before but the little screw that held it on the tumbler as well!

CHAPTER XVI

FURTHER CURIOUS HUNTING EXPERIENCES

Travelling through the wilderness—Find deep pool of water—Meet with two tsessebe antelopes—Shoot them both—Cover one of them with dry grass to keep off vultures—Ride back to waggon—Return to pool of water—Find tsessebe antelope gone—Never recovered—Journey to Bamangwato—Gemsbuck seen—Stalk spoilt—Long, stern chase—Gemsbuck wounded—Lost through glare of setting sun—Wildebeest seen—Return to waggon—Arrival of Count von Schweinitz—Lost gemsbuck found—Two hartebeests shot.

Towards the end of May 1884, I was travelling westwards through the uninhabited stretch of wilderness which lies between the Gwai and the Botletlie rivers. I had a roomy waggon for a home, a good span of oxen, some spare cattle and milch cows, and three salted[1] shooting horses. I had bade good-bye a month previously to the few Englishmen who were at that time living near the native town of Bulawayo, and was not destined to see another white face or hear my mother-tongue spoken for many months to come. My servants were a Griqua waggon-driver, a lad of the same nationality who looked after the horses, and two Kafir boys. But, besides these, I had with me, at the time of which I am writing, a few Masarwa Bushmen, who had accompanied me in the hope of

[1] That is, horses which had contracted and recovered from the most virulent form of horse sickness.

getting a supply of game meat, and whom I found very useful as guides from one pool of water to another, as well as to clear a path for the waggon by chopping down small trees and bushes wherever this was necessary; for we were travelling across country, towards the setting sun, without a road or track of any kind, where never a waggon had passed before.

One afternoon, leaving the Bushmen with the waggon, as there were a few bushes and small trees to be chopped down here and there, I rode on ahead, telling them to follow on my horse's tracks. After having ridden slowly forwards for about an hour and a half through country sparsely covered with low bushes and small trees, I waited until the waggon came in sight, and then rode on again. About an hour before sunset, I found myself approaching a deep depression in the ground, around which grew several large trees. Feeling sure that this hollow would prove to hold a good supply of water, I rode towards it, and suddenly caught sight of the head of a tsessebe antelope through the fringe of long grass which surrounded the pool. I immediately ducked down, and slipping off my horse's back, left him standing in the long grass, and crawled cautiously forwards.

On reaching the edge of the cup-shaped hollow, I saw beneath me a deep pool of water, some thirty yards in diameter, and between the circumference of the water and the ring of long grass which grew all round the top edge of the hollow was a piece of sloping ground some ten yards in width, free of grass or any vegetation whatever. On this bare ground, just opposite to me, stood two tsessebe antelopes. They were both standing motionless, with their heads turned away from me. Being on sloping ground, their hind-quarters were lower than their shoulders. I had not seen an antelope of any size for some days, and wanted meat badly for my native servants and dogs, and much regretted that my rifle was not a double-barrelled one, so that I might have secured them both.

One of the tsessebes was standing with its rump more squarely towards me than the other, so aiming just at the root of its tail, I fired, and saw at once that I had struck the unfortunate animal exactly right, as its hind-quarters immediately gave way, though it struggled towards the grass with the help of its forelegs. At the report of my rifle the unwounded antelope came galloping round the open ground surrounding the pool to within a short distance of where I was sitting, then, halting for an instant, turned and galloped back again. Just as it reached its stricken comrade, I had reloaded and was ready to fire again. Although this tsessebe was galloping pretty fast, it offered an easy shot, for it was almost broadside to me when I fired, and within sixty yards' range. As I pulled the trigger, down it went as if struck by lightning, and I felt very pleased at having secured a much needed supply of meat, close to the pool of water by which I had made up my mind we would camp that night, in order that none of it should be wasted.

On walking round to where the tsessebe last shot had fallen—the other one had struggled into the long grass—I found it lying flat on its side, and apparently just expiring. My bullet—a 360-grain hollow-pointed projectile, fired from a 450-bore Metford rifle—had struck it some six inches behind the right shoulder, and rather below the central line of the body. I turned the animal over, and seeing a bulge in the skin in the middle of its left shoulder, felt it with my fingers, and squeezed up the flattened and expanded cone of lead, which had mushroomed out to the width of a halfpenny, under the skin. As far as I could see, the prostrate antelope could not possibly have been the victim of a more perfect or more deadly shot. When I reached it, it was still breathing, but was limp and apparently at its last gasp. Seizing it by the lower jaw, I pulled its head backwards, and was about to cut its throat, when a dark shadow passed over the water below me. Looking up, I saw a vulture sweeping through the sky, whilst half a dozen more of these keen-eyed scavengers were close at hand. No, it would not do to cut the antelope's throat, and leave a great pool of blood on the bare ground where it lay; for I knew that had I done so the vultures would have torn the carcase to pieces whilst I was riding back to hurry up the waggon. I therefore let the animal's head swing back and fall to the ground, and set to work to cut grass with my pocket-knife. In ten minutes I had completely covered what I believed was the carcase of a dead animal with sheaves of long grass. Then I looked for the one I had first shot, and found it lying dead just beneath a small bush. I propped it up against the stem of the bush to make it look as if it was lying asleep, which I thought would protect it from vultures for the time being; and then mounting my horse, rode back to the waggon, which I brought to the pool about half an hour later, just as the sun was going down.

My men and the Masarwas had been extremely delighted to hear that I had killed two tsessebe antelopes. We pulled the waggon close up to the carcase of the one first shot, and then leaving the driver and one of the Kafirs to outspan the oxen, I led the way to where the other one was lying by the water all covered up with grass. There was the grass right enough, but it now lay on the bare ground, and there was no tsessebe antelope beneath it. The incomprehensible beast had got up and gone off. At first I thought a lion must have dragged the dead animal away immediately after I had left it. An examimation of the ground, however, soon showed that no lion had been there, but that the tsessebe, which I could have sworn was at the point of death, had got up and walked off. Well, I thought it couldn't have gone many yards, so we at once set about following it.

We followed it till dusk, but never set eyes on it again. At first we found blood here and there on the tracks, but after a time this ceased altogether. Then the spoor got mixed up with the tracks of other tsessebe antelopes, and then it got dark; so we returned to camp, and only cut up one animal after all. I went after the resurrected one the next morning with the Bushmen, but not knowing exactly which spoor to follow, we never got it. I have no theory to account for the escape of this animal. All I know is that the incident happened exactly as I have described it.

Nearly four years after the date of the incident which I have just related, in March 1888, I was travelling from Secheli's station towards Khama's old town of Bamangwato. Leaving my waggon in the shade of a cluster of tall, feathery foliaged mimosa trees which grew beside a pretty miniature lake of fresh, sweet rain-water, I rode out late one afternoon to look for game, and heading towards a long low line of ridges which ran parallel with the waggon road a few miles to the east of Selinya vley, rode slowly across an undulating expanse of country, everywhere studded, but nowhere thickly covered with thorn bushes of various kinds, sometimes growing singly, at others in clusters. The soil was soft and sandy, and irregularly covered with tufts of thick, tussocky grass; very heavy ground to gallop over.

I had ridden less than a couple of miles when I suddenly espied a single gemsbuck feeding amongst the scattered bushes, about five hundred yards ahead. Before the animal raised its head I slipped from the saddle and led my horse out to one side, till I got a thick cluster of thorn bushes between myself and the beautiful, long-horned antelope. Then remounting, I cantered quickly up to the cover, and again dismounting, pulled the bridle over my horse's head and left him standing.

On creeping round the bushes, and raising my head cautiously above a thick tussock of grass, I saw that the gemsbuck was still feeding quite unsuspiciously about two hundred yards away from my hiding-place; and as there seemed to be absolutely no wind, I at once commenced to crawl on my hands and knees towards a bush that I judged to be within easy shot of my intended victim. On reaching this I again looked up, and at first could not see the gemsbuck, but the next instant I saw it galloping away, and about three hundred yards off. Glancing towards where I had left my horse, I saw it had walked out from the cover of the bushes behind which I had left it, and by so doing had doubtless spoilt my stalk. Running back to it, I mounted hastily and commenced a long, stern chase.

The gemsbuck, a fine old bull, kept up a strong, steady pace, its long, bushy black tail swinging from side to side as it ran. The soft sandy soil and tussocky grass made the going very heavy, but I was well mounted and gradually gained upon the desert-born antelope I was pursuing, till at length little more than two hundred yards separated us. Perhaps I should never have got up to this gemsbuck at all had it run straight away from me, but it had continually kept swerving inwards, and this had enabled me to cut in on it. Twice I pulled in my panting horse, and jumping to the ground, fired at a distance of some 250 yards. Both these shots missed; but the third time I fired, having held well ahead of the fleeing antelope, as it swerved suddenly inwards, I heard the thud of my bullet that meant a hit, and soon after this the wounded animal began to slacken its pace very sensibly. Then the hunted beast led me into hard ground of limestone formation, heading straight down an open valley leading to a thickish grove of mimosa thorns, and exactly facing the great fiery disc of the setting sun, now very near the horizon. Gathering up the reins and encouraging my good horse with voice and spur, I pressed it to its utmost speed on the hard ground, and raced up to within thirty yards of the gemsbuck, whose strength was now evidently failing fast.

I ought to have galloped right past it, as I could, no doubt, very easily have done; but I foolishly pulled in to get a shot before it got in amongst the mimosa trees towards which it was heading. When I raised my rifle to fire, the red glare of the setting sun was full in my eyes, but I thought that as I pressed the trigger the foresight of my rifle was just on the black patch above the gemsbuck's tail. Then everything seemed a red blur, and for some few moments after I had remounted and again galloped forwards amongst the trees which the wounded antelope had just reached as I fired, I could see nothing distinctly. Not having heard my bullet thud, I did not know whether I had hit or missed, but galloped straight ahead through the open forest, and soon rode out into a broad valley quite free from trees or bush for a distance of several hundred yards. No gemsbuck was in sight, and as I knew that the wounded animal I was looking for could not have crossed this open piece of ground whilst I was riding through the narrow belt of thorn trees, I thought it must have turned either to the right or left in the shelter of the wood.

I first took a turn to the right, and was just coming round again to cut my horse's spoor in the open valley down which I had galloped just before my last shot, when I saw an animal running amongst the trees ahead of me. The sun had now set, and the light was already bad, especially beneath the shade of the trees; and as I went in pursuit, I thought I was after the wounded gemsbuck once more. I was, however, soon undeceived, for on galloping out into an open place, I saw an old blue wildebeest bull lumbering along in front of me. I at once pulled up, and again rode round to cut the gemsbuck's spoor; but it was now fast getting dusk, and I had somewhat lost my exact bearings, so I gave it up as a bad job and rode off westwards till I cut the waggon track, and finally reached my camp.

I was much annoyed, for a gemsbuck bull is always a beast worth shooting, and this particular one, which I had so unaccountably lost, had, I felt sure, carried a very fine head.

I had my supper and turned in, but I could not sleep for annoyance at losing the gemsbuck. Could I, I wondered, with the sun shining full in my eyes, have fired a little too high, and instead of hitting the gemsbuck at the root of the tail, have struck it in the back of the head or neck? Had I done so it would, of course, have fallen to the ground as if struck by lightning, and I might then have galloped close past it without seeing it, both because I was looking on ahead through the trees and because my sight was still blurred by the sun. Anyhow, I thought I would go back and solve the mystery the next morning.

It must have been about ten o'clock at night when my dogs began to bark, and presently I heard some one ride up to my waggon. It proved to be Count von Schweinitz, a German gentleman whom

I had met a short time before, and who, I knew, was about to proceed on a shooting trip to Mashunaland. He told me that he had left his waggons some twenty miles away at Batlanarma vley, and ridden on, as he knew I was not far ahead, and he wanted to have a couple of days' hunting with me.

I soon got my visitor something to eat, and whilst a sleeping place was being prepared for him, told him how I had lost a fine gemsbuck through firing at it with the setting sun full in my eyes. Count von Schweinitz wanted particularly to see some gemsbucks and hartebeests, as he knew that these animals were not to be got in Mashunaland. I informed him that I thought we would be sure to find hartebeests, but could not answer for gemsbucks, though I told him that if we could find the one I had wounded and lost, I hoped he would take its head.

At daylight the next morning we rode out with four of my Kafirs, and took my horse's track to where I had galloped after the wildebeest. Then I took a sweep round and cut the tracks of the gemsbuck, intermingled with those of my pursuing horse, and following them up, came on the beautiful antelope, lying dead just on the edge of the thorn trees where I had last seen it. It was just as I had surmised. My last bullet had gone a little high, and striking the gemsbuck in the back of the neck, had shattered the vertebrae and killed it instantly. It had, of course, fallen all of a heap in its tracks, and, impossible as it may seem, I had galloped past, and within three yards of the dead antelope, without seeing it. This, of course, could not have happened had not my sight been blurred for the moment by the glare of the sun. My horse probably saw the gemsbuck fall, and so did not shy as it passed it.

My first bullet, I found, had entered the gemsbuck's right flank, and ranging forwards, must have inflicted a wound which by itself would soon have proved fatal. The dead antelope carried a remarkably fine pair of horns, massive, widespread, and symmetrical. They measured 3 feet 5 inches, which is quite an unusual length for the horns of a bull gemsbuck, which are, as a rule, much shorter than those of the cow's. The horns of the latter seldom measure more than 3 feet 6 inches, though they have been known to reach a length of within half an inch of 4 feet.

After cutting off the head of the gemsbuck, which I gave to Count von Schweinitz, and leaving two boys to cut up the meat, we rode off to look for hartebeests. We soon found a small herd of these animals, and shot two of them, a bull and a cow. I then sent one of the two natives who had accompanied us to my waggon for four pack donkeys, and with their help carried all the meat, both of the gemsbuck and the hartebeests, to camp, which we reached early in the afternoon.

CHAPTER XVII

INCIDENTS OF A JOURNEY THROUGH THE NORTHERN KALAHARI

Southern Rhodesia—Country farther west still a primeval wilderness—Seldom traversed by white men—Scarcity of water—Remarkable rain-storm—Porcupine flooded out—Every hollow filled with water—All game in good condition—Many varieties encountered—Large herd of elephants—Four large bulls—Wariness of elephants—Lions roaring near camp—Search for them on the following morning—Large male seen and chased into thick bush—Successful encounter with a second male.

SOUTHERN RHODESIA, in which vast territory is comprised Matabeleland, Mashunaland, Manicaland, and part of Gazaland, is now a well-known country traversed by railways and supporting a considerable white population, the bulk of which, however, is confined to the mining districts and to the towns of Bulawayo, Salisbury, Umtali, and Gwelo. But between the western frontier of Southern Rhodesia and the swamps of the Okavango river there stretches a broad expanse of primeval wilderness which the recent development of European activity in all parts of Africa has left entirely untouched.

The reason for this is not far to seek, since the whole of this country is, in the first place, entirely without hills or indeed stone of any kind, and therefore cannot contain gold; and in the second, entirely without rivers, and therefore as a rule a sun-scorched waste, almost destitute of surface water, except during the rainy season.

Thus it has been left an unexplored wilderness which has seldom been traversed by white men, except on certain well-known routes, such as the old waggon trails from Tati to Pandamatenka and from Bamangwato to the Mababi river, and even on these I have travelled in dry seasons seventy and a hundred and twenty miles respectively without water.

Occasionally, however, when exceptionally heavy rains have fallen during the past wet season, this desert land becomes a very pleasant country to travel in. Such a year was 1884. Towards the end of May of that year, a full six weeks after the usual close of the wet season, the most extraordinary rain-storm I have ever experienced swept over the desert to the west of Matabeleland. I was at that time travelling slowly westwards by bullock waggon, following no track, but making my way across country under the guidance of Masarwa Bushmen from one pool of water to another.

One afternoon dense masses of black clouds gathered in the west, and presently spread over the whole sky. There was neither thunder nor lightning, but towards evening a strong wind sprang up, and soon afterwards a steady rain began to fall, at first light, but ever increasing in intensity, until soon after dark it was coming down in such a way that I thought it impossible that it could last long. But all through that night and until midday the following day, the heavy rain never ceased to fall. During the afternoon, however, the sky again grew lighter and the rain gradually ceased. By midnight the stars were shining from a cloudless sky.

Early the following morning I rode out to see the effect of this unprecedented downpour, and found the face of the country completely changed. On the sand ridges no difference was apparent, as the thirsty soil had easily absorbed all the rain that had fallen on it, but the intervening spaces where the Mopani trees flourish, and where the soil is a sort of light clay, had been transformed into broad, shallow lakes, from a few inches to two feet in depth. Riding across one of these flooded valleys, I came upon a porcupine seated disconsolately on the stem of a fallen Mopani tree—the first of these animals I had ever come across in the daytime.

The surface floods soon soaked away on the level ground, but every hollow became a lake or pond which held water for a longer or shorter time according to its depth, and when retraversing this same tract of country some five months later, I still found all the larger hollows fairly full, and was therefore able to travel at my leisure with ease and comfort through a country which, in ordinary seasons, would have been quite impassable by bullock waggon at that time of the year.

Under these conditions, I found this usually arid waste a very pleasant place to wander over. Game, though not very abundant, was still in sufficient numbers to enable me to keep my own people and the several families of Bushmen who had attached themselves to me in rude plenty. Owing to the favourable season, all grazing and browsing animals, including my own cattle, were in very good condition, and my larder seldom lacked the choicest portions of the giraffe, eland, gemsbuck, and springbuck, four of the best animals for the table, when in prime condition, which South Africa, or any other part of the world, can produce. Blue wildebeests were more plentiful than all other species of game, and on the broad, grassy plains which stretch westwards from Metsibutluku—the bitter water—often congregated in herds of from one to two hundred individuals. Here, too, large troops of zebras—Chapman's variety of Burchell's zebra—were often to be met with, as well as small herds of the Cape hartebeest, now quite a scarce animal, as it has been either exterminated in most parts of its former range or driven into the waterless deserts of South-Western Africa.

In the dense thorn jungles which lay a little to the north of my route, a large herd of elephants spent the whole year, as I saw their tracks when travelling westwards from Matabeleland, and again on my return eastwards some five months later. These animals were, however, very wary, never drinking twice running at one pool, and travelling immense distances every night. I twice followed their spoor for a whole day and slept on it without coming up with them. But besides this large herd of cow and young bull elephants, there were four immense old bulls (judging from their tracks), which frequented the same jungles but lived by themselves apart from the herd.

These old patriarchs I tried hard but unsuccessfully to find in the daytime, and I also watched for them at nights on several occasions at vleys at which they had been in the habit of drinking, but I never had the luck to hit off the right pool of water on the right night. Once they drank at a vley within a mile of the one at which I was watching, and I heard them at the water, but on this occasion I think they must have got my wind, as, although I was early on their tracks and followed them all day with the best Bushmen spoorers, I never got near them, and the next day rode home, shooting a fat giraffe cow on the way.

I may here remark that it is of little use, if you do not come up with elephants which have been frightened on the first day, to follow them any farther, as, when alarmed, these animals travel very fast and far at nights, and on the morning of the second day will, in all probability, be much farther off than they were when you first took up their spoor.

Of lions there were a few, but not very many, in this part of the country, and my one successful encounter with one of these animals during this season occurred late in the year, when I was once more nearing the western frontier of Matabeleland. My waggon was then standing beneath some tall, feathery leaved thorn trees near a large vley of water, beyond which stretched an open plain covered with a rather short growth of yellow grass for South Africa—as it was not more than about two feet in length. This open plain was skirted to the north by dense jungles of wait-a-bit thorns, and on its other three sides by open Mopani forest and scrub. My camp was on the northern side of the plain, quite close to the thorn jungles.

At this time I had been long absent from the farthest outpost of civilisation, and had not seen a white man's face or spoken a word of English for more than six months ; but I never felt lonely or low spirited, for I had plenty of books with me to read at nights, and hunting and collecting specimens of natural history filled all my time by day. I was, too, in perfect health.

One night I was reading in the waggon rather late, when a lion—the first I had heard for a long time—commenced to roar loudly apparently not very far away, and was immediately answered by several other lions roaring in unison. After this, and until I went to sleep, this roaring became almost continuous, but I could tell that there was one lion which always roared alone, and was answered by several others which all roared together. Presently, lulled by this grandest of all earthly music, I went to sleep.

I awoke just before daylight, and as the lions were still roaring, apparently within a mile of the waggon, I at once got up, and after drinking a cup of coffee, rode out just at daylight, accompanied by a mounted Griqua lad and several of my best Bushmen, to look for them. Twice after we had left the waggon their deep, menacing voices rolled out over the silent veld, and assured us that they were still in the open grass plain, but after the sun rose they became silent.

We had ridden for perhaps a mile and a half across the open plain, when I suddenly saw something dark appear above the long yellow grass some four hundred yards ahead of me, and knew at once that what I had seen was the maned shoulder of a lion. At this time I do not think he had seen us, but had just risen from the spot where he had been lately lying roaring, with the intention of making his way to the thorn jungles ahead of him. I was mounted on a very good, well-trained shooting horse, in splendid hard condition, and very fast, and I at once put spurs to him, and rode as hard as he could go, in the hope of getting up to the lion before the latter gained the shelter of the thorn jungle, where no horse could have followed him.

The noble quarry gave but one quick look towards the approaching horse, and then turned and galloped away through the grass at a great pace, making straight for a small island of forest and jungle lying in the open plain just outside the main bush. I was now going at racing speed, and was gaining fast on the lion, who did not appear to be exerting himself, though he got over the ground pretty quickly, going at an easy gallop, and looking like an enormous mastiff. He was very dark in colour, with a full dark mane.

Just before he got to the edge of the small isolated piece of bush, I ought to have pulled in and taken a shot at him at about 150 yards, but I thought he would halt at the edge of the cover and turn round and look at me, as lions, after having been chased across an open place on horseback, often do; but this one galloped straight into the cover, and I lost the chance. The patch of bush in which he now was, was not more than 100 yards long by 50 broad, but was only separated from the main jungle by an open piece of ground quite destitute of cover and about 60 yards across at the narrowest point. Having ridden round this isolated piece of bush without seeing anything more of the lion, I thought he must be hiding within it, and determined to send to the waggon for my dogs, which I knew would soon show me his whereabouts, as soon as the Bushmen came up.

They soon appeared with my mounted after-rider, who at once told me that, after I galloped forward, he had come on behind me across the plain, and had ridden right on to five lions lying in the grass, a big male and four females, which had trotted slowly away to a tongue of bush extending into the plain from the main jungle about a mile back.

I now rode round the piece of bush again, in which I thought that the lion I had chased was still hiding, with the Bushmen, in order to make sure that he was still there, and had not run straight through it and across the open into the solid jungle beyond, which he might just have had time to do without my seeing him, for I had pulled in for a moment near where he had disappeared.

Sure enough, we found his tracks emerging from the top end of the bush, and followed them across the open to the thick cover beyond, and as it would have been useless to look for him here without dogs, I galloped back at once with my after-rider to where the latter had last seen the other lions. "Was the male a big one?" I asked him. "Sir," he answered, "when he turned and stood looking at me from the top of that piece of rising ground, he looked like an eland bull!"

We had just passed the point of the tongue of bush I have previously alluded to, when my boy said in Dutch, "Daar's hij; pass op; hij zal ons jagd" ("There he is; look out; he will chase us"), and turning his horse's head, galloped away. I had not yet seen the lion, but I soon made him out standing looking at me, with his head held low. He was not more than eighty yards off, and I was just going to dismount and have a shot at him, when out he came with mouth held half open and ears laid back, jerking out with every breath a rolling thunderous growl. My horse knew the business well, and was round and off with the promptitude and speed of a well-trained polo pony, the lion close behind.

I think he got up pretty near us with his first furious rush, but then my horse got into his stride and gradually drew away from him, and when he had chased us for about 150 yards, he pulled up, at the same time ceasing to growl. It was the cessation of the roaring that let me know he had given up the chase, and pulling my horse in, I brought him round again as quickly as possible.

The lion was then standing looking at me, and as I approached he lowered his head, and at once commenced to growl again, whisking his tail rapidly from side to side without cessation. I knew he would charge again in a moment, so gave him no time to get his wind, but dismounting as quickly as possible, raised my rifle and took a quick shot for his open mouth. The bullet must have passed just below or on one side of his lower jaw, as it struck him in the chest, causing him to stand straight up on his hind-legs, and fall over backwards. He recovered himself immediately, but abandoning for the moment all thought of again charging, turned and trotted back towards the shelter of the trees he had left a short time before.

I was quickly in the saddle again and galloping

up behind him, as I feared to lose sight of him in the bush. He heard me coming, and whipping round with an angry roar, charged again in fine style, this time, however, chasing me for less than a hundred yards, and coming to a halt as before right in the open. I brought my horse round as quickly as I could, and again dismounting, fired as he stood facing me, and again hit him in the chest, when he at once turned and made for the bush, on reaching which he lay down under a large thorn tree. I now walked my horse towards him, and finding that he was apparently too far gone to get on his legs again, though he raised his great head and growled savagely as I approached, I came quite near to him, and gave him a third shot in the chest which killed him. He proved to be a fine lion just in his prime, in beautiful coat and with a very fair mane. He was, too, extraordinarily fat. The Bushmen took every particle of fat from the slain monarch, but left the rest of the carcase for the hyænas and vultures, which they would not have done had they been short of meat of other kinds.

I imagine that this lion was the lord and master of the four lionesses who were with him when my after-rider disturbed them, and that the single lion I had chased and lost was a depraved animal who wished to interfere with this domestic arrangement, but had been unable to allure any of the lionesses away from their rightful lord, and had not dared to put the matter to the ordeal of combat. This explanation would, I think, account for the continuous roaring which had gone on during the whole of the previous night.

CHAPTER XVIII

THE LAST OF SOUTH AFRICA'S GAME HAUNTS

Decrease of game in South Africa—Journey from Mashunaland to the East African coast—Find country full of game—Elephants—Great herds of buffaloes—Five old bulls—Bushbucks—Other antelopes and zebras—Curiosity of the latter animals—Wart-hogs, bush-pigs, and hippopotamuses—Numbers of carnivorous animals—Three lions seen—Fine male wounded, and subsequently killed.

DURING the twenty years succeeding my first arrival in South Africa in 1871, I had constantly wandered and hunted over vast areas of country, from the Cape Colony to far away north of the Zambesi, and in that time had seen game of all kinds—from the elephants, rhinoceroses, and buffaloes of the forest regions north of the Limpopo river to the wildebeests, blesboks, and springbucks of the southern plains—gradually decrease and dwindle in numbers to such an extent that I thought that nowhere south of the great lakes could there be a corner of Africa left where the wild animals had not been very much thinned out, either as a result of the opening up and settlement of the country by Europeans or owing to the extensive acquisition of firearms by the native tribes.

In the year 1891, however, when attempting, on behalf of the British South Africa Company, to discover a route free from the tse-tse fly between

THE LAST OF SOUTH AFRICA'S GAME HAUNTS.

Mashunaland and the East African coast, I walked into a country still teeming with big game, for no white man, as far as I am aware, had ever hunted there before the time of my visit,[1] and the fell plague of rinderpest, more potent for mischief than many legions of human game-destroyers, had only recently commenced its ravages, thousands of miles away on the plains of Masailand. Moreover, the natives living in this low-lying, fever-haunted district were few in number and almost destitute of firearms.

Elephants still wandered over this tract of country, often in large herds, as their tracks and pathways leading in all directions plainly showed. But these animals, whose fatal possession of ivory has made them an object of pursuit to man in South-East Africa ever since the days when the ancient Arabian traders carried gold and ivory to King Solomon, appeared to have inherited a timid and restless disposition, which, in spite of a present immunity from persecution, kept them always on the move.

All other animals were, however, singularly tame and confiding. Great herds of buffaloes feeding in the reed beds along the rivers or lying in the shade of the scattered thorn trees allowed a near approach before taking alarm, and some of the old bulls which were frequently encountered either alone or in little bands of four or five together would scarcely take the trouble to get out of one's way. I remember, when first descending from the broken country at the head of the Mutachiri river, where there was but little game, into the level coast plains, the first buffaloes I encountered were five old bulls, which were lying in the shade of some palm scrub on the bank of the river, whose course I was following.

[1] The Portuguese who travelled occasionally between the Pungwe river and Massi-kessi never hunted or left the footpath, along which they were carried in hammocks.

As I walked towards them they raised their great armoured heads and looked curiously at the first human being with a hat and shirt on they had probably ever seen. My small retinue of native servants was just then some little distance behind, and not until I was within fifty yards of them did first one, then another of these massive black bulls rise from his bed. But not immediately to run off, for they stood their ground and still for some time stared inquisitively—one might almost have said menacingly—with outstretched noses and horns laid back on their necks. However, in a long experience of African buffaloes, I have not found old bulls of this species either savage or aggressive when not molested—at any rate, when they are feeding or resting in ground sufficiently open to allow them to see anything approaching; though a sudden charge by a buffalo lying in long grass or thick jungle, which has either been previously wounded by a hunter or mauled by lions, is not an uncommon incident of African travel.

On the occasion of which I am speaking, when I was not more than thirty yards from the five old bulls, one of them actually came trotting towards me. I then took off my hat and waved it, shouting out at the same time. Then the old fellow turned and trotted away, and soon breaking into a heavy, lumbering gallop, was quickly followed by his companions. Later on, the same day, another solitary old buffalo bull allowed me and my native followers to walk past within eighty yards of where he lay without even troubling himself to get up.

After the buffaloes, the bushbucks were the tamest animals in this great natural game-park. These lovely little animals, whose rich dark brown coats are in this part of Africa most beautifully banded and spotted with white, would stand gazing at me, amongst the scrubby bush or open forest they frequent, and often allow a very near approach. The denizens of the open plains—blue wildebeests, tsessebes, Lichtenstein's hartebeests—were wilder and more wary than the buffaloes and bushbucks, but still tame compared with their much-hunted relatives in other parts of South Africa; whilst waterbucks, reedbucks, oribis, and zebras (Burchell's) were all very tame and confiding, and the latter, if they did not get one's wind, very inquisitive, as I have found them to be in other unfrequented districts.

One day I was resting with my native attendants and taking a midday meal on one of the large ant-heaps with which many parts of South-East Africa are studded, when a herd of perhaps a hundred zebras came up over the open plain to see what was going on. Led by a gallant-looking old stallion, the whole troop advanced slowly to within about a hundred yards of where I and my boys were sitting. Then they halted, and for a long time all stood quite still with ears pricked and eyes turned towards us. After a time the leader came walking slowly forward, and was soon followed by a few other adventurous spirits, the mass of the herd remaining where they were. I was myself so absorbed in watching this novel and interesting sight that I did not observe that one of my Kafirs (who took no interest in anything but dead zebras) had stood up behind me, until I saw the most venturesome of our visitors turn round and trot back to their companions. I then told all my boys to sit down and keep quite quiet; but although the old stallion and a few of the bolder spirits amongst his followers came forward again, they would not approach nearer than about seventy yards from us, the whole troop moving up slowly behind them.

I suppose I must have sat watching these beautiful animals for upwards of an hour, and they did not finally trot away until we had got our things packed up and were preparing to move in their direction.

I found both the wart-hogs and the bush-pigs, too, either very tame or very stupid; and several hippopotamuses, which were disporting themselves in small muddy lagoons, were at my mercy, had I wished to interfere with them; but on this trip I killed very few animals, nor ever fired a single shot except when obliged to do so, in order to secure a supply of meat for myself and my native attendants.

In a country so well stocked with antelopes, zebras, and buffaloes, carnivorous animals, it may well be supposed, were not wanting, and, indeed, in no part of Africa probably were lions, leopards, hyænas, wild dogs, and jackals more plentiful than they were in the neighbourhood of the lower Pungwe river at the time when Mr. Rhodes's pioneers first entered Mashunaland.

But all carnivorous animals are almost entirely nocturnal in their habits, and therefore only occasionally encountered in the daytime; and on the occasion of my first visit to this district I saw neither lions, hyænas, nor leopards, though the two former animals roared and howled nightly round my camp, and the grunting cry of the latter was often heard. Nor was I much more fortunate in this respect on my second visit to the same part of the country in 1892; for though I spent six weeks travelling and hunting between the Pungwe river and Lake Sungwe during October and November of that year, I only saw three lions, though there was not a single night during the trip on which I did not hear some of these animals roaring, sometimes close to camp, at others in the distance. On several occasions, too, I heard three different troops or families of lions roaring on the same night.

On the day when I saw the three lions, I had left camp with a few native followers very early in the morning, and was walking across an open plain studded with large ant-heaps, from which the long grass had been for the most part burnt off. On my right was a small river whose banks were fringed with a thick growth of scrubby bush. My course lay parallel to this river, but outside the strip of bush. Suddenly I came in sight of two lions at a distance of 400 or 500 yards out on the open plain. They were advancing at a slow walk towards the river and had been previously hidden from our view by some large ant-heaps. These two lions saw us at the same moment that we saw them, and at once halted and stood watching us. Telling my native attendants to sit down and remain where they were until my return, I commenced to walk towards the lions, hoping that they would allow me to approach within shot before running off, as I knew that these animals, which in many parts of Africa are very shy and wary, had very little fear of man in the Pungwe river district at that time. However, before I had advanced fifty paces, both lions turned round and commenced to walk slowly towards a small patch of long yellow grass which had escaped the last grass fire. They walked away from me at a very slow and leisurely pace. One seemed a monster, the other either a female or a young male with no mane.

I now commenced to run towards them, but had not gone far, when a third lion, that had previously been hidden by a large ant-heap, was suddenly revealed to me. He had evidently been walking over the plain about a hundred yards to the right of the other two lions, and not having seen me, did not understand why these latter had first come to a halt and then turned round and walked back again in the direction from which they had just come. When I first saw the third lion he was standing turned away from me and looking at the other two.

Quickly swerving to the left, but without stopping, I almost immediately put a large ant-heap between us, and then ran to it at my utmost speed. This ant-heap was quite twenty feet in diameter at the base, and ten or twelve feet in height. I quickly climbed half-way up it and then looked round the side, and saw that the single lion was still standing watching the other two, which were at that moment just entering the patch of long grass of which I have already spoken.

I now edged myself in a sitting position to the side of the ant-heap nearest the lion and prepared for a shot. He was facing half away from me and something more than two hundred yards off; but there was not so much as a blade of grass in the shape of cover on the level burnt plain between us, and had I attempted to get nearer to him he would certainly have seen me at once and then trotted after his companions. So, steadying myself and taking a careful aim with the 200-yards' sight, I fired. My bullet must have passed close beneath the brute's chest—I think behind his forelegs—as I saw it knock up the dust just beyond him. He at once sprang to the spot where the bullet struck the ground and again stood still, facing now exactly away from me, without apparently having taken any notice of the report of my rifle—a 450-bore single-barrelled Gibbs-Metford.

Extracting the empty cartridge and pushing a fresh one into the breech, as silently and quickly as possible, I fired again, this time taking a fuller sight and aiming for the centre of the lion's somewhat narrow hind-quarters. The dull thud which answered the report of the rifle assured me that I had hit him, but I never saw a lion before make so little fuss about a wound. He gave one spring forwards, accompanied by a loud growl, and then stood still again. But only for a moment. Then he came trotting round towards where I sat on the side of the ant-heap, turning first to one side then to the other, and evidently searching for what had hurt him, and I am sure that had he made me out he would have charged instantly. However, I was dressed only in an old felt hat, a cotton shirt, and a pair of shoes, and my scanty garments and bare, sunburnt limbs were all so weather-stained, and harmonised so well with the neutral tints of my immediate surroundings, that he never saw me.

I had thrown the empty cartridge out of my rifle before the lion turned, but had no time to reload before he commenced to trot towards me, for, knowing that the very slightest movement on my part would attract his attention, I sat perfectly still, feeling sure that in case of a charge I should have ample time to slip the cartridge, which I held ready in my hand, into the breech of my rifle before he got to me. However, he never discovered me, though he approached to within a hundred yards of the ant-heap on the side of which I was sitting. He then stopped, and after first looking towards me, turned round and once more stood facing exactly away from me.

This was my chance, so hastily loading and putting down the 200-yards' leaf sight, I again fired at him, and again heard my bullet strike. With a loud growl he sprang forwards, and then went off at a gallop. He turned almost immediately and, running almost broadside to me, made for a large ant-heap with some bushes growing at the top of it. Before he reached it I fired again and knocked him down, but after having lain still for a few moments he got up and half-ran, half-dragged himself to the ant-heap and disappeared behind the bush on its summit.

I now walked round and reconnoitred the ant-heap behind which the lion had disappeared, and found that just beyond it there was a small patch of unburnt grass quite six feet high, in which, no doubt, he was hiding. To have approached this patch of long grass across the open plain would, I felt sure, have meant facing a fierce charge at close quarters, for the wounded lion had shown every sign of being a savage and determined animal.

About two hundred yards to the left of the place where the lion was lying was another ant-heap, at the foot of which grew two good-sized trees, and as I thought I might be able to see something from the top of one of them, I went back to where I had left my Kafirs, and taking one of them with me, made a circuit and came up behind the trees. My native attendant quickly climbed to the top of one of them, but declared he could see nothing of the lion, although he said that the patch of grass in which it was lying was very small. He then began to come down the tree again, talking all the time.

He had got about half-way down when two wart-hogs which had been lying asleep somewhere near us, disturbed by his voice, got up and went trotting straight towards the spot where the lion was lying. They did not enter the grass, but passed close to it, and the lion must have heard them coming and made ready at once to repel another attack, for the Kafir suddenly saw it standing just within the edge of the grass. "Sir, sir, I can see the lion," he called to me in his own language. "I can see nothing," I answered. "Come up the tree a little way," he said, "and you will be able to see it." I told him to come down low enough to reach the rifle I handed to him, and then climbed into the lower branches of the tree. When about ten feet above the ground I could see the lion's head and the outline of its back indistinctly through the grass. First aroused by the near approach of the wart-hogs, he was no doubt now listening to us talking.

I got a little higher up the tree, but although from this position I commanded a somewhat clearer view, I could not steady myself to fire, so I came lower down and fired a shot with the 200-yards' sight. This shot missed the lion altogether, but it had an excellent effect, as the angry brute at once charged out of the grass and came straight towards where he had heard the talking. At first he showed signs of partial paralysis of the hind-quarters, but gathering strength with every stride, he was soon coming along at a great pace, growling savagely and evidently prepared to make things uncomfortable for the first human being he met. I let him come on to within about fifty yards of the tree in which I was perched, and then shot him right in the chest with an expanding bullet, which tore open his heart and killed him almost immediately.

This was the last of the thirty-one lions I have shot, and the first and only one of these animals that I ever shot from a tree. He was a fine full-grown animal, just in his prime, with a good mane for a coast lion, very thick set and heavy in build, and enormously fat. My first two bullets had struck him close together just below the tail, and either would probably have killed him had it been a solid projectile, but being expanding bullets they had probably not penetrated beyond the stomach.

We found subsequently, on examining the place where he had been lying in the grass at the foot of the ant-hill, that he had vomited great lumps of the meat and skin of a wildebeest on which he had been feasting the preceding night. My third bullet had struck him too far back, behind the kidneys, and passing just below the backbone, had momentarily paralysed his hind-quarters, causing him to fall when hit and subsequently to show weakness in the hind-legs.

CHAPTER XIX

HOW I SPENT CHRISTMAS DAY 1879

Travelling through the desert—Large number of bullocks—Long distances between permanent waters—Heavy sand—Start for Mahakabi—Intense heat—Sufferings of the poor oxen—No water at Mahakabi—Search for water with Bushmen guides—Another disappointment—Ride all night—Reach the Luali river—Bullocks lost—Dick's account of the catastrophe—Fear the worst—Ride to Shoshong for assistance—Return to Klabala—Meet waggons.

TRAVELLING south through the desert countries lying between the Mababi river and Khama's old town of Shoshong, during the month of December 1879, we had found water plentiful as far as the Botletlie. Farther south, however, but little rain appeared to have fallen, and it was not without difficulty that we crossed the desert stretch between that river and the wells of Tlakani.

Our party was a large one, as we were travelling in company with a number of Khama's people who had been hunting in the Mababi country during the past season, and with whom we were on very good terms. These people were under the command of Tinkarn, one of Khama's most trusted chiefs, a man who had been a hunter from his youth upwards, and who from the life he had led had always been closely associated with the wild Bushmen of the desert, whose language he spoke fluently, and over whom he exercised a strong influence.

Tinkarn and his people had five waggons with them and we white men four, two of which belonged to me, one to Mr. H. C. Collison, and one to a mutual friend, who had lost himself and died of thirst, poor fellow, some few months previously in the dreary wastes which lie between the Chobi and the Zambesi rivers.

I had with me two young Cape colonists, Messrs. Miller and Sell, so that we were four white men together. Having full spans of sixteen oxen for each waggon, as well as some spare animals, we had some 150 bullocks with us altogether, as well as eight or ten shooting horses.

South of Tlakani there was no permanent water nearer than the wells of Klabala; the deep pit of Inkowani having ceased to hold water since the emigrant Boers had deepened it during their memorable but disastrous journey through these same deserts in the winter of 1878.

In this country of railways, the distance between Tlakani and Klabala—not much over one hundred miles probably—may seem very small, but as the track between the two places lies through a level expanse of soft desert sand through which a heavy South African bullock waggon can only be dragged at an average rate of from a mile and a half to two miles an hour, it meant four days and four nights at least of constant travel to get through it. Tinkarn, however, had learned from the Bushmen that good rains had fallen not long before between Inkowani and Klabala, and felt sure that our live stock would get a drink at the pools of Mahakabi, in which we had found a good supply of water in the previous April.

As it would be a terrible pull to get our waggons through even as far as these pools, we gave our cattle a three days' rest at Tlakani, where the wells were luckily full, before starting southwards again.

I must here say that in the winter season, when the nights are long and cold, and the sun not intensely hot during the daytime, a picked span of bullocks in good hard condition will sometimes manage to pull a waggon along for four days and four nights without drinking, but in very hot weather no bullocks that I have ever seen can work for more than half this time pulling heavy waggons in deep sand and without water.

Christmas time is about the hottest season of the year in South Africa, unless heavy rains happen to be falling, and at the time of which I am writing the heat was simply terrific. The country around us was an absolutely dead level in all directions, everywhere clothed with a sparse covering of low thorny bushes, whose little grey-green leaves and hard black twigs, over which little hook-shaped thorns are profusely scattered, afforded but little protection from the cruel sun. Early in the day the sand became so hot that it was quite impossible to keep the palm of one's hand upon it for more than a few seconds at a time, nor was it possible to hold one's hand on any piece of iron exposed to the sun's rays. The sand itself was so deep and soft, that our heavy bullock waggons sank in it to a depth of several inches, over the felloes of the wheels, in fact; and as our long caravan moved slowly and painfully forwards, both bullocks and waggons were almost hidden from sight in a thick cloud of fine dust which rose from the trampled ground into the still hot air. When the sun set the relief was immense, but still the heat thrown up from the scorched sand was very great, and it was only for one short hour between dawn and sunrise that the temperature became pleasantly cool.

It was about four o'clock on the afternoon of December 23 that we finally left Tlakani, after having carefully filled our water-casks and given all the bullocks and horses a good drink. At sundown we outspanned, made a hasty meal of dried eland meat roasted on the ashes, washed down with a cup of tea, and then inspanned again. All that night we trekked on with only two short intervals of rest, and when day broke on the morning of December 24, our oxen had done ten hours' actual pulling through the heavy sand and covered some fifteen miles since leaving Tlakani. All this day we travelled slowly onwards through the frightful heat, giving the bullocks an hour's rest after every two hours' pull. The terrific heat of the cruel pitiless sun told upon the straining oxen very rapidly, for it must be remembered that nothing but steady hard pulling by every member of each span, all pulling in unison, could move the heavy waggons through the deep sand, and nothing made of flesh and blood could work very long in such a temperature without drinking.

Towards the close of the long day it became a pitiful sight to look at the poor oxen, as they toiled slowly and painfully along, with lowered heads and tongues hanging from their gasping mouths. The hot air they breathed was full of fiery dust, which rose in clouds from their feet and hung suspended in the breathless atmosphere long after the last waggon had passed. This hot dust no doubt very much aggravated the terrible thirst from which our bullocks were now suffering, and kept them continually gasping and coughing.

At last the dreadful sun turned blood-red as it neared the western horizon, and then soon sank from view behind the interminable landscape of stunted thorn bushes. When outspanned during the day, the bullocks had made no attempt to feed, but had only stood about in clusters amongst the shadeless thorn scrub; I was in hopes, however, that they would graze a little at sunset, albeit the grass was scorched and scant. But they were too parched to do so; and so, hungry, weary, and terribly thirsty, the poor brutes were once more yoked to the heavy waggons just as the short twilight of the early tropic night was giving place to a bright moonlight, for it wanted but a couple of days to full moon. The whole of this second night we travelled slowly southwards, with short intervals of rest.

I kept awake once more throughout the night, in order to time the periods of travel and the intervals of rest. As we were four Europeans, we might have kept awake turn and turn about, and turned in for a sleep in one of the waggons when not on duty; but when travelling through the desert I am always too anxious to be able to sleep, whilst making a push from one water to another, and always make a point of timing the treks myself, and keeping the waggon-drivers and leaders up to the mark; for these latter naturally get worn out during such journeys, and often are so tired that when a halt is called, they just throw themselves down where they stand and lie there like logs till it is time to move on again.

During the night we passed the deep limestone well and shallow pan of Inkowani, both of which were perfectly dry, and presently Christmas Day 1879 dawned upon us, and the cruel sun was soon once more shining over the desolate wilderness around us. By this time it had become evident that our bullocks could not possibly pull the heavy waggons much farther. One or other of them was constantly lying down, and had to be mercilessly beaten or its tail twisted or bitten before it could be induced to get up again and struggle on a little farther. Although the waggons of our Bamangwato friends were much less heavily laden than ours, their bullocks were much inferior, and on the whole in quite as sorry a plight.

About ten o'clock it became impossible to get the waggons along at all, and we had to give up the idea of reaching the pools of Mahakabi, from which we were only about six miles distant, with them, as we had hoped to have done. We therefore outspanned, and prepared to drive all our cattle and horses to the water, let them have a good drink and feed there, and return to fetch the waggons in the afternoon. Collison was not very well, so he and Sell remained with the waggons, whilst Miller and I—both of us mounted—and all our coloured boys, with the exception of the waggon-drivers, accompanied Tinkarn and his people to Mahakabi, taking all our cattle, horses, and dogs with us. Tinkarn, I think, only left a couple of boys to look after the five waggons belonging to his people. I let him start first with all his people and their troop of cattle, Miller and I following with our own herd, driven by our own boys, about a quarter of an hour or twenty minutes later. I rode my own favourite shooting horse "Bob," and led Collison's best nag "Big Bles," his after-rider, a Mangwato boy, named Dick, being mounted on his second horse. I had had a cup of coffee when we outspanned just before daylight, but had eaten nothing since the previous evening, and had not even tied a piece of "biltong" on my saddle, when leaving the waggons with the oxen, as I had hoped to get back again before sundown, and was besides too full of anxiety to think much about food just then.

Although the bullocks were unable to drag our heavy waggons any farther through the deep sand, they stepped out briskly enough along the road when unencumbered, and evidently knew that they were being taken to water. We were just approaching the first of the two pools of Mahakabi, and could see the cattle of our Mangwato friends standing round about it, when I saw Tinkarn coming riding back to meet me. "Metsi utin?" ("Is there water?"), I asked. "Metsi haio" ("There is no water"), he answered; almost immediately adding, "But we shall find water; I have two Bushmen here who will show us water." From the appearance of the grass, it was evident that a heavy shower of rain must have fallen over this part of the country about a month before our arrival, and Tinkarn told me that there must then have been a good supply of water in the Mahakabi vleys, which, however, had been very rapidly sucked up by the intense heat which had lately prevailed. When the Mangwatos' troop of cattle first reached the nearest and biggest vley, there was still a little water in it, but the thirsty beasts just rushed into the shallow pool, and of course soon trampled it into mud. Two Bushmen, however, had been found at the water, who, of course, knew Tinkarn and feared him, as one of Khama's most influential headmen, and these savages reported that heavy rain had fallen farther to the east during the last moon, and thought that a certain vley they knew of would probably still have some water in it. If there should prove to be no water there, said they, they would guide us to the place where the road from Shoshung to Pandamatenka crossed the Luali river.

It was now past midday, and the heat intense. Our horses, as well as the oxen, had been nearly forty-eight hours without drinking, but as they had done no work during that time, they were not suffering like the latter animals. However, I did not like to go away with the cattle, and perhaps have to take them right through to Luali, without letting Collison know what had happened, so I sent Miller back to the waggons, telling him to give the horse he was riding a few pannikins of water as soon as he got there, as our two largest casks had, I knew, been scarcely touched. Should the vley spoken of by the Bushmen prove to contain a good supply of water, I told Miller I would rest the oxen there until after midday on the 26th, and drive them back to the waggons, after they had had a good drink, on the afternoon of that day, in time to start for Klabala the same evening. Should I not turn up by that time, however, I told him not to expect me for at least another twenty-four hours, as he would then know I had had to go on to Luali.

Having bade good-bye to Miller, I started Dick (who was mounted) and all our boys with our cattle on the track of those belonging to Tinkarn and his people, who had already set off eastwards under the guidance of the Bushmen. After a very hot and weary tramp, we at last reached the vley where our guides had hoped to be able to show us water. As in the pools of Mahakabi, so here there were still a few gallons of liquid left, but not enough, unfortunately, to be of any use, as the thirsty oxen just rushed into it and trampled it into mud immediately.

There was now nothing for it but to push on for Luali as speedily as possible during the cool of the night. Soon the scorching sun once more went down, but as the moon was near the full, we had no difficulty in keeping a good line through the open thorn scrub, and got on at a good quick walk, as our thirsty cattle stepped out briskly, and weary though they must have been, showed no signs now of flagging. About midnight we called a halt, and off-saddling the horses—about six of Khama's headmen were mounted—lit fires, round about which the oxen were collected in two herds, the one composed of those belonging to the Mangwatos, from which I kept ours a little separate. We rested for about an hour, during which time I sat talking with Tinkarn. My boys had all lain down near the fires and gone fast asleep, as soon as they had seen the cattle begin to lie down, and I would fain have followed their example, but was afraid to do so lest any of the thirsty beasts should wander away. Luckily, the bright moonlight enabled me to keep an eye on all the cattle as they lay scattered about in the thin bush, from where I sat. Presently Tinkarn suggested that we should saddle up again and get on towards the river. He had been giving me a lot of interesting information about the desert Bushmen, their modes of hunting, etc., and asked me to ride with him, instead of remaining behind with my own troop of cattle.

This I agreed to do; so, after waking up Dick and all my boys and telling them to come on with the cattle at once, I rode forwards, always leading Collison's horse "Big Bles," on the tracks of the Mangwatos' cattle, which had trampled broad paths in the soft sandy ground, that were very plainly discernible in the moonlight. I soon joined Tinkarn, who was right in front with the two Bushmen, and his pleasant companionship and cheery talk helped very materially to relieve the tedium of the long, weary ride. At last, just as day was dawning on the morning of December 26, we reached the little Luali river just where the waggon road crossed it. Here there was plenty of good water, so Tinkarn, the Bushmen, and I had a refreshing drink, before the thirsty cattle had fouled it, for though there were several good-sized pools amongst the rocks of the river's bed, there was no running stream. The Mangwatos' cattle were close behind us, and my own troop I thought would not be far behind them. However, when an hour had passed and they had not arrived, I began to feel uneasy; but Tinkarn reassured me, saying that Dick and the herd-boys must have loitered round the fires after we had left, but were bound to be here before very long, as they had drunk nothing since leaving the waggons, and their very lives now therefore depended on their getting to the water quickly. I said I would wait till midday, and then, if they had not turned up by that time, ride back on the cattle tracks to look for them. In the meantime the only thing to do was to rest, as we had no food of any sort with us, and were therefore unable to satisfy our hunger. I was very tired and sleepy, as well as hungry, having had no rest whatever for three consecutive nights, nor any food for more than thirty-six hours, so when I lay down in a sort of little cave amongst the rocks, where the sun would not reach me the whole day, I soon went off into a deep dreamless sleep, from which I was awakened late in the afternoon by Tinkarn, who informed me that Dick had just turned up, riding Collison's spare horse, but without the cattle.

I soon learned what had happened. "After you woke me and the herd-boys at the place where we rested in the night," said Dick, "I saddled up my horse, and then said to my companions, 'Let us go; the master has gone on with Tinkarn, and all the Mangwato cattle have started.' But some of the herd-boys said, 'No, Dick, let us rest a little longer, for we are very tired. Then we will drive the cattle on fast, as we can see the tracks of the big herd that has gone on ahead very plainly in the moonlight.' I was tired too," said Dick, "and did not think a little delay would matter, so I tied my horse to a tree and sat down again by one of the fires. Our cattle were still all lying down then. It was very foolish of me to sit down again, for, as you know, I had led my master's oxen for two nights previously through the deep sand, and was therefore very tired and sleepy. After sitting down again I don't remember anything, sleep must have overcome me, as well as my companions. When at last I woke again, the fires had all gone out, and I could see that the dawn was just breaking. The oxen were gone. 'Wake, wake,' I cried to my companions. 'The oxen have got up and gone away.' Then we took up their tracks, which led us away to the north and had not followed on the spoor of the Mangwatos' cattle. I remained with the rest of the boys, following on the tracks of the cattle until the sun stood there"—pointing to a part of the heavens which the sun must have reached at about 10 A.M.—"and then I thought I must let the white man, my master's friend, know what had happened. Ki peto" ("that is all"). "And how about the herd-boys, will they not all die of thirst?" I asked Dick; for, as they had been walking in the sun for the greater part of the preceding day, I knew from experience that, if they had not yet reached water, they were probably all dead by now; as, although a man may live for three or four days without water during the winter season, no man that is born of a woman can live much more than two days, if walking hard all the time, when exposed to the intense heat of the sun during the hottest time of year in the deserts of Western Africa. "If God wishes it," said Dick, "the sun has now killed them all; but I do not think they are dead. When we all halted in the middle of the night, you remember there was no wind; but when I awoke before dawn this morning there was a light wind blowing from the north; and our oxen, on getting up from where they had been lying, instead of following on the tracks of the other cattle, went off in a bee-line dead against the wind. I think, therefore, that they must have smelt water and were making straight for it. The boys that I left following them up on foot thought so too. They were terribly thirsty when I left them, but thought their only chance for life was to stick to the cattle tracks they were following, as they did not think they would have the strength to retrace their steps to where we rested last night and then follow up the tracks of the Mangwato cattle to the Luali river, as I have done on horseback."

This was Dick's story, and how much or how little to believe of it, I did not know. He had always been a good, trustworthy boy, and a great favourite with his master. I never imagined that he and all my boys would have gone to sleep again after I had roused them, but I felt more angry with myself than with them, for not having actually seen my cattle started before riding forward. As, according to Dick's account, he must have ridden at least twelve miles on the tracks of our cattle without their having come to the water which he thought they had smelt whilst the herd-boys slept, I could not believe it possible that they had really scented water. Tinkarn, however, whose experience was far greater than mine in such matters, stoutly maintained that cattle, when thirsty, could scent water at extraordinary distances, and arguing from the abstract to the concrete, thought that had the lost oxen not done so, they would assuredly have followed up the tracks of his own herd and arrived by themselves at the Luali river.

Tinkarn and his people were now, after the day's rest, about to start back with their cattle to the place where their waggons had been left standing in the desert, but I did not care to go with them, and take the chance of my oxen having found water, and having then been driven back to the waggons. Supposing the oxen and the herd-boys had died of thirst—or been killed by the sun, as the Kafirs express it—what was to happen to our waggons then? Collison, Miller, Sell, and the four waggon-drivers would, I knew, be all right, as well as the horse that Miller had ridden, as they would go on to Klabala with Tinkarn, but our waggons would in that case have to remain standing in the desert with no one to look after them for several days at least. This would be known to the two Bushmen who had guided us to the Luali, and be communicated by them to other Bushmen, who, I feared, might rob the stranded waggons before I could get back to them with fresh cattle from Shoshong.[1]

I soon made up my mind what to do. Shoshong itself was about sixty miles from where I then was at the crossing of the Luali river, and there was a good waggon track leading to it, so I resolved to ride there that night, borrow four spans of bullocks either from the white traders living on the station or from Khama, and after getting something to eat, start back with them at once on the desert road by which we had been travelling from the Botletlie river. Should my oxen have found water, and after having drunk, been driven back to the waggons on the night of the 27th, I should meet them on the road, and no harm would have been done; whilst, on the other hand, should the worst have happened, and our four spans of bullocks and the poor herd-boys prove to have succumbed to thirst, heat, and fatigue, I should be able to reach our waggons before they had been long deserted, and take them into Shoshong with the spans that had been lent to me.

Sixty miles, much of it in heavy, sandy ground, is a good long ride, so I resolved to take my friend's horse "Big Bles," a very powerful animal, in excellent condition. My own horse "Bob" I entrusted to Tinkarn, and sent Dick back to the waggons with him also.

The full moon was just rising as I bade good-

[1] The chief town of Khama's people, the Bamangwato.

bye to Tinkarn and my Mangwato friends, and rode off on my lonely journey. All our shooting horses had been well looked after during the past season, and well fed daily on half-boiled maize, and "Big Bles" was not only a very powerful animal, but accustomed to hard work, and in splendid hard condition. Keeping up an average pace of about seven miles an hour—a very good one in heavy, sandy ground—and only off-saddling twice during the whole journey, I reached Shoshong about an hour before daylight on the morning of December 27. I rode straight to the store of a trader named Jim Truscott, and roused him, as well as another old friend named Fred Drake. My story was soon told. No food had passed my lips since the evening of December 24—some sixty hours—and with the exception of the sleep I had had at the Luali river during the 26th, I had had no rest either during all that time. I was thin and hard naturally from the life I had been leading, but I suppose I looked unusually worn and haggard, as Truscott insisted on my lying down on his bed at once, whilst he had some food prepared for me, and Fred Drake undertook to get the oxen together that I required, and kindly offered to go back with me to where I had left the waggons beyond Klabala.

At the time of which I am writing, South Africa was a very different country to the South Africa of to-day. Gold had not then been discovered on the Witwaters Rand, and there were therefore comparatively but few Englishmen living even in the Transvaal; whilst north of the Limpopo there were no European settlements whatever, and the few white traders and hunters who earned a precarious livelihood amongst the native tribes might have been counted on the fingers of one's two hands. Amongst these few scattered whites a bond of brotherhood existed such as cannot endure under more civilised conditions. Any white man in distress was sure of the warmest sympathy and most generous assistance on the part of all the few others of the same colour scattered here and there over a vast country. But now the times are changed. What was once the "far interior" has been opened up to the civilisation of Western Europe, and the old-time traders and hunters, with their indifferent morals, unbusiness-like habits, but hearts of gold, have passed away from South Africa for ever.

By ten o'clock Fred Drake had got together four spans of good oxen, all lent by the few white men on the station, and had also got a cart and eight oxen to carry some water-casks and provisions. I had gone fast asleep on Truscott's bed as soon as I had had something to eat, and they let me sleep on till midday. Then I had another meal, and at about 1 P.M. started back for my waggons with Fred Drake. We travelled very quickly with the light cart and fresh oxen, even during the heat of the afternoon, and keeping at it all through the night and the next day, were nearing the wells of Klabala on the afternoon of December 29 when we heard a waggon whip crack close ahead of us, and presently saw the fine cloud of dust rising above the low trees which we knew portended the arrival of a waggon. I thought it must be Tinkarn's waggons. We pulled up, and Drake and I jumped off the cart and walked on ahead. As soon as we saw the front oxen I knew them for the leaders of my own fine Damara span, and very soon we were shaking hands with Collison, Miller, and Sell.

The explanation was simple. Our oxen, when they wandered away from the resting-place on the night of December 25, had found their way to water at last before midday on the 26th. Whether they really smelt it, or were made aware by a certain freshness in the air that water lay in the direction from which the wind was blowing, or whether they only hit off the water by chance, I cannot say, but they reached a vley or pool in which there was a good supply of recent rain-water. The herd-boys who followed them had, it appeared, had a very hard time of it, and on coming to a small vley in which there was only mud but no water, a short time before reaching the larger pool, two of them had declared that they could go no farther, and had thrown themselves down and rolled in the mud, and would doubtless have died there, had not their comrades, who shortly afterwards reached the larger pool with the cattle, carried them back some water in a calabash and revived them. The cattle were driven back to the waggons on the night of the 26th, and arrived there before Tinkarn's cattle returned from the Luali river. Collison at once gave the order to inspan, and pushing on through the heat of the day, reached Klabala on the night of the 27th, Tinkarn and his people turning up a few hours later. At Klabala the cattle were given a rest till the afternoon of the 29th, and soon after again making a start for Shoshong, met me coming back with my unnecessary relief spans—as it turned out.

Well, all's well that ends well; though I hope I may never experience such an uncomfortable Christmas again as the one I spent in the desert in the year 1879.

CHAPTER XX

NOTES ON THE MASARWA: THE BUSHMEN OF THE INTERIOR OF SOUTH AFRICA

First Bushmen seen by author in 1872—Armed with bows and arrows—Large areas of country uninhabited except by Bushmen—The Masarwa—Origin of the word "Vaalpens"—Dwarf race mentioned by Professor Keane—Notes on the language of the Bushmen north of the Orange river—Apparently very similar to that spoken by the Koranas—The author's faithful Korana servant—The Nero family—Physical dissimilarity between the Koranas and the Masarwa—Stature of Bushmen met with north of the Orange river—Probably a pure race—The Bakalahari—Livingstone's account of them—Khama's kindness to them—Habits and mode of life of the Masarwa—Their weapons—Bows and poisoned arrows—Food of the Bushmen—Bush children tracking tortoises—Terrible privations sometimes endured by Bushmen—Provision against famine—A giraffe hunt—Rotten ostrich egg found by Bushmen and eaten—Fundamental difference of nature between Bushmen and civilised races not great—Personal experiences with Bushmen—Their marvellous endurance—Skill as hunters and trackers—Incident with lion—Family affection amongst Bushmen—Not unworthy members of the human race.

In previous chapters I have often referred to the Masarwa Bushmen, the remnants probably of one of the oldest and most primitive races of mankind still surviving on the earth, and as my personal knowledge of these people is very considerable, I think that a few notes concerning their habits, language, and mode of life will prove of interest, if not to all who are likely to glance over the pages of this book, at any rate to some few amongst them who believe that "the proper study of mankind is man."

The first Bushmen I ever saw were met with on the banks of the Orange river on January 4, 1872, in the country then occupied by the Korana chief Klas Lucas and his people.

In my diary of that date I made the following notes of this experience:—

"*January* 4, 1872.—Whilst poking about along the river, looking for guinea-fowls, I came upon a Bushman's lair amongst the trees by the water's edge. A few boughs woven together and forming a sort of canopy was all they had in the way of a habitation; the only weapons they possessed were rude-looking bows and neatly made poisoned arrows, some about two and a half feet in length, fashioned from reeds, whilst others were only a foot long. Their language seemed even fuller of clicks and clucks than the Korana, and altogether to a casual observer they appeared to be very few steps removed from the brute creation. The following day three more Bushmen came to the waggon begging for tobacco; they were taller and better looking than those I had first seen."

During the following month (February 1872) I met with a good many more Bushmen, and hunted with them in the Southern Kalahari to the west of the Scurfde Berg. At that time these people had no firearms of any kind, but they all carried small toy-like bows and bark quivers containing poisoned arrows.

During the twenty years succeeding my first meeting with Bushmen on the banks of the Orange river, I met with scattered communities of this primitive race throughout every portion of the interior of the country, where Bantu tribes had not been able to establish themselves owing to the aridity of the soil and the scarcity of water in sufficient quantities to satisfy the needs of a settled population possessed of large herds of cattle, sheep, and goats.

Thus at least nineteen-twentieths of the whole of the enormous area of country included in the Bechwanaland Protectorate are entirely uninhabited except by the descendants of the aboriginal Bushmen, the more civilised Bantu living crowded together in a few large towns. Khama's old town of Shoshong, which was abandoned more than twenty years ago, was said to contain 20,000 inhabitants, practically his whole tribe.

In the last Annual Report of the Transvaal Native Affairs Department, it is stated that the Bushmen living in the valley of the Limpopo in the Northern Transvaal are known as Maseroa, and are distinct from the ordinary South African Bushmen.

All the Bushmen I have seen, whether those living on or near the Orange river, or along the eastern border of the Kalahari, or throughout the Bechwanaland Protectorate, from the Chobi river to Lake N'gami and the Botletlie, and from thence to the Limpopo, appeared to me to be very much the same in appearance and absolutely identical in their ways of life and the fashion of their dress and weapons. Here and there no doubt there has been a certain admixture of Bantu blood amongst them; but seeing how little they vary as a rule both in appearance and in habits and manner of life in widely separated areas, I think that for the most part they must be a pure and distinct race throughout the greater part of the countries they inhabit.

The name given by Khama's people to the Bushmen living in the country ruled over by that chief, which is spelt "Maseroa" in the Report above referred to, is pronounced—at least so it always seemed to me—Ma-sarr-wa (with the "r" very much rolled), and the singular—the word signifying "a Bushman"—ought, I should think, to be Li-sar-wa.

The name "Vaalpens," often applied by the Boers to Bushmen, signifies "grey belly," and has been given to them because, having no huts, but sleeping as they do in the open, they often lie so close to the fire on cold nights that they blister themselves on their shins and abdomens. The skin thus burnt peels off and is replaced by new skin of a lighter colour than that of the rest of the body. Bushmen may often be seen with their legs and bellies covered with such unsightly scars, and it is such blistered patches of skin on their abdomens which has earned them the name of "Vaalpens," or "grey belly."

Although I have travelled in the Zoutpansberg, Waterberg, and Dwarsberg districts of the Northern Transvaal, I have never met with or heard of the dwarf race spoken of by Professor Keane in his book on *The Boer States*. These people, Professor Keane says, are the only genuine Vaalpens, and are almost entirely confined to the above-named and adjacent districts of the North Transvaal as far as the banks of the Limpopo. Professor Keane further says that these people call themselves "Kattea," and that they are almost pitch-black in colour, only about four feet high, and quite distinct both from their tall Bantu neighbours and from the yellowish Bushmen.

It would be interesting to learn where Professor Keane got his information concerning this remarkable race of people. Personally, I find it difficult to believe in their existence, as I have been acquainted with so many Boers who had hunted for years in the very districts in which they are said to exist, or to have existed, and yet have never heard any one of them speak of a dwarf race of black Bushmen. Moreover, I have myself met with Bushmen of the same type as those I have seen in other parts of South Africa, both in the Waterberg district of the Transvaal to the south of the Limpopo and also in the desert country not far to the west of the Dwarsberg.

I believe that the researches of the late Dr. Bleek, the well-known philologist, tended to show that there was little or no affinity between the languages spoken by the Bushmen inhabiting the south-western districts of the Cape Colony and the Hottentot tribes living in the same part of the country. On the other hand, the well-known missionary, the late Dr. Robert Moffat, wrote: "Genuine Hottentots, Koranas, and Namaquas meeting for the first time from their respective and distant tribes could converse with scarcely any difficulty." The Bushmen, however, Dr. Moffat said, "speak a variety of languages, even when nothing but a range of hills or a river intervenes between the tribes, and none of these dialects is understood by the Hottentots." As bearing upon the subject of the affinity or otherwise of the language spoken by the Koranas living in Griqualand and along the Orange river with that of the Bushmen of the interior of South Africa, I must now make an extract from a book written by myself and published in 1893 (*Travel and Adventure in South-East Africa*) relating to this question.

Although I cannot but consider that the facts which I then brought forward were really of some value, I do not think that they have ever been noticed by any one interested in the study of the origin and affinities of the various native races in South Africa, and I am anxious, therefore, to put them on record once more.

The passage I refer to reads as follows:—"In 1871 a Korana boy named John entered my service, and went to the interior with me the following year; and as he had previously learned to speak Dutch from a Griqua master, I could converse freely with him. In 1873, when elephant-hunting in the Linquasi district to the west of Matabeleland, we saw a great many Masarwas (Bushmen), and noticing that their language, full of clicks and clucks and curious intonations of the voice, was similar in character to that I had heard spoken by the Koranas on the banks of the Orange river in 1871, I asked John if he could understand them, but he only laughed and said, 'No, sir.' During the next two years, however, John had a lot to do with the Masarwas; and one day, towards the end of 1874, as we were returning from the Zambesi to Matabeleland, I heard him conversing quite familiarly with some of these people. 'Hullo, John,' I said, 'I thought you told me that you could not understand the Bushmen?' 'Well, sir,' he answered, 'at first I thought I couldn't, but gradually I found that I could understand them, and that they understood me, and, in fact, I can say that with a few slight differences these Bushmen speak the same language as my people on the Orange river.' A Griqua family too, the Neros, who for many years lived in Matabeleland, all spoke Sasarwa (the language of the Masarwas) with perfect fluency, and they all assured me that they had had no difficulty in learning it, as it was almost the same language as that spoken by the Koranas." Now surely these facts are worthy of note. My boy John (who ran away from the Griqua master whose slave he then was and came to me in 1871) followed my fortunes for twenty-five years, and was always a most faithful servant, and in his younger days a very good elephant hunter. He is still alive to-day, and long ago christened himself John Selous.

John was born (probably about the middle of the last century) and brought up on the banks of the

Orange river, being a member of the Korana clan ruled over by Klas Lucas. He is an absolutely pure Korana by blood, of a pale yellow brown in colour, beautifully proportioned, with small, delicately made hands and feet, and the sparse-growing peppercorn hair which I have often seen amongst full-blooded Koranas, but only rarely amongst the Bushmen living in the countries north and west of the Transvaal, who are, moreover, darker skinned than the majority of the Koranas of the Orange river, though very much lighter, as a rule, than Bantu Kafirs.

John, speaking as his native tongue one of the most extraordinary of known languages—a language full of clicks and clucks and curious intonations of the voice, and absolutely impossible of acquirement by a full-grown European—travelled with me some eight hundred miles to the north of the country where he was born on the banks of the Orange river, and there met with a race of wild people living in the desert country immediately south of the Zambesi, who he found, much to his surprise, spoke a language so similar to his own mother-tongue that, after a very little intercourse with them, he was not only able to understand what they said, but to talk to them with perfect fluency. Is not this a most remarkable fact, well worthy the attention of philologists?

When John first told me that, by listening attentively to the Bushmen inhabiting the country immediately to the south of the Chobi and Zambesi rivers, he soon discovered that they were speaking a language very similar to his own, he concluded his explanation by saying in Dutch: "Ik kan maar say daat's de selde taal" ("I can just say it's the same language").

The Nero family, with their dependents, numbered some eight or ten persons, amongst whom was a pure-blooded Korana woman named "Mina," a lady most bountifully endowed with all the physical characteristics peculiar to the Hottentot race. These people all came originally from Griqualand, and they all spoke Dutch in addition to Sintabele (the language of the Matabele) and their mother-tongue, which they told me was Korana. I have heard all these people over and over again talking with the most perfect ease and fluency with the Masarwa Bushmen inhabiting the country to the west of Matabeleland, and they all assured me that they had had no difficulty in learning Sasarwa, as it was practically the same as the language spoken by the Koranas living in Griqualand and along the Orange river.

The apparent uniformity of the language spoken by the scattered families of Bushmen living in widely separated areas of country in the interior of South Africa is somewhat remarkable. My boy John could converse without any difficulty not only with the Masarwas we met with in the valley of the Limpopo, but also with those we came across in the country between the Chobi and Mababi rivers, several hundred miles farther north, although there was never any intercourse between these widely separated clans.

In 1879 I became very well acquainted with Tinkarn, one of Khama's headmen, who has a very thorough knowledge of, and great influence over, the Bushmen living throughout the country over which that chief exercises jurisdiction. I first met Tinkarn in the neighbourhood of the Mababi river, and subsequently travelled with him from there to Shoshong, and later on again met him on the Limpopo. The Masarwa in the Mababi undoubtedly spoke the same language as those living only a couple of days' journey farther north, with whom I heard my boy John talking in 1874, and these latter, according to John, spoke the same language as the Bushmen living in the Limpopo valley near the mouth of the Shashi. Farther west, I have listened to Tinkarn conversing not only with the Masarwa of the Mababi, but also with Bushmen living on the Botletlie river, and in many places in the desert between there and Shoshong, and also with some of these people living on the Limpopo. Tinkarn told me that he had learned the language of the Bushmen when he was a child, and I always thought that he spoke to all of them in the same language, not in a number of dialects. At any rate, he was perfectly fluent with all of them.

Although, however, there would seem to be strong presumptive evidence that all the various families or tribes of Bushmen living scattered over the more arid regions of South-Western Africa to the north of the Orange river speak a language, or dialects of a language, which is essentially the same as that spoken by the Koranas, yet, speaking generally, all the Bushmen I have seen differ considerably in physical appearance not only from pure-blooded Koranas—very few of whom are left to-day—but also from the descriptions I have read of the dwarf race of Bushmen that used to inhabit the Cape Colony. It is these latter whose language was studied by Dr. Bleek, and pronounced to be fundamentally different to that of the Hottentot tribes inhabiting the country near Cape Town. That, prior to the incursion of the tall, dark-coloured Bantu tribes from the north, the whole of Africa south of the Zambesi was inhabited by a race akin to the Bushmen of the Cape Colony is, I think, proved by the similarity of the rock-paintings in Mashunaland and Manicaland—which I think that I was the first to discover—to those existing in caves in many parts of the Orange and Cape Colonies.

I have never seen any pigmy Bushmen. Those I met with on the Orange river and in the country to the west of Griqualand in 1872, as well as a small number I saw near the Vaal river above its junction with the Orange in the same year, may not have been as tall as the average of the Masarwa farther north, but I feel sure that all the men were well over five feet in height.

Speaking generally, I should say that the Bushmen that I have seen—and they were many—whilst they were considerably lighter in colour and shorter and more slightly built than Kafirs, were at the same time darker skinned than most Koranas, and neither so thickset nor so short of stature as the average of those people.

The average height of the Masarwa men I have met with in the country extending from the western border of Matabeleland to Lake N'gami would certainly, I think, be over 5 feet 4 inches, and I have seen many of these people standing quite 5 feet 8 or 9 inches, and a few even 6 feet.

I have, however, occasionally seen men amongst them of a distinctly Korana type, short and stout built in figure, very light in colour, with small black glittering eyes, high cheek-bones, and hair growing in small tufts. There were two young men of this type amongst the Masarwa Bushmen living near the Mababi river in 1884. They reminded me very forcibly of the life-sized figure of a Cape Colony Bushman in the Museum of the Jardin des Plantes in Paris, though they were, I think, nearly if not quite five feet in height. From time to time, no doubt, members of various Bantu tribes have fled to the desert for refuge from their enemies and amalgamated with the Bushmen, and this may account for the greater stature observable amongst certain clans of Masarwas, when compared with full-blooded Koranas, or with the Bushmen of the Cape

Colony, and the very general absence of the peppercorn growth of the hair in the former which is general in the latter; but if further investigation should definitely establish the fact that there is a very close similarity between the very peculiar languages spoken by the Koranas on the Orange river and all the scattered Masarwa clans that wander over the arid country stretching from the Limpopo to the Chobi river, there must be a very close racial connection between the two peoples. On the whole, I am inclined to believe that the greater part of the Bushmen I have met with were of pure race, with very little, if any, admixture of Bantu blood in their veins.

I never remember to have noticed any marked tendency to that wonderful development of the buttocks (*steatopygia*) in Masarwa women which is so characteristic a feature in pure-bred Korana women after they have reached middle age. Bushmen and Bushwomen, however, lead terribly hard lives, and do not often get the chance to become really fat, in the districts in which I have met with them. Should they do so, the men noticeably—far more so than the women—put on more flesh on the buttocks than do well-fed Europeans; but this is the case with the men of all the Bantu races as well. All the members of the royal family of Matabeleland, both male and female, who had passed middle age showed a most extraordinary development of the thighs and buttocks.

In addition to the yellow-skinned Bushmen, however, who are without doubt the oldest aboriginal race in South Africa, there are—or were—also to be found living in the eastern part of the Kalahari a few scattered communities of a race known to the Bechwanas as Bakalahari—they of the desert.

Speaking of these people, Dr. Livingstone wrote long ago, in that most admirable book *Missionary*

Travels: "The Bakalahari are traditionally reported to be the oldest of the Bechwana tribes, and they are said to have possessed enormous herds of the large horned cattle mentioned by Bruce, until they were despoiled of them and driven into the desert by a fresh migration of their own nation. Living ever since on the same plains with the Bushmen, subjected to the same influences of climate, enduring the same thirst and subsisting on similar food for centuries, they seem to supply a standing proof that locality is not always sufficient of itself to account for difference in races. The Bakalahari retain in undying vigour the Bechwana love for agriculture and domestic animals. They hoe their gardens annually, though often all they can hope for is a supply of melons and pumpkins. And they carefully rear small herds of goats, though I have seen them lift water for them out of small wells with a bit of ostrich egg-shell or by spoonfuls."

I used to think that the Bakalahari were a mixed race formed by the amalgamation of broken Bechwana tribes with the desert Bushmen. But I believe there is no warrant for this. Though all those I have seen spoke the language of the Bushmen as well as Sechwana, there can be no doubt that Dr. Livingstone was quite right in saying that, although the Bakalahari have lived a life of terrible hardship and privation for centuries in the desert, they still remain in character true Bechwanas, with all the love of that race for agriculture and stock-breeding.

Under the kind and just rule of Khama many Bakalahari have given up their nomadic life and once more become a settled agricultural tribe. They were supplied with seed-corn and given cattle, sheep, and goats to look after, and in 1879 I found large communities of these once miserable outcasts living near the wells of Klabala, cultivating large areas of ground, and growing so much Kafir corn and maize that, except in seasons of severe drought, they would never again have been likely to suffer from the famine against which their immediate ancestors had constantly struggled. These people, too, were tending considerable herds of cattle, sheep, and goats belonging to Khama, a portion of the increase of which was given to them every year.

I do not think there is any instance on record of a tribe or family of the aboriginal yellow Bushmen having given up their wild free life in the desert and taken to agricultural or pastoral pursuits.

In habits and mode of life true Bushmen seem to be the same wherever they are met with, and the Masarwa—the Bushmen of the interior of South Africa—certainly resemble very closely in these respects the descriptions I have read of their now almost extinct kinsmen of the Cape Colony. They build no huts, but merely erect temporary small shelters of boughs with a little dry grass thrown on the top. They neither sow nor reap any kind of grain, nor do they possess any kind of domestic animals, except small jackal-like dogs, which cannot bark. They obtain fire very rapidly with two pieces of wood. One of these is held flat on the ground by the feet of a man sitting down, whilst the other, the end of which has been placed in a small notch cut for its reception, is whirled rapidly round between the open hands, until the fine wood dust produced by the friction begins to smoulder, when it is placed amongst some dry grass and blown into flame.

The dress for men, women, and girls amongst the Masarwa is the same as that which used to be worn by the Bechwana and Makalaka tribes before these latter had come in contact with Europeans. They obtain iron-headed spears and earthenware cooking pots from the neighbouring

Kafir tribes in exchange for the skins of wild animals, their only native weapon being the bow and arrow. Their bows are very small and weak-looking, and their arrows are unfeathered, being made of light reeds into the ends of which bone heads are inserted. These bone arrow-heads are always thickly smeared with poison, which seems to be made from the body of a grub or caterpillar mixed with gum. At least, in the bark quivers of the Bushmen whose belongings I have examined, I have usually found, besides their arrows and fire-sticks, a small bark cylinder closed at one end, in which were the bodies of grubs or caterpillars preserved in gum, which I was told contained the poison they smeared on their arrows.

The Masarwa living immediately to the west of Matabeleland have long since discarded their bows and poisoned arrows in favour of firearms, but twenty or thirty years ago these curiously toy-like but very effective weapons were in general use amongst the Bushmen living in the deserts to the south and west of the Botletlie river.

Except that they do not eat grass, Bushmen are almost as omnivorous as bears. Besides the flesh of every kind of animal from an elephant to a mouse (which is acceptable to them in any and every stage of decomposition), they eat certain kinds of snakes, fish, lizards, frogs, tortoises, grubs, locusts, flying ants, wild honey, young bees, ostrich eggs, nestling birds of all sorts, and various kinds of berries, bulbs, and roots. Bushwomen may often be met with miles away from their encampments, wandering alone over the desert wastes they inhabit, searching for edible roots and bulbs, which they dig up with pointed sticks. The children, too, begin to forage for themselves at a very early age, and I have seen little mites, apparently not more than two or three years old, crawling on their hands and knees on the tracks of tortoises. It was explained to me that these reptiles make light scratches on the ground with their claws as they walk along, and these almost imperceptible marks the infant Bushmen are taught to follow. No wonder they grow up to be good game trackers!

In many parts of the countries the Bushmen inhabit not only does game periodically become scarce or almost non-existent, but all other sources of food supply are liable at times to fail them as well.

At such times these wild people sometimes endure the most terrible privations, and no doubt numbers of them succumb yearly to slow starvation.

I have often met with families of Bushmen all the members of which were in such a terrible state of emaciation that it seemed a marvel that they were still alive. In such cases the flesh appeared to have almost completely wasted away from their legs and arms, leaving nothing but the bones encased in dry yellow-brown skin, whilst their faces looked like skulls covered with parchment, though the small black eyes still glittered from the depths of their sockets.

Whenever I have encountered Bushmen in this condition, they were never actually without food, but, in default of anything better, seemed to have been living for a long time past on certain kinds of berries, which were so innutritious that very large quantities had to be eaten to support life at all. The consequence was that the bellies of these slowly starving savages were always enormously distended, giving them a most grotesque though pitiable appearance.

If some large animal such as a giraffe or elephant be killed and given to a starving Bushman family they will all manage to get to the carcase, though it be miles away and they appear to be in the last stage of emaciation. Once there, it is with the men a case of "J'y suis, j'y reste," and they will not move again until every bit of the meat is eaten. The women and children have to fetch water every day, though it may be miles distant. However wasted and apparently near death Bushmen may be, once they get alongside of a dead elephant they recover flesh and regain their strength in a marvellously short space of time.

When hunting in the Linquasi district to the west of Matabeleland, in 1873, I often noticed large pieces of rhinoceros and giraffe hide which had evidently been placed by human hands high up in the branches of trees. These slabs of hide, the Bushmen told me, had belonged to animals killed by their people, and had been placed in the trees out of the reach of hyænas as a provision against starvation in times of famine.

I was once riding behind some hungry Bushmen looking for giraffe in the country between the Mababi and Botletlie rivers, when they came on a single ostrich egg lying on the ground. It was then late in September, and this egg had in all probability been laid in the previous May or June, and had lain on the ground in the broiling sun ever since.

My gaunt and hungry guides seemed greatly excited over their find, and each of them in turn held it up and shook it close to his ear. Then I saw they were going to break it, so I moved to one side, as I expected it would go off with a loud explosion. It was, however, long past that stage, all the contents of the egg having solidified into a thick brown-coloured paste at the one end. I never would have believed, if I had not experienced it, that so much smell could have been given off by so small an amount of matter. As I once heard an

American lady remark of the atmosphere of a small mosque in which we had been watching some dancing Dervishes at Constantinople, it gave off "a poor odour"—one of the poorest, I think, I have ever encountered, in her sense of the word, though by many people it might have been thought too rich.

With the Bushmen, however, an egg in the hand was evidently considered to be worth more than a problematical animal in the bush, and they at once sat down, and taking turn and turn about, slowly and with evident relish licked up the fœtid contents of the treasure which fortune had thrown in their way. Up to this time we had not even seen the fresh track of a giraffe, but not long afterwards we sighted a magnificent old bull, which I managed to kill for them after a hard gallop through some very thick and thorny bush.

When I met with the first Bushmen I ever saw on the banks of the Orange river, in 1872, I was a very young man, and regarding them with some repugnance, wrote in my diary that they appeared to be very few steps removed from the brute creation. That was a very foolish and ignorant remark to make, and I have since found out that though Bushmen may possibly be to-day in the same backward state of material development and knowledge as once were the palæolithic ancestors of the most highly cultured European races in prehistoric times, yet fundamentally there is very little difference between the natures of primitive and civilised men, so that it is quite possible for a member of one of the more cultured races to live for a time quite happily and contentedly amongst beings who are often described as degraded savages, and from whom he is separated by thousands of years in all that is implied by the word "civilisation." I have hunted a great deal with Bushmen, and during 1884 I lived amongst these people continuously for several months together. On many and many a night I have slept in their encampments without even any Kafir attendants, and though I was entirely in their power, I always felt perfectly safe amongst them. As most of the men spoke Sechwana, I was able to converse with them, and found them very intelligent companions, full of knowledge concerning the habits of all the wild animals inhabiting the country in which they lived. I found the Bushmen very good-tempered people, and they are undoubtedly the best of all the natives of South Africa to have with one when in pursuit of game, as they are such wonderful trackers, and so intimately acquainted with the habits of every kind of wild animal. To be seen at their best they must be hungry, but not starving. They will then be capable of marvellous feats of endurance. I have known a Bushman run on elephant spoor in front of my horse for five hours, only very occasionally slowing down to a walk for a few minutes. He ran till it got dark, and as we had neither blankets nor food, which had been left with the Kafirs far behind, we lit a big fire, beside which we sat all night, not daring to lie down and sleep, for fear lest lions should kill my horse, which we had to watch whilst it fed round near the fire. When we took up the elephant tracks again the next morning, we had been twenty-four hours without food, and it was late in the afternoon before we were making a meal off elephant's heart. During the two days this Bushman must have walked and run for at least eighty miles without food or sleep, and he never showed the least sign of exhaustion. Living as they do in families or small communities, Bushmen have not developed any warlike qualities, and I cannot imagine any of them I have known being anxious "to seek the bubble reputation even in the cannon's mouth"; but for all that they are certainly more courageous with dangerous game than the generality of Kafirs. A friend of mine was once out looking for game on horseback, accompanied by a single Bushman. The Bushman, who was walking in front of the horse, suddenly spied a lion lying flat on the ground watching them, and less than fifty yards away. Raising his left hand as a sign to my friend to stop, he pointed at the crouching animal with his spear, at the same time retiring slowly backwards until he stood beside the horse. "Tauw ki-o" ("There is a lion"), he quietly said; but my friend for the life of him could not see it. The Bushman then again advanced, and taking the horse by the bridle, led it a few paces forwards, when his master at last saw the lion, and firing from the saddle, disabled it with the first shot, and finished it with a second. It was a fine big animal, but without much mane. My friend said it was the lion's eyes that he first saw, and then the twitching of its tail. He was very much pleased with the coolness and staunchness of the Bushman, quite a young man. Oh, if I had only had that Bushman for a gun-carrier on a certain day in 1877, when the most magnificently maned lion I ever saw in my life suddenly showed himself within twenty yards of me, and the wretched Makalaka who was carrying my rifle and was just behind me, instead of putting it into my outstretched hand, turned and ran off with it! Had I killed that lion, its skin would have been my trophy of trophies, but—kismet! it was not to be.

In 1874, 1877, and again in 1879, during which years I shot a great number of buffaloes along the Chobi river, and followed many of them into very thick cover after having wounded them, I always employed Bushmen to act as my gun-carriers, and better men for such work it would have been impossible to find, for not only were they always cool and self-possessed in any emergency, but the quickness of their eyesight, and their intimate knowledge of the animals we were pursuing, gave them a great advantage over the staunchest of gun-carriers drawn from any Kafir tribe.

Although the wives and children of Bushmen lead very hard lives, especially when food is scarce, and have always to keep the encampment supplied with water no matter how far it has to be carried, I have never seen them ill-treated, and I have seen both the men and the women show affection for their children. In fact, the Bushmen of South Africa, although they have never advanced beyond the primitive stage of culture attained to by their distant ancestors at a very remote period of the world's history, are ethically much the same on the average as the members of all other races of mankind, which shows how little the fundamental nature of man has changed throughout the ages, and during the evolution and destruction of many civilisations. I have known Bushmen to be very grasping and avaricious, and to show an utter want of sympathy or kindness towards a fellow-man in distress; but has civilisation eliminated such defects of character in all members of the most highly cultured societies? Murder, robbery, rape, adultery, are crimes against the Bushman's code of morals, just as they are with more civilised peoples, and they are probably less frequently practised amongst primitive than amongst civilised races. A Bushman will resent an injury and be grateful for a kindness just like an Englishman, a Hindu, or a Red Indian. Whenever I was told, as I often was in South Africa, that all natives were black brutes who could not understand kindness and were incapable of gratitude, I always knew that the masterful gentleman or fair lady who was speaking to me had no kindness in their own natures, and that never in all their lives had they given any native the slightest reason to be grateful to them.

The Bushmen are the only really primitive race in South Africa, but, rude and uncultured though they may be, I cannot look upon them as degraded savages, but rather as a race whose development was arrested long ago, by the circumstances of their surroundings; but whose members, nevertheless, are beings whose human hearts can be touched and whose sympathies can be aroused by the kindness of another human being, however widely separated the latter may be from themselves in race and degree of culture. Well and truly has it been said by one of England's most illustrious sons, "One touch of nature makes the whole world kin."

INDEX

THE END